George Buehl

The Death of Socialist Realism in the Novels of Christa Wolf

2nd, unchanged edition

PETER LANG
Frankfurt am Main · Bern · New York

CIP-Kurztitelaufnahme der Deutschen Bibliothek

Buehler, George:
The death of socialist realism in the novels of
Christa Wolf / George Buehler. − 2., unveränd.
Aufl. − Frankfurt am Main ; Bern ; New York :
Lang, 1986.
  (European university studies ; Ser. 1, German
  language and literature ; Vol. 787)
  ISBN 3-8204-7477-3
NE: Europäische Hochschulschriften / 01

Library of Congress Cataloging-in-Publication Data

Buehler, George, 1943−
  The death of socialist realism in the novels of
Christa Wolf.

  (European university studies. Series I, German
language and literature, ISSN 0721-3301 ; vol. 787
= Europäische Hochschulschriften. Reihe I, Deutsche
Sprache und Literatur ; Bd. 787)
  Bibliography: p.
  1. Wolf, Christa−−Criticism and interpretation.
2. Socialist realism in literature. I. Title.
II. Series: Europäische Hochschulschriften. Reihe I,
Deutsche Sprache und Literatur ; Bd. 787.
[PT2685.036Z56 1986]   833'.914   86-18626
ISBN 3-8204-7477-3

ISSN 0721-3301
ISBN 3-8204-7477-3
© Verlag Peter Lang GmbH, Frankfurt am Main 1986

Table of Contents

Chapter VI

Chapter I

The Function of Literature in the German Democratic Republic

On May 8, 1945 Germany submitted its unconditional surrender
to the victorious Allies. The nightmare of the National Socialist era had finally ended. Rarely had a nation paid so dearly
for its reprehensible delusion of grandeur and world conquest.
Millions of victims of the perverse Hitler mania were strewn
on distant battlefields stretching from the burning sands of
the Sahara to the frozen steppes of Siberia. At home, the
German industrial, technological and military might lay in
ruins. The survivors of the aforegone madness gazed in horror
and disbelief at the desolation that had turned their homeland
into a virtual moonscape.

Compounding the physical suffering experienced by the post-
war survivors in their day-to-day struggle for existence was
the mental anguish endured by the growing realization that the
fatherland had been subjected to military occupation. Indeed,
as East-West relations began to cool, Germany served as the
political barometer of the developing rift between the United
States and the Soviet Union. The increasing polarization of
the two super powers was subsequently reflected in the abandonment of the Four Power Administration of Germany and the
establishment of a Bi-Zone, the Eastern Zone under Soviet
domination and the Western Zone under the administration of
the three Western allies. Thus, each zone became ever more
closely aligned and identified with its respective military
protector to the point that each region was compelled to
adopt the political system of its "big brother." As a result,
two politically antithetical German "entities" had emerged
by 1948 whose hostility toward one another echoed the cold
war enmity between the two super powers. This de facto existence of two Germanies, one a capitalist system under Western
influence and the other a socialist state under Soviet domination, was formalized in 1949 by the founding of the Federal
Republic of Germany (FRG) and the German Democratic Republic

(GDR).

Long before the official founding of the GDR on October 7, 1949, a fundamental social, economic, cultural and political transformation had taken place in the Soviet Occupied Zone. In an effort to prevent a recurrence of the lunacy of 1933-1945, to cleanse the inhabitants of the Eastern Zone from their contamination with decadent Western ideology and to make disciples of the East Germans to the precepts of socialism, a "tabula rasa" policy was implemented. Indicative of the complete dismantling of the old order and its replacement with a new "Basis" were the reforms instituted by the Red Army, the Soviet Military Administration and the German communists following the surrender of Germany:

1. Enteignung der Betriebe von Kriegsverbrechern und aktiven Nationalsozialisten. Dadurch gingen 8% der Industriebetriebe, die 39% der industriellen Bruttoproduktion erzeugten, in Volkseigentum über; 22% der Industrieproduktion wurde Eigentum der UdSSR (in Form der 'Sowjetischen Aktiengesellschaten,' der SAGs) aufgrund der Reparationsansprüche dieses von deutschen Faschisten verwüsteten Landes.

2. Enteignung allen landwirtschaftlichen Privatbesitzes über 100 ha sowie des Grundbesitzes von führenden Nationalsozialisten; zwei Drittel des Landes wurden an ca. 550000 landlose Bauern, Landarbeiter und Pächter verteilt (Bodenreform).

3. Überführung der Bodenschätze und Bergwerksbetriebe in Staatseigentum (dies erst 1947).[1]

Complementing the transition from a private to a state-owned economic order as a precursor to socialism was the founding of the "Kulturbund zur demokratischen Erneuerung Deutschlands" on July 4, 1945 to promote an intellectual regeneration of the German people. Motivated by a genuine desire to atone for the mistakes of the past, the "Kulturbund" dedicated itself to a "democratic renewal of Germany" through a cultural and scientific renaissance at all levels. Specifically, the founding declaration of the "Kulturbund" stated:

> Der "Kulturbund zur demokratischen Erneuerung Deutschlands" setzt sich die Aufgabe, die heute eine der höchsten nationalen Aufgaben der Intelligenz ist: alle deutschen Männer und Frauen zu vereinen, die des ehrlichen, unbeugsamen Willens sind, zur geistigen, kulturellen Erneuerung Deutschlands mit Einsatz ihrer ganzen Kraft beizutragen. Die besten Deutschen aller Berufe und Schichten gilt es in dieser schweren Notzeit deutscher Geschichte zu sammeln, um eine deutsche Erneuerungsbewegung zu schaffen, die auf allen Lebens- und Wissensgebieten die Überreste des Faschismus und der Reaktion zu vernichten gewillt ist und dadurch auch auf geistigkulturellem Gebiet ein neues, sauberes, anständiges Leben aufbaut...[2]

The "Kulturbund," according to this statement, was founded for the purpose of advancing the highest principles of human dignity and freedom--free from allegiance to any ideology or political party. However, this provision was soon violated as an ever increasing segment of the membership of the "Kulturbund" belonging to the Communist Party turned the former supra political entity into a forum for the dissemination of communist ideology. As early as February 1946, communist members of the "Kulturbund" advocated "das erfolgreich zu gestalten, was heute der Hand des Künstlers bedarf; der Neuaufbau Deutschlands aus den Trümmern und Ruinen, wobei der schaffende Mensch im Mittelpunkt steht."[3]

The seeds of political control over a previously independent literature had been sown in this seemingly innocent demand which was brushed aside by the great majority of the "Kulturbund" as mere rhetoric of overzealous Party functionaries. Surely no one seriously contemplated a direct linkage between

a political party and literature. However, this attitude of
benign neglect and nonchalance toward the ever increasing effort of the communist members to politicize literature soon
came to haunt the advocates of an apolitical "Kulturbund."
Following the merger of the East German section of the Social
Democratic Party (SPD) and the German Communist Party (KPD)
into the Socialist Unity Party (SED) on April 21, 1946, the
heretofore camouflaged intention of the communists to subject
literature to political ends was revealed in public pronouncements. Accordingly, a communiqué of the Party Conference of
the newly merged SED declared its goal as: "Kulturelle Erneuerung Deutschlands; Forderung von Literatur, Kunst und
Wissenschaft."[4] It now became clear that the arts and sciences
in the Soviet Military Zone had lost their former independence
and had been linked to the political process. Henceforth,
the role and scope of the arts and sciences on East German
soil would be subservient to the needs of the state as defined
in large measure by the functionaries of the SED.[5]

The blueprint for the subordination of the arts to the political process had been prepared long ago by the progenitors of
the communist ideology. Friedrich Engels was among the first
to reject the concept of the independence of literature which
permitted the author to depict reality through impartial eyes.
Engels discarded any notion of a neutral depiction of life as
an incomplete and perverse perception of the role and scope
of the literary process. Instead, Friedrich Engels mandated
that every work of art and literature must epitomize the inherent conflict that characterizes the transition from the
old order of suppression and exploitation to the new socialist era of equality: "Die rebellische Auflehnung der Arbeiterklasse gegen das Milieu der Unterdrückung, das sie umgibt,
ihre Versuche--konvulsivisch, halbbewußt oder bewußt--,
ihren Status als menschliche Wesen wiederzuerlangen, gehören
zur Geschichte und müssen darum auf einen Platz im Bereich
des Realismus Anspruch erheben."[6]

Wladimir I. Lenin was even more adamant in his demand to
reduce literature to a "Bestandteil der organisierten, plan-

mäßigen... Parteiarbeit."[7] Indeed, Lenin viewed the subordination of literature to the political process as a politically
condoned, necessary and appropriate precondition to the successful realization of the socialist order. Accordingly,
Lenin delegated to the arts and literature the vital task of
carrying out the spade work in preparing the masses for a new
way of life. In this scheme, literature assumed the role of
harbinger of the impending socialist society by portraying the
"Entwicklung der besten Vorbilder, Traditionen und Ergebnisse
der bestehenden Kultur, ausgehend von der marxistischen Weltanschauung und den Lebens- und Kampfbedingungen des Proletari-
ats in der Epoche seiner Diktatur."[8] This function of literature as an ancillary tool of the government was not perceived
as exploitation by Lenin but rather justified by his belief
that in this role literature fulfilled its primary and most
appropriate function--the promotion and fostering of the ongoing class struggle.

It should not have come as a total surprise to the inhabitants of the Soviet Occupied Zone, therefore, that the Soviet
Union would export Engels' and Lenin's concept of the role and
scope of literature to its newly conquered territory. Accordingly, Major Dymschitz, Chief of the Department of Culture of
the Soviet Military Administration, provided an important clue
pertaining to the direction in which East German thinking and
literature was expected to turn for guidance and regeneration
on July 1, 1947: "Leider stellen sich die deutschen Leser
nicht mit genügender Klarheit vor, welch ungeheure geistige
Reichtümer ihnen die Überwindung der Grenzen nationaler Be-
schränktheit und besonders das aktive Studium der Kultur der
Sowjetvölker verheißt."[9]

Heeding this cue from Major Dymschitz, the Socialist Unity
Party proclaimed its cultural and literary "Anschluß" to the
Soviet Union during its First Party Conference on January 25-
28, 1949. In a remarkable turnabout, therefore, the independent status of the arts and sciences had suddenly been subjected to complete political control. From this day forth,
the role and scope of literature in the Soviet Occupied Zone

was modelled after the grand design of Engels and Lenin, declared a resolution of the First Party Conference, in order to
achieve on East German soil a comparable transformation from
oppressive capitalism to the blessings of socialism as had occurred in the Soviet Union. The formula for the total regeneration of the German psyche called for absolute renunciation of
the past: "Nur im schärfsten Kampf sind die Überreste des
Nazismus in Literatur, Wissenschaft und Kunst zu überwinden.
Auch die Erscheinungen des Neofaschismus, der Dekadenz und der
formalistischen und naturalistischen Verzerrungen der Kunst,
die nur den Zerfall des monokapitalistischen Systems wider-
spiegeln, sind unversöhnlich zu bekämpfen."[10]
Step by step, the Soviet model of the function of literature was subsequently transplanted to the Soviet Occupied Zone.
In accordance with the precepts of Engels, the new literature
of the Eastern Zone was delegated the specific function of
denigrating the immediate German past as a case in point of
capitalist brutality, suppression and perversion whose justi-
fiable downfall was brought about by the Soviet forces of
peace, justice and equality. Indeed, the heroic struggle and
sacrifice of the Soviet people in freeing the Germans from
oppression was to serve as the centerpiece of the new literature. The inviolability of this prerequisite for literature
within the borders of the Soviet Occupied Zone was articulated
by Fritz Erpenbeck, the new minister of culture, in June 1949:
"Ein Kunstwerk kann nur entstehen auf der inhaltlichen Grund-
lage des gesellschaftlichen Wahren. Mit anderen Worten: ein
Werk, das nicht die großen gesellschaftlichen Tendenzen der
Realität gestaltet, also den Klassenkampf wahrhaft widerspiegelt, kann niemals ein Kunstwerk sein."[11] The artists and
writers were thus accorded the singular distinction to serve
as harbingers of the impending new social order as Lenin had
demanded. Literature was to serve as the catalyst for inspiring the masses to the cause of socialism. The new literature
of the GDR was to portray the new principles of brotherhood and
human equality that would characterize the impending era of
the socialist society. As architects of the future society

on East German territory, the authors of socialist realism
works would fulfill Lenin's precepts for literature:

　...gestaltend mitzuwirken bei der Entfaltung
　der sozialistischen Menschengemeinschaft, bei
　der Verwirklichung einer neuen Stufe des Sozi-
　alismus. Das bedeutet für die Kunst, teilzu-
　nehmen an der Ausprägung des geistigen Antlitzes
　der sozialistischen Persönlichkeit, an der Ent-
　faltung des sozialistischen Bewusstseins, der
　weltanschaulich-ethischen Werte und der Schön-
　heitsvorstellungen der neuen Gesellschaft, da
　gerade die Kunst es mit ihren spezifischen
　Mitteln vermag, auf jene komplexe Weise die
　Gedanken- und Gefühlswelt der Menschen zu beein-
　flussen, auf die es bei der allseitigen Formung
　der sozialistischen Persönlichkeit ankommt.
　Die Wirkung der sozialistischen Kunst im Gesell-
　schaftsganzen beruht in erster Linie darauf,
　einen unersetzbaren Beitrag zur Ausbildung
　der Haupttriebkraft der gesellschaftlichen
　Entwicklung, zur ständigen Übereinstimmung
　der gesellschaftlichen und persönlichen In-
　teressen zu leisten.[12]

A chronological overview of official Party and government
pronouncements concerning the function of literature in the
GDR following its founding in 1949 illustrates that the role
and scope assigned to literature by the politicians has not
deviated appreciably from its prefounding days to the present.
While Western literature perceives its role as the pursuit and
depiction of the essence of the human condition, the primary
function of literature in the GDR is that of promoting the
ideals and policies espoused by the political infrastructure.
This subservient relationship of the arts to the state is in
large part due to the heavy government subsidies paid to the
artist. As a result, literature in the GDR is not perceived
as an independent entity by most political leaders, but rather
as an ancillary tool of the state. In this subservient role

many politicians regard literature as little more than a
mouth-piece for official government policy and an ally and
"Mitkämpfer" in the continuing struggle to build the socialist society. This viewpoint was expressed openly and unabashedly by Otto Grotewohl in 1951 during the "Formalismus-Kampagne:"

> Literatur und bildende Künste sind in der Poli-
> tik untergeordnet, aber es ist klar, daß sie
> einen starken Einfluß auf die Politik ausüben.
> Die Idee der Kunst muß der Marschrichtung des
> politischen Kampfes folgen... Was sich in der
> Politik als richtig erweist, ist es auch unbedingt
> in der Kunst.[13]

In accordance with its assigned role and in faithful obedi-
ence to Lenin's prescription for literature, the Socialist Unity Party enrolled the services of the arts as a useful tool for
the purpose of popularizing decrees emanating from the political hierarchy. Thus, the arts "served" the government by ex-
plaining, defending and rallying public support for government
policies. This was achieved by producing artistic and literary
works that depicted the gradual transition from the post-war
state of destruction and desolation to a resurgence of pride
in the accomplishments of GDR workers in the gradual establishment of the new society. As "Bahnbrecher" and "Mitkämpfer" for
a new order under difficult circumstances, authors of socialist
realism literature contributed their good will and moderate
talent toward achieving Stalin's ultimate goal for every art-
ist--to function as an "Ingenieur der menschlichen Seele."
Stalin's prescription for literature as "servant to the state"
was subsequently dutifully incorporated into the program of
the SED:

> Die Kunstwerke dienen der moralischen Ver-
> änderung des Menschen im Geiste des Sozialis-
> mus. Sie regen zu großen Taten für den
> Sozialismus an, erwecken in ihnen die Liebe
> zur Arbeit, bereichern das geistige Leben des
> Volkes, bilden die rationalen und emotionalen
> Fähigkeiten des Menschen der sozialistischen

Gemeinschaft und erziehen ihn zu großer Lebensfreude.[14]

Government officials joyfully hailed the adoption of this
precept of socialist realism as the North Star for all subsequent literature produced in the GDR. They criss-crossed the
GDR proclaiming the good news, extolled the virtues of socialist realism as a revolutionary art form and exhorted one and
all to incorporate these noble principles into their works:

> In unserer Epoche der großen gesellschaft-
> lichen und technischen Umwälzungen, der He-
> rausbildung neuer, wahrhaft menschlicher
> Beziehungen zwischen den Menschen sind un-
> sere Künstler vor die schöne Aufgabe gestellt,
> in ihren Werken diesen neuen Lebensinhalt,
> dieses sozialistische Lebensgefühl zu ge-
> stalten. Die Kunst unserer Epoche, die uns
> ermöglicht, diese Aufgabe zu erfüllen, ist
> der sozialistische Realismus... Wir sind
> für einen Realismus, der - von sozialistischen
> Positionen aus - die ganze Fülle des Lebens
> aufnimmt und künstlerisch verallgemeinert.[15]

Literature and politics had entered a new interdependent
relationship in the GDR. While the body politic functioned
primarily in an administrative capacity by chartering the
political course of the new republic and by formulating specific goals designed to keep the ship of state on course, literature performed the more difficult "task" of inculcating
these ideas into the minds and hearts of the general public.
The master-servant relationship between the political hierarchy
and socialist realism writers is evident by the specific
"Auftrag" GDR writers have to incorporate into all literary
works:

> Der Auftrag besteht darin, daß sie das Neue
> im Leben, in den gesellschaftlichen Bezie-
> hungen der Menschen, in ihrem Kampf um den
> sozialistischen Aufbau, um die sozialistische
> Umgestaltung des gesamten Lebens künstlerisch

gestalten, daß sie durch ihre künstlerischen
Leistungen die Menschen begeistern und dadurch
mithelfen, das Tempo der Entwicklung zu be-
schleunigen und vorwärtszubringen.[16]

This "Auftrag" of socialist realism literature to function
as "Ingenieure der menschlichen Seele" in promoting the new
socialist society was incorporated into official GDR policy by
the First Party Conference of the SED in 1949: "Die kulturelle
Aufgabe, Menschen mit einer neuen gesellschaftlichen Erkenntnis
und einer neuen Einstellung zur Arbeit zu erziehen, ist nur zu
erfüllen, wenn alle Schriftsteller und Künstler ihre ganze
Kraft und Begeisterung diesem Werk widmen."[17]   Thus, the Soviet
model of the role of literature had been transferred to the GDR.
The non-negotiable nature of this master-servant relationship
between state and literature was subsequently conveyed in no
uncertain terms by Paul Wandel, the minister of education, to
the assembled writers of the Second Conference of the "Kulturbund," held on November 23-26, 1949:

> Wir wollen keinen Zwang auf künstlerisches Schaffen
> legen, keine Verbote oder etwas Ähnliches aussprechen
> [...] Aber es wird - und ich spreche das mit genü-
> gendem Nachdruck aus - in der nächsten Zeit für
> manche fühlbar werden, daß anstelle der früheren
> feudalen und kapitalistischen Auftraggeber neue
> Auftraggeber getreten sind... Wer nicht versteht,
> das zu gestalten, was den neuen schaffenden, schö-
> pferischen Menschen wirklich Freude, Erbauung,
> Kraft, Optimismus und Zuversicht gibt, der muß
> seine Auftraggeber in jener vergehenden und zer-
> setzenden Welt suchen, der er sehr oft seine
> Impulse schöpft.[18]

In accordance with this pronouncement, Otto Grotewohl at
the same conference enlisted the writers of the GDR as "Kampf-
genossen der Regierung" in the establishment of the new socialist society while the Soviet writer, Nikolai Tichonow, stressed
the "staatliche Funktion" of literature. Similarly, Johannes
R. Becher extolled the new role of socialist realism writers

as a "Werkzeug der Wandlung" while Kuba urged the authors to
venture into town, country and factories to contribute in prac-
tical ways to the alleviation of real problems. Bodo Uhse even
went so far as to denounce "das verlogene Schlagwort von der
'Freiheit der Kultur'" and called for "einen anderen Ton" in
literary works. The entire proceedings were capped by Johannes
R. Becher's reminder of Stalin's warning: "Wenn der Feind sich
nicht ergibt, muß er vernichtet werden."[19] The unmistakeable
message to all may be summarized succinctly in the Biblical
adage: "Let him who has ears, listen."

The battle lines had been drawn. From this day forward GDR
authors were classified according to their labor either as proponents or opponents of the "great experiment" and subsequently
as friends or enemies of the peoples' state. Ironically, this
"love it or leave it" mentality rekindled memories of the "wer
nicht mit mir ist, ist gegen mich" syndrome of the Hitler era,
thereby accentuating the fact that both the old and new political order used embarrassingly similar means to achieve their
political ends. As had been the case before, the net effect
of this decree was literally a parting of ways for many authors
residing in the GDR. Those who could not reconcile their artistic principles with the political demands of the communists
left the GDR for the Federal Republic while those who embraced
the new role of literature fervently espoused these principles
in their works. Perhaps Anna Seghers expressed most eloquent-
ly the motive of the great majority of writers who chose to
remain in the GDR upon her return to the German Democratic
Republic from her exile in Mexico:

Als ich aus der Emigration zurückkam, fuhr
ich vom Westen her quer durch Deutschland.
Die Städte waren zertrümmert und die Menschen
waren im innern genau so zertrümmert. Damals bot Deutschland eine 'Einheit' von
Ruinen, Verzweiflung und Hunger. Aber es gab
auch Menschen, die nicht vom Elend betäubt
waren und zum erstenmal Fragen aussprachen,
die auch alle drückten: Was ist geschehen?

Wodurch geschah es? - Daraus ergab sich die
nächste Frage: Was muß geschehen, damit das
Grauen nie mehr wiederkommt? [...] Das war der
Augenblick, in dem die deutschen Schriftsteller auf den Plan treten mußten, um so
klar und vernehmlich wie möglich Rede und
Antwort zu stehen. Durch die Mittel ihres
Berufes mußten sie helfen, ihr Volk zum Begreifen seiner selbstverschuldeten Lage zu
bringen und in ihm die Kraft zu einem anderen, einem neuen friedvollen Leben zu
erwecken.[20]

Others, like Erwin Strittmatter, were convinced that socialism as envisioned for the GDR by its leaders offered a viable
alternative to the vicious cycle of war and exploitation that
had plagued Europe and Germany for centuries. Since all other
forms of government in Europe to that point in history had
failed to bring about peace and tranquility, Strittmatter was
prepared to cast his lot with the socialists as the only remaining hope for mankind to bring about this elusive dream:

Wir werden eine gute Kunst und Literatur
schaffen, wenn wir die Hilfe der Partei in
Anspruch nehmen, wenn wir uns von ihrer kol-
lektiven Weisheit den Weg weisen lassen. Wir
müssen akzeptieren, daß unsere Arbeit ihre
Funktion hat in dem großen Plan, der unser
aller Leben bestimmt.[21]

Indeed, a surge of optimism and confidence pervaded the
GDR writers who had remained in the GDR. They were convinced
that the characteristics of socialist realism literature offered them the best opportunity to bridge the gulf that had
existed through the ages between the author and his readers.
While other forms of literature had always addressed an audience comprised of the educated and elite, socialist realism literature catered to all segments of the population and the
lower classes in particular. For the first time, therefore,
literature extended a direct invitation to the downtrodden

to become a part of the mainstream of life by participating
in an activity that had previously been reserved for the upper
classes. Here was the opportunity, as Alfred Kurella stated
·in 1960, to form a lasting partnership between the author and
the broad spectrum of the population:

Im Prozeß dieser Diskussionen [...] festigt sich
das Bündnis zwischen Arbeiterklasse und
Künstler, formt sich immer mehr das geistige
Antlitz der Arbeiterklasse, bildet sich immer
klarer unter Künstlern die Orientierung auf
ihren Auftraggeber, die Arbeiterklasse, heraus.
Auf diese Weise - kann man sagen - wird die
Trennung von Kunst und Leben bei uns in der
Deutschen Demokratischen Republik ein für
allemal überwunden werden.[22]

To foster this new relationship between literature and the
working class, socialist realism writers produced works dealing with topics of primary interest and concern to the masses.
Thus, the problems encountered on the job became the focus of
numerous works of the 1950's and 1960's. Whether in the steel
mills, chemical works or collectives in the country, the conflicts to be resolved were everyday problems experienced by
the workers. Mechanical breakdowns, the unavailability of
crucially needed components of production, the lethargy of a
coworker harboring neofascist tendencies that threatened the
harmonious working relationship of the group were the focus
of these works. The central theme of an untold number of literary works of this period belabors the problems of a "Brigade"
faced with the near catastrophic prospect of not fulfilling its
assigned quota, thereby endangering not only its own well-being
but even the very foundation of the state. To resolve these
crises situations, the collective wisdom of the group is tapped.
In group discussions, the workers analyze the causes of their
problems, offer alternative solutions to them and then one by
one dedicate themselves to overcoming the hardships encountered
through personal sacrifice and greater zeal for the common
good. In true socialist harmony, the hardships are turned

into triumphs as the various members of the "Brigade" close
ranks to accomplish nearly impossible tasks. This collective
effort brings out the best in each individual and serves to
promote genuine friendship, trust, and mutual respect for each
other that culminates in a new sense of pride for their individual and collective achievements. Such a depiction of the
transformation from selfishness to selflessness in the home,
the work place and public arena that culminates in the evolution from a capitalist to a socialist society is the center
piece of socialist realism literature as advocated by Anna
Seghers: "Wir wünschen uns Bücher... die den Menschen verständlich machen, in welcher Richtung, durch alle Konflikte
hindurch, die Lösung liegt."[23]

True socialist realism literature, then, is didactic literature. It never leaves the reader in a state of bewilderment, despair or hopelessness. Instead, the reader is guided
to the proper answer along politically and humanistically
approved paths in order to bring about the needed regeneration
in the reader as exemplified in the work. In stark contrast
to Western literature, therefore, socialist realism is a positive, upbeat literature that depicts man as the master of his
fate. During times of personal doubt, uncertainty and even
despair, the GDR citizen can turn to socialist realism literature for spiritual sustenance and revitalization, knowing
full-well that every true socialist realism writer abides by
the credo: "Es gehört zu meinem Beruf, daB ich sowohl die
Leute, die ich darstelle, wie die Leute, die mich lesen, nicht
ratlos sitzen lasse."[24]

A striking example of the new relationship between the
political hierarchy, the writers and the workers is offered
by the Bitterfeld experience of 1959. The youth brigade
Nikolai Mamai, employed in the aluminum works in Bitterfeld,
had requested that the writers of the GDR devote their talents
to an even greater degree to the presentation of problems of
immediate concern to the workers. The youth brigade objected
to the works of many writers as mere fabrications of the mind,
subsequently lacking the necessary authenticity of the real

life of workers at home and on the job. At the same time
many workers aspired to improve their station in life by becoming writers themselves. As a result, a mutually beneficial
experiment was proposed:

1. sollten die Schriftsteller, die Kopfarbeiter,
   in die Betriebe gehen, mit Brigaden zusammen-
   arbeiten und die Arbeitsbedingungen an Ort und
   Stelle studieren;

2. sollten die 'Kumpel', die Handarbeiter, 'zur
   Feder greifen', um dadurch einerseits die all-
   täglichen Kämpfe und Fortschritte im Produk-
   tionsbereich zu dokumentieren und sich anderer-
   seits durch die eigene Schreibtätigkeit, die
   literarische Produktivität zu den 'Höhen der
   Kultur' emporzuarbeiten.[25]

The Bitterfeld experience epitomized in many ways the
strengths and weaknesses of socialism and its perspective of
the literary process. On the one hand it is certainly a credit
to the socialist doctrine of the equality of man that it would
respond so quickly and decisively to the wishes of the working
class to be represented and included more fully and accurately
in the works of literature. Even more noteworthy is the positive response of the politicians to the request of the workers
to gain entry to the literary profession as a symbolic gesture
of their full integration into society at all levels. Consequently, Walter Ulbricht's blessing of the concept of the
Bitterfeld Conference as a fulfillment of legitimate rights
of the workers and responsibility of the writers to the masses
must be viewed positively:

Wir sind der Meinung, daß es gerade 'die Ce-
genwartsaufgabe des Schriftstellers ist',
das Neue in der gegenwärtigen sozialistischen
Umgestaltung, in der Entwicklung des gesam-
ten wirtschaftlichen und kulturellen Lebens,
der neuen Beziehungen der Menschen, des neuen
gesellschaftlichen Lebens zu gestalten.[26]

The nearly three hundred worker-writers were ecstatic with

the overwhelming support extended to them by the professional
writers and the political hierarchy, leading one of these
worker zealots to proclaim:

> Heute ist der Kampf des freien Arbeiters in
> der sozialistischen Produktion die Grundlage
> unserer gesamten gesellschaftlichen Entwick-
> lung. Dabei kann nur der Schriftsteller Er-
> folg haben, der den Menschen in der Produktion
> kennt, mit ihm fühlt und mit ihm lebt. Ja,
> die größte Unterstützung bekommt unsere lite-
> rarische Entwicklung durch den Arbeiter selbst,
> wenn er zum Autor wird. Kumpel, greif zur
> Feder, die sozialistische Nationalkultur
> braucht dich.[27]

No matter how well-intentioned the goals of the First
Bitterfeld Conference may have been, the legacy of that experience is one of disillusionment and naiveté. More than that,
it is an indictment of the simplistic concept attributed by GDR
politicians to the role and scope of literature as perceived
throughout the centuries. Surely, the art of producing liter-
ature--even for political expediency--cannot be debased to the
degree suggested by the Bitterfeld experiment. Writers cannot
be herded into factories to be "sensitized" to the struggles
of man against machine, nor can they be dispatched to the collectives to gain greater empathy with those pitted against the
forces of nature in their unending quest for bounteous harvests.
A writer is a writer exactly because he is by nature more "sensitive," more "perceptive," more "empathetic," more "in tune"
with the hopes and fears, the joys and sorrows, the inner and
outer longings of his fellow man. Furthermore, the true writer
possesses the rare gift to communicate these characteristics in
a universally meaningful manner. The art of producing true literature, therefore, may be best defined as an "inherent gift"
possessed by only a few individuals. It is not a "skill" or
"craft" that can be taught in a few easy lessons to workers
who may aspire to become "writers" as is inferred by the Bitterfeld experience.

While the aftermath of the First Bitterfeld Conference may
have paid a few political dividends, the literary results must
be labelled an exercise in unmitigated mediocrity. The works
of both the professional and lay writers of this period are
characterized by a pervasive lack of originality, lack of character development and crude style. Work after work is mired
in endless description of the step by step rebuilidng process
of specific machinery and entire factories, an intolerably
detailed and boring accounting of statistics of productivity,
of a multitude of competing brigades, and worst of all, by
totally predictable plots that would even test the patience
of Job. In effect, the post-Bitterfeld era of literature may
be characterized as prefabricated, formula-based writing in
which only changes in names, products, dates and titles dis-
tinguish one work from another.

Even the Party functionaries lamented the deplorable state
of literature during the period of the Sixth Party Conference
of the SED in 1963. While paying lip service to the enthusiasm
displayed by the worker-writers in their literary efforts, the
Party urged the lay writers to expand their intellectual and
literary horizons in an effort to escape from the literary
morass of the last several years and called for greater depth
and breadth in socialist realism works:

Die im Kunstwerk gestalteten Erkenntnisse und
Gefühle dienen der moralischen Veränderung der
Menschen im Geiste des Sozialismus. Sie regen
sie zu großen Taten für den Sozialismus an, erwecken in ihnen die Liebe zur Arbeit, bereichern
das geistige Leben des Volkes, bilden die ratio-
nalen und emotionalen Fähigkeiten des Menschen
der sozialistischen Gemeinschaft und erziehen
ihn zu echter Lebensfreude...
Die Sozialistische Einheitspartei Deutschlands
setzt sich dafür ein, daß der sozialistische Realismus mit tiefem Ideengehalt, mit mehr Phan-
tasie und echtem Neuerertum, mit der ganzen
Weite seiner schöpferischen Möglichkeiten in den

verschiedenen Schaffensformen, Stilen und Gat-
tungen diese Aufgabe erfüllt.[28]

The Second Bitterfeld Conference of 1964 predictably steered
away from the course set at the first conference five years
earlier. Despite the literary fiasco, Walter Ulbricht declared
the experiences of the "Bitterfeld Weg" a huge success in that
it had won for the workers full amalgamation into society
through the "Erstürmung der Höhen der Kultur." Now that complete access to all echelons of society had been achieved for
all GDR citizens, it was argued, the task of producing works
of literature might be more properly returned to the professional writers. These writers, advised Ulbricht, should continue
to contribute their artistic talents to the noble task of advancing the cause of socialism:

> Die fachlich-künstlerischen, kulturpolitischen,
> wissenschaftlichen, ideologischen und selbst-
> verständlich auch ökonomischen Fragen der Kul-
> turentwicklung müssen zu einem vollständig aus-
> gebildeten System verbunden werden, das allen
> Funktionären, aber auch den Künstlern und den
> jeweiligen Bereichen als konkretes Arbeitspro-
> gramm dienen kann.[29]

The Second Bitterfeld Conference was by no means a renunciation of the function of literature as it had been ordained
during the pre-founding years of the GDR. It only represented
a retreat from the policies espoused during the First Bitterfeld Conference in which the workers were to carry the torch
of socialist realism literature. That task had now been returned to the professional writers in an effort to upgrade the
quality of literary works. Thus, the role and scope of literature had remained constant while the task to accomplish this
goal had been reassigned from the layman to the professional.
To this end, Walter Ulbricht in his main address at this conference reminded the writers of the awesome responsibility
vested in the power of the pen: "Ich sage offen: Wie gut und
wie schnell es bei uns vorwärts geht, das hängt in einem hohen
Grade von Ihrer zielstrebigen und guten Arbeit ab, von Ihren

Romanen und Dramen, Gedichten und Liedern, Bildern und Skulp-
turen."[30]

It was no coincidence that Walter Ulbricht himself delivered
the main address at the Second Bitterfeld Conference. His
presence in word and deed added weight to the unalterable role
that literature had played in the past and was to play in the
present and future in the GDR. Through his personal pronouncements Ulbricht put to rest the murmurs of discontent among many
writers for greater freedom of expression and independence in
exercising their profession. Thus, the frustration experienced
by many writers as a result of the restrictions imposed on them
by the criteria of socialist realism and the embarrassment of
the "Bitterfeld" experience nurtured an intense yearning for
intellectual exchange and debates with their counterparts in
the Federal Republic pertaining to theories and trends in literature. However, this longing on the part of GDR writers for
a more congenial climate between East and West in the area of
the arts was rebuked by Ulbricht as utterly inappropriate and
foolish:

> Es geht nicht darum, daB wir uns, wie manche
> behaupten, 'für die unmittelbare und direkte
> Auseinandersetzung mit der spätbürgerlichen
> Kultur und Kunst' zu schwach fühlten und sie
> deshalb bei uns keinen Platz hatte. Es geht
> darum, daB wir keine Sackgassen und Irrwege
> brauchen, um eine unserem Leben entsprechende
> Kunst zu schaffen.[31]

The final authority on this topic had spoken. As in the
past, literature in the GDR would continue its "service" function to the state. No internal or external pressure would
succeed in swaying it from this designated course. After all,
there was a job to be done. The socialist society was far from
complete. While the GDR had come a long way since 1949, it had
a longer way to go before it fulfilled its full aspirations as
a socialist society. Therefore, the continued cooperation,
commitment and contribution of every citizen of the GDR to the
fulfillment of this goal was sought and expected from those

who worked with their hands and those who worked with their
minds:

> Kunst und Literatur müssen sich wie jede andere
> gesellschaftlich notwendige Tätigkeit als nütz-
> lich erweisen. Sie tun dies durch ihre Resultate,
> also durch ihre Werke, deren Genuss dazu anregt,
> an der Gestaltung des eigenen und des gesellschaft-
> lichen Lebens mitzuarbeiten.[32]

With the introduction of the NÖSPL (Neues ökonomisches
System der Planung und Leitung) in 1964, the GDR had entered
into a new phase of its socio-economic development. While the
first fifteen years of the formal existence of the GDR had been
a continuous struggle to earn official recognition by the world
as an independent nation, to rebuilding a devastated industry,
and to charter a new political course under the watchful eye
of the Soviet Union, that work had now been completed. The
GDR had gained legitimacy as a sovereign state in the East and
West. The economy had been rebuilt to the point that the GDR
now belonged to the major industrial giants of the world. In
the area of international athletic competition, the GDR had
stunned the world with its spectacular success through its
disproportionate accumulation of gold, silver and bronze medals
in the Olympic games, thereby further enhancing its legitimacy
as a sovereign state.

Through hard work and great sacrifice, the people of the
GDR had risen from the ashes of World War II and within the
span of fifteen years had succeeded in providing for themselves
the highest standard of living of any Eastern Block nation.
While these achievements were genuine cause for pride and celebration, the inevitable comparison with their West German
counterparts revealed a glaring disparity in overall industrial
productivity and standard of life. Thus, the NÖSPL was specifically designed to close the gap between the GDR and FRG in
this area. "Increased productivity" became the slogan of an
entire nation in an all-out effort to catch up with and even
surpass their German counterparts on the other side of the Elbe
despite all of the built-in advantages enjoyed by the Federal

Republic in the areas of natural resources, population and the
Marshall Plan. The entire nation was mobilized to out-perform
the FRG in industrial productivity as they had done in sports.
The task of uniting the people in this common endeavor, as usual,
fell to the artists and writers. Consequently, the Seventh Party
Conference in 1967 enlisted the services of the GDR writers in
the transformation of the "entwickelte gesellschaftliche System
des Sozialismus" to its successful conclusion: "Die Perspektive
der Künste in unserer Republik ist bestimmt durch ihre Funktion
bei der Vollendung des Sozialismus."[33]

While the GDR did not succeed in outstripping or even equalling
the per capita productivity of the Federal Republic, it has
achieved a noticeable increase in the quality of its literature.
Even though most literary works still adhere to the guidelines
of socialist realism and conform to Party directives to promote
the fulfillment of the socialist society, many literary works
of the late 1960's and 1970's emerged from the level of pure
propaganda to achieve the status of genuine literature. No
longer are the works of the more prominent GDR writers laden
with burdensome statistics of competing brigades in their zeal
to outperform each other for the good of the impending socialist
society. Gone is the predictable type-casting of earlier days
and the inevitable triumph of the positive hero over material
and human impediments. Instead, character development, realistic personal and group conflicts have become the hallmark of
the new GDR literature. The headway made by the writers in improving the quality of their works was subsequently acknowledged
by the Eighth Party Conference of the SED. At the same time,
however, the writers were cautioned to retain the proper perspective in all their works:

Unser Ziel ist und bleibt die Erziehung gebilde-
ter und überzeugter Erbauer des Sozialismus, die
vom Geiste des proletarischen Internationalismus
erfüllt sind. Diesem Ziel sind wir ein gutes
Stück näher gekommen.
Unsere Schriftsteller und Künstler haben in
den letzten Jahren viele neue Werke geschaffen.

Die sozialistische Literatur, die Film,- Fern-
seh- und Theaterkunst, die Musik und bildende
Kunst streben nach Parteilichkeit und hoher
Aussagekraft. 'Sie zeichnen das Bild der Menschen, die unser sozialistisches Leben bewuBt
gestalten, deutlicher. Das erscheint uns als
der wichtigste Fortschritt.' Solche schöpferischen
Leistungen, in denen die Werktätigen die Gegenwart, ihre Probleme, Gefühle und Gedanken gestaltet finden, vermitteln ihnen Freude, An-
regung und Selbsterkenntnis.[34]

The advent of the Honecker era brought a further liberalization and increased independence to heretofore tightly controlled
segments of GDR life. Tangible evidence of real concessions
made by the government to the youth of the GDR in the name of
peace and tranquility could be seen by the appearance of longer
hair styles, blue jeans and the increased tolerance of rock
music. Tolerance of these fads that were scorned only a few
years earlier as "decadent" Western immorality reflected a new
sense of security and confidence prevailing in the GDR. GDR
citizens as a whole exhibited a new pride in their nation and
felt a greater confidence to express their opinions without
fear of being turned in by a "Spitzel." Slowly but surely the
nearly impossible happened--the people of the GDR cautiously
began to criticize government policies without being silenced.
While all criticism had to be "constructive" and, therefore,
limited to exposing weaknesses in individuals rather than Party
doctrine, the GDR, nevertheless, had taken a giant step forward
in its political maturity.

It is difficult to ascertain with any degree of certainty
whether the boldness to criticize public officials and their
policies began in the public sector and was subsequently incorporated into literature, or whether the growing criticism
in literature fostered greater independence of thought among
the public. Perhaps it is most accurate to say that they complemented one another. At any rate, much of GDR literature
slowly began to exhibit a refreshing independence of thought,

wit and charm that taunted many a Party bureaucrat and, therefore, would have been censored only a few years earlier. While
some critics attacked this trend toward a less constrained form
of socialist realism and called for an immediate suppression of
any practices in conflict with pure socialist realism principles,
the Honecker regime decided to lure the GDR writers back into
the mainstream of socialist realism tenets by means of a "carrot"
policy:

> ...die ganze Schönheit unseres Lebens meister-
> haft zu gestalten... Das setzt eine enge Verbin-
> dung der Künstler mit dem Leben und ihr bewuBtes,
> tiefes Verständnis für die Entwicklungsprozesse
> unserer Gesellschaft voraus. Dann werden die
> Schriftsteller und Künstler ohne Zweifel nicht
> nur die richtigen, unserer sozialistischen Gesell-
> schaft nützlichen Themen in den Mittelpunkt ihres
> Schaffens stellen, sondern auch die ganze Breite
> und Vielfalt der neuen LebensäuBerungen erfassen
> und ausschöpfen.[35]

Despite this apparent trend toward greater amelioration and
accomodation between the political and artistic communities, it
was obvious that these two forces were on a collision course.
How much freedom could the political hierarchy permit the writers
before all vestiges of socialist realism disappeared from literature and art? How long would it be before the "antics" of
Wolf Biermann became the norm? Was it not already too late to
stem the tide of "revisionist" literature a la Ulrich Plenzdorf's
"Die neuen Leiden des jungen W.," Volker Braun's "Die Kipper"
and Christa Wolf's "Nachdenken über Christa T."? What would be
the repercussions of such works if they were not checked quickly? Could they be the forerunners of an army of Robert Havemanns
or Rudolf Bahros? How much longer would it be until the dam of
political restraint broke completely?

The answer to these questions was quite clear. The brakes
had to be put on before it was too late. The only uncertainty
was the degree of the clampdown. How far should the clock be
rolled back to restore the "proper" relationship between the

arts and politics? The answer to this question was supplied
by Erich Honecker himself in May 1973 during the Ninth Plenary
Session of the Central Committee of the SED. In a stern lec-
ture directed at all artists and writers in the GDR, Honecker
deplored the anti-social current inherent in many artistic
works which represented a clear violation of socialist criteria:
"Die in verschiedenen Theaterstücken und Filmen dargestellte
Vereinsamung und Isolierung des Menschen von der Gesellschaft,
ihre Anonymität in bezug auf die gesellschaftlichen Verhältnisse
machen schon jetzt deutlich, daß die Grundhaltung solcher Werke
dem Anspruch des Sozialismus an Kunst und Literatur entgegen-
steht."[36]

Six months after these pronouncements by Erich Honecker, the
Seventh Writers' Conference was held. It was clear from the
beginning of this conference that Honecker's message had reached
each person in attendance. Thus, the tone of the conference was
set by Anna Seghers, the president of the "Schriftstellerverband
der DDR," in her opening address:

> Die sozialistische Kunst öffnet den Sinn für
> Frieden und für Gerechtigkeit. Das muß aus
> unserer Arbeit herausklingen, wie verschieden
> auch unsere Darstellungsarten sein mögen und
> die Stoffe, die sich die Künstler aussuchen.
> Wenn das klar geworden ist, können wir disku-
> tieren, ob diese oder jene Darstellungsart,
> dieses oder jenes Thema der Gesellschaft hilft,
> so zu werden, wie wir es wünschen. Fangen
> wir gleich auf diesem Kongreß damit an.[37]

It was apparent from these remarks that a compromise had
been reached. On the one hand there was to be absolutely no
deviation from the "Grundhaltung" of literature in promoting
the "neue sozialistische Persönlichkeit" and the completion of
the socialist society as Honecker had demanded. Allegiance to
the Party and state always would continue to be a non-negotiable characteristic of all works of art and literature. On the
other hand, the artists and writers were accorded greater freedom in expressing their "Parteilichkeit" to the state.

This new breathing room led to feverish experimentation in
form and content in GDR art and literature. Topics ranging
from the fantastic to the sublime, from the ludicrous to the
tragic were offered to the public in a format spanning the gamut
from realism to the abstract, from the authorial mode of narration to stream-of-consciousness. Thus, GDR art and literature
had taken another leap forward. A notable convergence with
Western literature in form and content had taken place.

Five years later the Central Committee of the SED condoned
this new ameliorating relationship between literature and politics in its "GruBschreiben an den VIII. SchriftstellerkongreB"
held in May 1978. As before, the Party demanded absolute allegiance from its writers in promoting the fulfillment of the
socialist state. At the same time, however, it reaffirmed its
relaxed attitude toward the manner in which literature was to
pursue this goal:

> Vor allem jene Werke finden groBe Beachtung und
> Verbreitung, die gesellschaftlich bedeutsame
> Vorgänge der Geschichte und der Gegenwart er-
> fassen, dem Schöpfertum der aktiven Erbauer des
> Sozialismus künstlerischen Ausdruck verleihen
> und sich durch Parteilichkeit, Volksverbundenheit
> und hohen sozialistischen Ideengehalt auszeichnen.
> Unsere Partei bringt allen Bemühungen der Schrift-
> steller Verständnis und Aufmerksamkeit entgegen,
> die unsere sozialistisch-realistische Literatur
> bereichern und ihre ideologische Wirkungskraft
> verstärken. Wie sich das Leben im Ringen um die
> Verwirklichung unserer sozialistischen Ideale
> verändert, so verändern sich auch die Inhalte,
> Themen und Gestaltungsweisen der sozialistisch-
> realistischen Literatur. In unserer Gesellschaft
> haben alle literarischen Bemühungen ihren Platz
> und ihr Wirkungsfeld, die dem Frieden und dem
> Humanismus, der Demokratie, der antiimperiali-
> stischen Solidarität und dem realen Sozialismus
> verpflichtet sind.[38]

It seems that the great majority of writers belonging to
the "Schriftstellerverband der DDR" are satisfied with this
compromise. They genuinely want to contribute to a regeneration of man, and for the most part, are in agreement with the
political philosophy of socialism. Thus, there seems to be no
activist element among GDR writers that wishes to "bring down"
the political system, as some Westerners mistakenly proclaim.
The general contentment of GDR writers with their assigned
role as advocates of the state is reflected in the recent declaration of the delegates to the Eighth Writers' Conference to
the Central Committee of the SED:

> Das Wohl der sozialistischen Gesellschaft braucht
> und fördert die kameradschaftliche Zusammenarbeit.
> Sie überwindet den Gegensatz von Geist und Macht.
> Wir bekräftigen deshalb unser Bekenntnis zur
> Deutschen Demokratischen Republik, die das huma-
> nistische Erbe bewahrt und die revolutionären Er-
> rungenschaften unseres Volkes schützt und mehrt.
> Wir bekräftigen unser Bekenntnis zur Politik der
> Sozialistischen Einheitspartei Deutschlands, deren
> Beschlüsse auf dem VIII. und IX. Parteitag das
> gesellschaftlich Nötige und Mögliche weitblickend
> formuliert haben. Wir rufen alle Schriftsteller
> unseres Landes auf, die Erfüllung dieser Beschlüsse
> durch gemeinsame Arbeit für eine Literatur zu för-
> dern, die den Idealen des Kommunismus verpflich-
> tet ist und den realen Sozialismus stärkt.[39]

While such subservience by writers to any political philosophy is alien to Western notions of the role and scope of literature, most GDR writers accept their service role as a legitimate expectation of the state. Yet, Western skeptics continue
to ask: How many of the GDR writers truly support the statements of solidarity with Party politics emanating from these
conferences? How many would wash their hands from all political associations if given the chance? How many would advocate
a·total separation of literature from politics and demand complete independence for their profession?

Any specific response to these questions is pure speculation.
The fact is that no one knows. The only reliable clues pointing
to the real feelings of GDR writers toward socialism are provided
by those authors who have left their homeland and now reside in
the West. These writers, almost without exception, have remained
loyal to socialism while criticizing the current imperfections
of that system. Consequently, the "Gruβschreiben der Delegierten
an das ZK der SED" must be seen as more than lip service of the
"servant" to his "master." The members of the "Schriftstellerverband der DDR" seem committed to the goals set forth by the
SED. They may not like all of the restrictions put upon them
as artists, but they take seriously their obligation and opportunities to contribute to the establishment of a new socialist
society:

> Die Verantwortung des zeitgenössischen Autors
> in der sozialistischen Gesellschaft ist unab-
> trennbar mit seiner politischen und mora-
> lischen Verantwortung für den Sozialismus ver-
> bunden. Er kann ihr nur gerecht werden, wenn
> er sich bewuβt in die Gesellschaft stellt, an
> ihrer Entwicklung aktiv teilnimmt und nicht aus
> ihr heraustritt.[40]

This chronological overview has demonstrated the steadfast
adherence of socialist realism literature to its service function
to the state. From the onset of the Soviet military occupation
in 1945, to the founding of the German Democratic Republic in
1949, to the establishment of the "entwickelte sozialistische
Gesellschaft" in 1964, to the present, literature in the GDR
has served as "Wegweiser," "Vorkämpfer" and "Urheber der neuen
sozialistischen Persönlichkeit." It is dedicated to the depiction of the transformation of mankind from callous, self-centered
individuals into benevolent, group-oriented advocates of socialism. Indeed, if one were to strip all of the political ramifica-
tions from socialist realism literature, the remaining characteristics of the positive hero in the service of mankind are
strikingly reminiscent of the ideals espoused by Lessing, Schiller
and Goethe. Unfortunately, the tenets of socialist realism do

not condone the depiction of these noble characteristics apart
from the proper political frame. Consequently, writers of socialist realism literature must always be on guard to fulfill
the primary function prescribed for them by the political hierarchy:

> Impulse zu geben zu einem klassenbewußten
> sozialistischen Denken, Fühlen und Ver-
> halten, zu Handlungen schließlich, die
> der Einheit von individuellen und gesell-
> schaftlichen Interessen gemäß sind und damit
> auf die Festigung und Entwicklung der sozi-
> alistischen Lebensweise orientieren, die es
> letztlich dem einzelnen und der Gemeinschaft
> ermöglicht, die von Sozialismus geschaffenen
> materiellen und kulturellen Werte auch zur
> Grundlage des eigenen schöpferischen Lebens
> zu machen.[41]

Chapter II

The Nature of Socialist Realism

Despite the overwhelming number of works dealing with the
general topic of socialist realism,[1] there remains a genuine
state of bewilderment among experts and laymen alike as to the
precise nature of this literary phenomenon. The cause for this
confusion and uncertainty pertaining to the specific characteristics of socialist realism may be attributed in part to the
fact that no one has provided an all-encompassing, satisfactory
definition of this term. Compounding the problem is the fact
that neither Marx nor Engels expounded in any great detail on
literary theory[2] while Lenin's pronouncements on this subject
are generally restricted to "Parteiliteratur" rather than literary theory per se. In the absence of an unquestioned point
of reference, therefore, past definitions of socialist realism
focused only on particular aspects of this concept while omitting
others. This hit-or-miss approach has escalated the ongoing
debate over the necessary criteria for an acceptable definition
of socialist realism.

A. The Founding of Socialist Realism in the USSR

The first definitions of socialist realism surfaced during
the formative years of this concept in the Soviet Union. In
1933 P. Rožkov argued that the emergence of socialist realism
was a natural result of historical dialectics. As the dialectical process of historical materialism had fostered a change
in the political sphere from Czarist Russia to Soviet communism,
argued Rožkov, a corresponding modification in the perception
and depiction of reality in literature had occurred: "Der
Sozialistische Realismus ist der konkrete Ausdruck des dialektischen Materialismus in der Kunst, ähnlich wie der historische
Materialismus der konkrete Ausdruck des dialektischen Materialismus in der Geschichte ist."[3]

Rožkov's characterization of socialist realism as a product
of the times was supported by Andrej Ždanov, Stalin's minister
of culture, during the first All Union Conference of Soviet

Writers in 1934. Ždanov's definition of socialist realism is
particularly noteworthy in that he was the first person to advocate the exploitation of this new literary method for political purposes:

> Der sozialistische Realismus... fordert vom Künst-
> ler wahrheitsgetreue, historisch konkrete Darstel-
> lung der Wirklichkeit in ihrer revolutionären Ent-
> wicklung. Wahrheitstreue und historische Konkretheit
> der künstlerischen Darstellung muß mit den Aufgaben
> der ideologischen Umgestaltung und Erziehung der
> Werktätigen im Geiste des Sozialismus verbunden
> werden.[4]

Socialist realism, as the name suggests, according to Ždanov,
was not to strive to present a realistic or objective depiction
of reality but rather a reality as seen through socialist lenses.
This aspect of Ždanov's definition has remained the cornerstone
of socialist realism literature to this day.

Socialist realism literature by definition, therefore, is
bound to a "Weltanschauung" characterized by the evolution from
bourgeois capitalism to socialism and eventually to communism.
This perception of reality is deemed the only correct and therefore "scientific" view of the world. Any interpretation of
reality in conflict with the socialist realism "Weltanschauung"
is automatically labelled as "unscientific" and summarily discarded as a "revisionist" plot to undermine the proper course
of history. Thus, André Stil, the leading spokesman for the
French Communist Party pertaining to literary theory during the
1950's, also emphasized the service function of socialist realism literature. In order to qualify a work of literature as
a work of socialist realism, it must

> 1) eine wissenschaftliche Auffassung von der Welt
> zum Ausdruck bringen und mit den historischen Tat-
> sachen übereinstimmen; 2) exakt die Aktion und den
> politischen Kampf der Arbeiterklasse wiedergeben,
> der sich unter der Führung der Partei vollzieht;
> 3) den Optimismus aufzeigen, d.h. die Perspektive
> der sozialistischen Gesellschaftsentwicklung und

nicht irgendwelche abstrakte Zustände der Freude;
4) den Menschen verstehen und lieben lehren; 5) ein
HöchstmaB an ideologischem Wert erreichen, jedoch
nicht durch ständiges Sich-berufen auf die politische Argumentation, was unweigerlich zum Schematismus führen würde, sondern durch die Schilderung
des Lebens selbst.[5]
A remarkably similar characterization of socialist realism
was advocated by S. Aaronovich during a conference on socialist realism sponsored by the British Communist Party for the
specific purpose of delineating more clearly this thorny issue.
Edward Mozejko aptly summarizes the pertinent elements of socialist realism advanced by Aaronovich as follows:

a) Der Sozialistische Realismus muB in seiner Form
national und in seinem Inhalt sozialistisch sein;
national bedeutet, daB jede Nation ihre eigenen
Merkmale, ihre eigene Geschichte und ihre besondere
Psyche hat, was dazu verpflichtet, die klassische
und volkstümliche Tradition in der Entwicklung
der Nationalkultur eines jeden Volkes zu berück-
sichtigen; in GroBbritannien impliziert die Definition 'national in der Form' den Kampf gegen
die Invasion der amerikanischen 'Lebensweise'. Sozialistisch heiBt, daB die Kunst für die Sache
der Arbeiterklasse zu kämpfen hat.
b) Der Sozialistische Realismus muB eine getreue
und historisch konkrete Widerspiegelung der Wirklichkeit sein; der Schriftsteller, der sich dieser Methode bedient, muB ständig auf die Wahl des Details
bedacht sein, um eine naturalistische Darstellung
der Ereignisse zu vermeiden, die gewöhnlich das
Bild der Wirklichkeit verzerrt; zum anderen darf
er nicht vergessen, daB die Kunst, ähnlich wie die
Wissenschaft, aufgrund von Beobachtungen und Erfahrungen Verallgemeinerungen schafft. Eine historisch
konkrete Darstellung ermöglicht stets die Schaffung
eines bestimmten Gesellschaftstyps in der Literatur

und vermeidet somit den Schematismus.

c) Der Sozialistische Realismus zeigt die Wirklichkeit in ihrer stetigen Entwicklung; dieses Merkmal
ist eng mit dem vorhergehenden verbunden, denn eine
getreue und historisch konkrete Darstellung der Wirklichkeit ist ohne eine nähere Erklärung ihrer Entstehung, Veränderung und Entwicklung unmöglich.

d) Der Sozialistische Realismus hat eine erzieheri-
sche Aufgabe in der Gesellschaft zu erfüllen; er
soll den Leser im Geist des Kampfes um den Sozialismus erziehen. Dieses Merkmal setzt die Einbe-
ziehung der revolutionären Romantik in den Sozialistischen Realismus voraus.

e) Das fünfte Merkmal des Sozialistischen Realismus
schließlich ist die Widerspiegelung des Typischen.
(Aaronovich wiederholt hierbei die bekannte For-
mulierung Malenkovs aus dessen Referat anläßlich
des XIX. Parteikongresses in Moskau 1952.)[6]

Finally, Hans Koch, the renowned literary critic residing
in the GDR, is content to limit his definition of socialist
realism to the service function first advocated by Ždanov:
"Die Methode des sozialistischen Realismus ist die Methode des
künstlerischen Schaffens vom Standpunkt der revolutionären Arbeiterklasse und der historischen Entwicklung des Sozialismus."[7]

This overview of definitions of socialist realism demonstrates
the inadequacy of past efforts to deal systematically with the
essence of this literary phenomenon. While all critics acknowledge the function of socialist realism to be the advancement of
socialism, few of these experts enumerate the specific criteria
by which this goal is to be achieved. Consequently, the reader
is left in a benign state of neglect concerning the genesis,
evolution and precise criteria ascribed to socialist realism
in the GDR. It is the purpose of this chapter to provide satisfactory answers to these questions in order to enable any reader
of GDR literature to determine to what degree the work at hand
conforms to or deviates from the precepts of socialist realism,
thereby putting an end to the bewilderment and confusion surround-

ing this concept as expressed by Ernst Fischer:

> Außerdem weiß man in Diskussionen (concerning socialist realism-G.B.) oft nicht, wovon die Rede ist: von der 'Gesinnung' des Autors oder von seinen künstlerischen Ausdrucksmitteln, von seiner 'Thematik' oder 'formalen' Kriterien, von 'Politik' oder 'Kunst'. Es gab und gibt einander widersprechende ästhetische Definitionen des 'sozialistischen Realismus'[8]

It is of central importance to begin this discussion with the understanding that socialist realism is not the result of a natural evolution of one literary movement into another, nor is it the product of a reaction of one literary period to another. The genesis of socialist realism occurred totally out of context of the literary environment. Socialist realism is quite simply the product of political fiat.

The beginning of socialist realism can be traced directly to the totalitarian order imposed upon the Soviet people under the regime of Joseph Stalin. Stalin was less patient than his predecessor W.I. Lenin in permitting the Russian people a gradual adjustment to communist policies instituted after the October Revolution in 1917. In 1930, Stalin ordered an immediate speedup in the "derussification" process of the Russian populace and a transformation to the new "Soviet" prototype as envisioned by the communist ideology. It was clear to Stalin that the hoped for metamorphosis of the Russian proletariat and peasants to inspired advocates of communism required extraordinary measures. To achieve this goal, nothing less than a complete psychological regeneration of the Russian populace was required. The central question confronting the rulers of that vast nation was: What are the most effective means of transforming the great masses of the Soviet Union from disinterested, apathetic bystanders to ardent supporters of communism?

The answer to this question came in December 1930 when Stalin informed Demjan Bedny, a revolutionary Soviet writer, that the herculean task of transforming widespread Soviet apathy toward communism into active proponents of the new political ideology

had been assigned to literature. In order to bring this monumental assignment to a successful conclusion, a drastic change
in the role and scope of literature had to be implemented. Literature could no longer be permitted to pursue an independent
"l'art pour l'art" policy as had been the case up to this time.
Instead, all works of literature were henceforth expected to
adhere to narrow guidelines established by the state.

In order to ensure that all writers adhered to the guidelines
set forth by the political hierarchy, the Soviet Writers' Association was founded at the request of the state. This writers' association should not be equated to a writers' union or
similar organizations that exist for the purpose of securing
individual and/or collective rights for their membership. The
Soviet Writers' Association did none of these things. On the
contrary, the purpose of this association was to provide a con-
venient mechanism by which the government could scrutinize the
literary output of its members, identify and take appropriate
action against any dissidents, and disseminate its directives
to all the writers of the Soviet Union. Thus, the creation of
this writers' association enabled Stalin to kill two birds with
one stone. While the formation of the writers' association appeared to be a magnanimous gesture by Stalin to Soviet intellec-
tuals and men of letters to advance their literary interests,
this forum was used as a means of suppressing dissent and directing the new literary method according to the dictates of the
state. In this new role literature in the Soviet Union played
the primary role in transforming the Russian people into proponents of the socialist cause. With one clean stroke Stalin
had succeeded in relegating the writer to the role of "Ingenieur
der menschlichen Seele," a role heretofore alien to the literary profession in that country.

The blueprint, which the "Ingenieure der menschlichen Seele"
were forced to follow in transforming the character of the Soviet
society, was labelled "socialist realism." Although it is impossible to pinpoint with absolute certainty the first appearance of this term, all indications point to May 20, 1932 as the
date of its formal introduction to the public. On this day

I. Gronskij, the chief editor of "Izvestija," the official newspaper of the government, delivered a speech to an assembly of
various literary groups. In this speech Gronskij proclaimed
socialist realism as the new literary method within which Soviet
writers were to find their artistic expression. Three days later
on May 23, 1932, the "Literaturnaja Gazeta" (The Literary Newspaper) published Gronskij's pronouncements, thereby marking the
first written appearance of this term.[9] On May 29, 1932 another
article entitled "Za rabotu" (Let's Get to Work) appeared in
this same newspaper in which all Soviet writers were exhorted
to make the concept of socialist realism a success by adopting
this new literary method in their works.[10] In October of the
same year, Stalin met with a number of Soviet authors in the
home of Maxim Gorkij. During this meeting Stalin himself en-
dorsed the merits of socialist realism and coined the phrase
"Ingenieure der menschlichen Seele" as an appropriate characterization of the new function of Soviet writers as contributors to
the effort to restructure the mental and social fabric of the
Soviet society.

During the First All Union Writers' Conference held in August
1934, socialist realism was adopted as the official literary
method for all Soviet writers. The form and content of socialist
realism were codified under the watchful eye of Andrei Ždanov,
the secretary of the Leningrad Communist Party. Complete authority was given to the Communist Party in determining the appropriate subject matter and style of socialist realism literature
during the time of its inception and in the future. Thus, it
was already decided at this conference that socialist realism
literature would "liberate" itself from the influence of Western
literature by means of a thorough cleansing from such negative
elements as eroticism, alienation, negativism, despair and psychological intrigue while emphasizing such positive characteristics as the joy derived from hard work and the satisfaction
experienced from contributing to the building of a socialist
society. To this end, the writers were exhorted to look to the
great classics for inspiration. As the classicists strove for
the attainment of the highest ideals in man and society, so the

writers of socialist realism were urged to portray the regeneration of man who was dedicated to the establishment of socialist
ideals.

The official definition of socialist realism adopted by the
First All Union Writers' Conference was taken from the founding
document of the Soviet Writers' Association. It reflected precisely Stalin's directive to subjugate literature to the needs
of the state: "Als die grundlegende Methode der sowjetischen
schönen Literatur und der Kritik fordert der Sozialistische Realismus vom Künstler eine wahrheitsgetreue, historisch korrekte
Darstellung der Wirklichkeit in ihrer revolutionären Entwicklung."[11]

Thus, it is clear that the genesis of socialist realism was
the result of political maneuvers by Joseph Stalin in an effort
to reshape the Soviet society rather than the result of intrin-
sic or extrinsic literary causes. Consequently, socialist realism must be understood as a literary method that even today is
controlled by politicians whose primary concern is the attainment of political goals through literary means. Socialist realism literature by definition can not be apolitical literature.
As its name indicates, it is directly tied to the socialist
ideology whose goals it is pledged to extol.

Following the adoption of socialist realism during the First
All Union Writers' Conference, it became clear that the nature
of this new literary phenomenon had already been determined by
an organizational committee that was cleverly stacked in favor
of the political interests advocated by Joseph Stalin. The
four-member committee consisted of three professional politicians, A. Ždanov, K. Radek, N. Bucharin, and only one writer,
M. Grokij, who alone boldly advocated universally recognized and
respected literary techniques in implementing socialist realism:
"Der Mythos ist Erfindung. Erfinden heißt, aus der Summe dessen,
was real ist, den grundlegenden Sinn herauszuholen und ihn
bildlich darzustellen--auf diese Weise erhalten wir Realismus."[12]

Despite Gorkij's efforts the three politicians presented a
solid front in carrying out Stalin's mandate to subordinate socialist realism to Party politics. They remembered very clearly

Stalin's pronouncement to the assembled writers in Gorkij's home
on October 26, 1932 concerning his concept of socialist realism:
"Der Künstler soll vor allem das Leben darstellen. Wenn er unser
Leben wahrheitsgetreu schildert, dann muß er das wahrnehmen,
muß er das zeigen, was zum Sozialismus führt. Eben das wird
Sozialistischer Realismus sein."[13] In conformity with these
views, Ždanov called for a "realistic" presentation of life.
Realism in this context, however, did not refer to a naturalistic reflection of life but rather the Marxian sense of "real,"
which is defined as the correct interpretation of reality in
its evolution from a capitalist to a socialist order. All socialist realism literature, therefore, was obligated to portray
this evolutionary process no matter what specific aspect of life
it illustrated. In a similar manner, Radek stressed the importance of transcending the scope of previous periods of literature
such as 19th century poetic realism and naturalism which were
satisfied with a mere reflection of reality in their works. Socialist realism literature on the other hand was to be future-
oriented. The focus of socialist realism was not on mere depiction of reality as it is, but rather on its transformation to
"what could and should be," thereby unveiling the transition of
all societies toward socialism.

The most ardent disciple of the Stalinist view to subordinate
literature to the role of an adjunct tool of the state was found
in N.A. Dubroljubov. Dubroljubov interpreted the function of
literature purely as a sophisticated propaganda tool of the
state. As such, socialist realism literature had the sole function of popularizing government policy in an aesthetically pleas-
ing and palatable manner. Socialist realism literature was to
serve as a transformer of the minds and hearts of the populace
according to government needs. Therefore, the depiction of
happy, healthy, robust people engaged in the many needed tasks
to achieve the new socialist society relied on the effect of
mass psychology to convert the antagonistic and undecided elements within the population to jump on the bandwagon and to
become converts of socialism. These proposals by Dubroljubov
served as the basis for the inception of the "positive hero" as

a key component in socialist realism literature.

Having established the function of socialist realism as an instrument of the government in the conversion process of the Soviet society to socialism, the question remained as to the best means by which this goal could be achieved. What specific characteristics could socialist realism literature utilize to make the strongest possible impact on the Soviet citizens? Since socialist realism literature was aimed primarily at the great masses of the Russian people, it was obvious that the form of this literary method would have to be rather simple and direct. Therefore, such complicated stylistic modes of narration as stream-of-consciousness and narrated or interior monolog were immediately discarded as inappropriate and even counterproductive to the goals of this literary method. Instead, the early advocates of socialist realism called for a reflection of reality along the lines of 19th century poetic realism. Belinskij in particular insisted on a portrayal of reality through an abundance of pictures as an effective method for transmitting the central ideas to unsophisticated readers. In contrast to poetic realism, however, these "pictures" should not reflect a middle class or bourgeois perspective but rather the viewpoints of the great masses of the world in general and those of the Soviet Communist Party in particular.

Socialist realism, therefore, was predicated upon the proposition that the highest form of art and literature is a realistic reflection of reality. For this reason the concept of "Widerspiegelung" of reality plays a central role in the mode of presentation of socialist realism works. It is crucial, therefore, to have a proper understanding of the Marxist use of this term.

Throughout history literary philosophers have engaged in endless debates concerning the precise nature of reality, culminating in Immanuel Kant's treatises to determine the essence of "das Ding an sich." While it was generally established by philosophers that reality is indeed composed of specific anatomical characteristics, it is also commonly accepted that there exists a reality beyond these physical traits. This reality is determined by the individual's perspective, point of view or lenses by which the object, concept or political philosophy is perceived. Thus, the concept of the New Testament God is on the one hand worshipped by millions of Christians as the creator and sustainer of all that exists while others perceive this same concept as the preposterous imagination of weaklings, unable to cope with reality.

Likewise, the same socio-political system may at the same time be extolled fanatically by some, while others are sworn to its eradication at all cost. It is merely a difference in perspective that serves as the determining factor in perceiving the same entity in antithetical ways. In a similar manner, the proponents of socialist realism claim the right to view reality from a socialist perspective in which history is interpreted as a continuous struggle between the upper and lower classes. Seen from this vantage point, the untold revolutions and uprisings through the ages provide convincing testimony to this interpretation of history. Slowly but surely, the socialists claim, the proletariat of the world has succeeded in liberating itself from the oppression of its masters as was the case in the Soviet Union during the October Revolution. Accordingly, it is the mission of socialist realism to spread the good news of the past victories, to encourage the elimination of suppression wherever it still exists, and to portray the vision of a life of equality, justice and fraternal brotherhood in the impending socialist societies of the world. This admittedly tainted perspective of history is characterized by the term "Parteilichkeit." It too is a central component of socialist realism, and any work that does not adhere to this viewpoint deviates from the "correct" perspective of historical evolution.

Another characteristic established as a mainstay of socialist realism during its founding days is its emphasis on dealing with the "typical" or "das Typische" of life. Instead of dealing with elements of the exotic, the fantastic or bizarre so characteristic of Western literature, socialist realism attempts to portray ordinary, everyday aspects of life from which the reader may gain insight in solving his problems. Socialist realism literature, therefore, is pedagogical in nature in that it attempts to teach its readers how to cope with daily hardships in a way that will enhance the quality of life of the individual and the community. This positivist approach to life is exemplified in the character of the "positive hero" who is confronted with a myriad of typical problems which he learns to overcome in a manner consistent with socialist mores, thereby earning the respect of both his fellow man and the Party. The underlying lesson to the reader is to emulate the actions of this "hero" and thereby to earn similar accolades in individual and collective efforts.

Closely aligned to the characteristic of the "typical" in socialist realism is the requirement for "Volkstümlichkeit" or "national traits." The emphasis on national traits in socialist realism literature must be understood within the context of its didactic framework. The progenitors of socialist realism did not place a high priority on expanding the minds of their readers by familiarizing them with unique or unusual lifestyles in foreign lands, cataclysmic events or adventures of the mind. The primary concern of Stalin, Ždanov and Gronskij was the education of their readers about past and current events and conditions in the Soviet Union that are of relevance to them. By focusing on the national scene, socialist realism works imparted a greater urgency and impelling need for all Soviet citizens to participate actively in the eradication of remaining social and economic problems in the USSR, thereby improving their personal station in life and contributing to the establishment of a true socialist society.

B. The Emergence of Socialist Realism in the GDR

The emergence of socialist realism was sparked by a remarkably similar set of circumstances in the German Democratic Republic as had been the case in the Soviet Union. As we have seen, socialist realism in the USSR was the result of the drastic transition from Czarist Russia to Soviet communism. Specifically, socialist realism was introduced by a new political order to accelerate the transformation of the old Russian mentality to the new Soviet spirit according to the precepts of Marxism/Leninism. In parallel fashion socialist realism made its appearance in the GDR as the direct result of the replacement of national socialism by communism following the defeat of Germany in World War II. As in the case of the Soviet Union, socialist realism was instituted by the new political order of the GDR for the expressed purpose of reshaping the "Weltanschauung" of its populace according to the new political reality. In short, history had indeed repeated itself.

Following the end of World War II, the German population residing in the Soviet Occupied Zone suddenly found itself in the astonishing position of having to undergo an immediate Saul to Paul political conversion. These Germans were not only expected to be miraculously cleansed of their former associations with Nazism but were impelled to embrace a sociopolitical system that was abhorrent to the overwhelming majority of East Germans. Even the most optimistic of the German and Russian bureaucrats were fully aware of the immense task before them. As in the case of the Soviet Union following the October Revolution, this overwhelming assignment called for similar extraordinary measures. Thus, it came as no surprise to students of Soviet history that the communists, when faced with the recurring task of transforming the mindset of an entire nation from totalitarian to communist ideals, would apply the same model on foreign soil that had proved to be successful within their own borders.

Indeed, the Socialist Unity Party wasted no time in initiating the adoption of socialist realism as the official mode of literature on East German soil following the termination of World War II. The urgency for the transplanting of socialist realism unto East German soil was motivated by the fear on the part of the communists that the generally liberal climate pertaining to the arts in the Soviet Occupied Zone after 1945 might strike deep roots in the hearts and minds of the writers and public which would make the task of reeducation more difficult as time went by.[14]

Following the model of the Soviet Union, a German Writers' Association (Schriftstellerverband) was organized ostensibly for the purpose of marshalling the collective wisdom of its members in setting the future course of GDR literature. In reality, however, the German Writers' Association served only as a rubber stamp to the guidelines and decrees that were formulated

during each Party Conference preceding every meeting of the
writers' association. As in the Soviet Union, therefore, the
founding of the German Writers' Association is not to be interpreted as a magnanimous gesture on the part of the political
hierarchy to encourage intellectual exchange among the writers.
On the contrary, the founding of the German Writers' Association
served the same purpose as its Soviet counterpart--to act as a
conduit for decrees from the SED to the writers, to chart the
direction of literature in the GDR, and to control the literary
output of its members.

In accordance with a scenario devised by government officials
of the Soviet Occupied Zone, the concept of socialist realism
was introduced during the first conference of the writers' association held on October 4-8, 1947. This first conference of the
writers' association served as a precedent for future meetings
by adhering precisely to the guidelines provided for it by the
"Bundes-Kongreß des Kulturbundes" on May 19-21, 1947. The agenda
of the first "Bundes-Kongreß des Kulturbundes" discloses the
pivotal role it played in determining the work of the first
writers' association conference, thereby providing a model for
all future writers' association meetings in the GDR. One by one,
members of the SED extolled the great achievements in the recent
literature of their Soviet liberators. Johannes R. Becher
praised the "Vorrang" of Soviet literature in the advancement
of human freedom and labelled the Soviet experience as a literary achievement worthy of imitation. Alexander Abusch went
further than Becher by proposing a lock, stock and barrel adoption of the Soviet literary model. Alexander Abusch denounced
the "Freiheit der Persönlichkeit" as a "Waffe der Mächte des
Rückschritts" and discredited all opposition to the emulation of
Soviet socialist realism as mere "Hetze" against the Soviet
Union.[15] Finally, Colonel Tulpanov of the Soviet Military Administration sternly conveyed the Soviet perspective and expec-
tations of the East Germans regarding the proposals made by
Becher and Abusch: "Für Deutschland und die ganze Welt gilt als
Prüfstein der Ehrlichkeit und der Konsequenz eines jeden
Demokraten, ich sage schon nicht von denen, die sich Sozialisten

nennen, sein Verhältnis zur Sowjetunion."[16] It was now clear
to everyone that the Russians would not tolerate any deviation
from the prescribed path of socialist realism literature as
formulated by them for internal and external implementation.
Thus, the foundation for the importation of socialist realism
had been laid. Accordingly, the German Writers' Association
did its duty and "adopted" socialist realism as the official
literary method within the Soviet Occupied Zone.

The new reality of post-war life under Soviet occupation
made itself apparent more quickly than most people had expected.
Already the first two-year plan for 1949/50 emanating from the
central government introduced far-reaching changes for GDR citizens in general and for writers in particular. The two-year
plan called for a new literature in the GDR through which dignity was restored to the human being. This new literature would
emphasize the importance of reeducation and total regeneration
of mankind by embracing a new humanism that rejected sterile
abstraction and existential dabblings found in Western literature.[17] The center piece of this new literature was the cultivation of the noble instincts in man which would culminate in the
establishment of a new socialist society. Alexander Abusch even
urged all artists to go to factories and villages to proclaim
the good news of the impending new society to all in his speech
"Die Schriftsteller und der Plan." Abusch implored the writers
to educate the public to the wave of the future and at the same
time to be receptive to the invaluable education afforded them
as a result of the direct contact with the common people.[18]

Thus, the concept of socialist realism had gained a substan-
tial foothold as official doctrine when the fledgling "Arbeiter-
und Bauernstaat" made its appearance on the world scene. Yet,
there remained a persistent element of non-conformists who
continued their "decadent" ways by their adherence to literary
experimentation in violation of socialist realism guidelines.
Obviously this dabbling in despised formalism could not be
tolerated. Consequently, an official anti-formalism campaign
was instituted in 1951 to wipe out the last vestiges of this
heresy. The irony of the attempt by GDR officials to cleanse

East German literature of all remnants of such despised Western
literary elements as the existence of powerful, anonymous forces
that intruded into the lives of individuals for no apparent
reason was reinforced by the very actions of this newest dicta-
torship of the proletariat:

> Es hat sich bei uns eine Kafkasche Atmosphäre
> entwickelt. Wahrhaftig, das merkwürdige, mir
> bislang schwer eingängige Genie des Verfassers
> von 'Der Prozeß' ist mir erst durch die Er-
> fahrungen der jüngst vergangenen Zeit verständ-
> licher geworden. Es ist eine unheimliche Reali-
> sation. Da werden Entscheidungen über einen ge-
> fällt, von denen man nichts erfährt; Beratungen
> werden über einen geführt, aber man kennt die
> Mitglieder des beratenden Gremiums nicht; irgend-
> wo liegen Akten, man weiß nicht, was in ihnen
> steht; der Rechtspruch bleibt in suspens, und
> man rätselt, an wen gegebenenfalls zu appellieren
> sei; der, von dem man vermutet, er habe ein
> wohlerwogenes Urteil gefällt, gibt öffentlich
> seiner Verwunderung darüber Ausdruck, daß aus
> geheimnisvollen Gründen das (von ihm exekutierte)
> Schauspiel nicht mehr am Leben sei, ist aber
> seither zu keiner weiteren Äußerung zu bringen...[19]

Despite the contradictions in literary theory and everyday
reality the political hierarchy succeeded in implementing socialist realism as the only legitimate literary method in the
GDR. Indeed, Marxist critics perceive socialist realism as
the most advanced form of literature in that it alone reflects
accurately the transition from a capitalist to a socialist society in conformity with Marxist dialectical materialism. Furthermore, these critics claim, socialist realism must be regarded
as the crown of literary achievement in that it for the first
time affords the writer the opportunity to blend his subjective
creativity with objective reality:

> Der sozialistische Realismus ist die erste
> künstlerische Methode, die den Gegenstand der

künstlerischen Aneignung adäquat historisch
zu fassen vermag, die sich auf eine in ihren
historischen Zusammenhängen erkannte, in ihrer
gesetzmäßigen historischen Entwicklung und revolutionären Veränderung begriffene gegen-
ständliche Wirklichkeit bezieht.[20]

Moreover, socialist realism is characterized as an adaptable
form of literature that reflects the evolving nature of reality.
Thus, as the conditions and methods of the class struggle change
with time, socialist realism adjusts its method of portraying
this reality in an appropriate format:

> Der Kunstfortschritt, der sich im Schaffen der
> Künstler in der entwickelten sozialistischen
> Gesellschaft kundtut, basiert darauf, daß sie
> jene Kraft bloßlegen, die nunmehr als lebens-
> und menschenbildende Kraft im Sinne des sozia-
> listischen Humanismus wirksam wird und in die-
> sem Bezug das Bild des Erbauers der neuen Gesell-
> schaft formen und gleichzeitig streitbar alles
> Überlebte kritisieren, das dem sozialistischen
> Aufbau im Wege steht. Daraus ergeben sich die
> neuen Inhalte, die neuen gesellschaftlichen
> Funktionen und aus beiden neue Formen und künst-
> lerische Techniken.[21]

What then are the distinctive features of GDR literature that
enable the reader to recognize a work of art as socialist realism
literature? What criteria have been designated by government
officials and literary critics as absolutely essential in literary works to fulfill the prerequisites of the concept of socialist realism?

1. Objective Reflection of Reality

The most fundamental prerequisite of socialist realism is the
concept of "objective reflection of reality" in its works. This
concept must in no way be confused with such terms as realism or
naturalism which denote a realistic, true-to-life or even photo-
graphic depiction of reality. While socialist realism literature also advocates the portrayal of reality by means of real-

istic images and pictures, this concept goes far beyond mere
stylistic concerns. The concept of objective reflection of
reality encompasses the entire philosophical perspective of
historical dialectical materialism from a Marxist viewpoint and
the subsequent reflection of reality within that context in literature and art. Thus, objective reflection of reality may be
defined as the artistic portrayal of life and reality in harmony
with the socialist interpretation of history as the evolution
from a capitalist to a socialist society. According to this
principle, the greater the correlation between historical events
and Marxist/Leninist ideology in works of art and literature,
the greater the degree of objective reflection of reality and
subsequently the artistic achievement. On the other hand, any
work of art or literature that does not conform to this basic
principle is denounced as anti-socialist realism propaganda and
cast aside as unworthy of serious consideration by virtue of
its false perspective of reality.

The concept of objective reflection of reality was derived
from Wladimir I. Lenin's theory of cognition which he formulated in his work "Materializm i empiriokriticizm" ("Materialism
and Empirical Criticism," 1908). In this work Lenin offers
the proposition that the material world exists independently
of and separate from man's consciousness. Yet, the material
world can be determined by means of man's consciousness of it.
Thus, the nature of this independent objective reality is perceived according to the nature of the consciousness of the human
being. This process of cognition involves three phases: first,
the perception of objective reality by the senses; second, the
interpretation and categorization of objective reality according to certain concepts and termini by means of abstract thought
processes; third, the verification of steps one and two and
application of the results in pragmatic settings.[22] While this
theory of cognition was intended primarily for the use of the
natural and physical sciences, Marxist ideologs adapted it to
the arts and humanities. Thus, literature, and in this case
specifically socialist realism literature by adopting the concepts of Lenin's theory, has become a vital instrument of cog-

nition by which mankind determines the nature of reality as it
applies to socio-political processes:

> In ihrer Auseinandersetzung vor allem mit spät-
> bourgeoisen Kunsttheorien verteidigte die
> marxistisch-leninistische Ästhetik schon bei
> ihren ersten Schritten die materialistische
> wissenschaftliche Einsicht, daß die Kunst
> ebenso wie die Wissenschaft die Wirklichkeit
> in einer spezifischen Weise widerspiegle und
> ein zuverlässiges Wissen von Lebensprozessen,
> Konflikten, gesellschaftlichen Zusammenhängen
> und Problemen geben könne.[23]

In the past, Marxist literary critics assert, the process
of cognition yielded a false perception of reality through
literature because the authors of literary works perceived reality from a bourgeois or aristocratic perspective. Consequently,
such a false perspective necessarily resulted in an incorrect
reflection of reality, since it was not based on the only
scientific and correct view of reality as embodied in Marxist
tenets:

> Das hieraus hervorgehende gesellschaftliche
> Bewußtsein ist in seiner Gesamtheit stets ein
> historisch bedingtes Abbild der bereits ange-
> eigneten, zum Objekt gewordenen materiellen
> Welt, sowohl der natürlichen als auch der gesell-
> schaftlichen, und es widerspiegelt diese Welt in
> verschiedenen Formen, die teils mehr oder weniger
> adäquat sind, wie die Wissenschaft mit ihren
> kognitiven Abbildern oder die realistische Kunst,
> teils mehr oder weniger verzerrt, wie z.B. die
> bürgerliche Ideologie, teils sogar phantastisch
> und illusorisch, wie in der Mythologie, Religion
> und im Idealismus.[24]

According to Marxist ideology, it is vitally important,
therefore, that false perceptions of reality be replaced with
the only correct interpretation of history as formulated in
Lenin's prescription by means of the "illustrative" and "form-

48

ative" components. In accordance with Lenin's theory, the concept of objective reflection of reality is characterized by an objective portrayal of the world in all its diversity and complexity. Transposed to literature, an author abiding by this concept must focus on the multitude of socio-economic and political processes that shape the nature of society. Thus, not only surface conditions must be considered in conveying reality, but instead the focus must be on the underlying causes of this reality to determine the true reasons for the surface reality. This "scientific" reflection of reality, Marxist critics assert, will uncover the forces at work in the inevitable transformation of the capitalist society to a socialist order. Therefore, the writer of socialist realism literature must concentrate on those aspects of the class struggle that portray most convincingly and persuasively this evolutionary process.

Socialist realism literature, however, is not satisfied with a mere illustration of the underlying causes of reality. The uncovering of the "real" causes of surface inequities and exploitation of individuals and entire nations must be depicted in a manner that serves as a catalyst for the transformation of this inequality to human equality. A central component of socialist realism literature, therefore, is its future-oriented nature in which the reader is "shown" the way out of the "real" to the "ideal" world. Thus, socialist realism literature is by its very nature transition-oriented. It constantly depicts the inadequacy of "what is" and points to the way it "should be" as was advocated by Lenin: "Das Bewußtsein des Menschen widerspiegelt nicht nur die objektive Welt, sondern schafft sie auch."[25] The vital nature of this characteristic in socialist realism is stressed repeatedly by literary critics in the German Democratic Republic:

> Von grundsätzlicher Bedeutung ist die Antwort
> auf die Frage nach dem Wahrheitsgehalt sozia-
> listischer Kunst. Sozialistisch-realistische
> Kunst sieht ihre Hauptaufgabe nicht nur in der
> Verfertigung von Abbildern der Wirklichkeit
> schlechthin. Sie ist an ganz bestimmten Abbil-

dern mit ganz bestimmter Wirkung interessiert.
Es geht bei der Abbildung der Wirklichkeit darum,
'die Welt so darzustellen, daß sie beherrschbar
wird.' Deshalb sollen die Abbildungen sozia-
listisch-realistischer Kunst 'praktikabel' sein,
also nicht nur Einsichten in das soziale
Getriebe gewähren, sondern zugleich sozialistische Impulse erzeugen. Wobei sozialistische Kunst sowohl die Lust am Erkennen
als auch an der Veränderung der Wirklichkeit erregen müsse.[26]

It is a central component of socialist realism literature,
therefore, to present both a "scientific" reflection of "what
is" and to anticipate "what will be" in order to satisfy the
concept of "objective reflection of reality." In this way,
socialist realism offers both an accurate diagnosis of the
dilemma and provides the cure for the ills of mankind. By
means of the element of "Antizipation" works of socialist realism portray the solutions to current problems as logical components of socialism. Thus, socialist realism literature, in
contrast to Naturalism, does not depict a passive reflection
of reality, but rather one that induces the reader to become
actively involved in the establishment of the new society. According to Bertolt Brecht, one should not perceive the objective
reflection of reality "nur als Abglanz der Wirklichkeit...,
sondern auch als aktiven Vorgang des Einwirkens auf die Wirklichkeit in der dialektischen Vereinigung von Erkenntnis und
Praxis."[27] Socialist realism, advocated Brecht, should strive
to transform "folgenloses Denken" of the public into "eingrei-
fendes Denken."[28]

By means of the concept of "objective reflection of reality"
the authors of socialist realism works contribute significantly
to the transformation of society by advocating in an artistic
manner the advancement of socialism. As such, socialist realism plays a key role in the overall plan of the political hierarchy in bringing about the downfall of capitalism and its replacement with socialism. This is the reason for the extensive

involvement of the highest government officials in directing
the function and nature of art and literature in the GDR. It
explains the great concern of the politicians over any trends
in literature that deviate from the prescribed course. It also
sheds considerable light on the need for censorship in the GDR
of certain works of literature or the banning of rebellious
authors from their native soil for violating these guidelines.

2. Partiality

The concept of partiality is an integral component of the
overall framework of objective reflection of reality and serves
as an indispensable ingredient in socialist realism. The theoretical basis of this concept can be traced back to Lenin's
essay "Parteiorganisation und Parteiliteratur" ("Party Organi-
zation and Party Literature") of 1905 in which he declared that
a free literature would be instituted in the Soviet Union that
would no longer serve the few who belonged to the "oberen Zehntausend" but instead would serve the "Millionen und aber Millionen Werktätigen" who shall determine the future of the Soviet
Union.[29] In this essay Lenin also lashed out against the
"bürgerlichen Karrierismus und Individualismus" of writers up
to that time and called for the establishment of a genuine
Party literature: "Nieder mit den parteilosen Literaten:
Nieder mit den literarischen Übermenschen: Die literarische
Tätigkeit muß zu einem Teil der allgemeinen proletarischen
Sache, zu einem 'Rädchen und Schräubchen' des einen einheit-
lichen, großen sozialdemokratischen Mechanismus werden."[30]
Finally, Lenin declared that the despicable bourgeois literature that is tied to the "Geldsack" must be liberated and replaced by a "wirklich freie, offen mit dem Proletariat verbun-
dene Literatur."[31]

Lenin's conception of a built-in "partiality" in literature
introduced a radical change to the role and scope of writers
as professionals and their relationship to their work and society. Whereas literary tradition up to that time had perceived the role of writers to lie in the presentation of personal, unbiased, impartial perceptions of the essence of the
human condition in the hope of contributing to a better under-

standing of life, Lenin's concept of partiality stripped the
authors of this independence and freedom to portray life as
they saw it. Instead, the imposition of the concept of partiality coerced them to filter their observations through the prism
of Marxist ideology. While Western reaction to the introduction
of this mode of literary presentation was viewed as the complete
subjugation of literature to the whims of political despots,
Soviet critics hailed Lenin's new criterion for socialist realism as a further advancement and refinement of the literary process. G. Kunicyn,[32] V.R. Sčerbina,[33] and L. Novičenko[34] extolled
the concept of partiality as a higher form of class consciousness. Indeed, communist partiality was viewed as the only legitimate literary mode since, in the eyes of its advocates, it
was the only perspective that was in harmony with the evolutionary process of class antagonism. All other perspectives are
summarily dismissed as revisionist plots to subvert the realization of socialist ideals.

Consequently, the concept of partiality became a key component of the objective reflection of reality as part of the
only scientific, correct and legitimate interpretation of historical materialism. Indeed, from a communist perspective, the
concept of partiality is merely a natural and logical extension
of its "Weltanschauung" that is legitimately incorporated into
its literature:

> Die Parteilichkeit der Literatur ist das natür-
> liche System der Gedanken und Gefühle des
> Schriftstellers, der dem Schicksal seines Vol-
> kes aufrichtig verbunden ist. Die Parteilich-
> keit der Literatur ist die organische Fähigkeit
> des Künstlers, die historische Entwicklung des
> Lebens so zu sehen, wie es in der Philosophie
> des Kommunismus zum Ausdruck kommt. Die Partei-
> lichkeit der Literatur ist der innige Wunsch des
> Schriftstellers, mit allen Mitteln seines Talents
> und seines Verstandes offen und überzeugt um den
> Sieg der großen Sache zu kämpfen, die im Partei-
> programm formuliert ist; um den Aufbau einer neuen

Gesellschaft. Und schließlich bedeutet die Parteilichkeit der Literatur Unnachgiebigkeit gegen-
über den Feinden des Kommunismus; sie ist eine
offene, prinzipielle Auseinandersetzung über
strittige Fragen der Kunst.[35]

This concept of Soviet socialist partiality was subsequently
exported to the German Democratic Republic. In the GDR, as in
the Soviet Union, socialist partiality is not at all perceived
as a restriction on the independence of the writer, but instead
is seen as a healthy partnership between the Party functionaries
and the writers. Each partner in this relationship provides an
essential service for the other. The Party, according to Kurt
Hager, educates the writers as to the proper political perspectives to be incorporated into literature while the authors illustrate these principles in socialist realism works:

Die Beschlüsse und Dokumente der Partei geben
den Künstlern eine zuverlässige Orientierung.
Sie helfen ihnen, sich in der Wirklichkeit
zurechtzufinden, die großen gesellschaftlichen
Zusammenhänge zu überblicken und die wesent-
lichen sozialen Entwicklungen zu erkennen...
Sie sind ein sicherer Kompaß zur tieferen Er-
kundung der Lebenswahrheit.[36]

While Kurt Hager described "partiality" as a mutually beneficial relationship between the SED and GDR writers, Werner
Jehser defines this concept as the "volle Übereinstimmung mit
Theorie und Praxis der revolutionären Partei der Arbeiterklasse,
mit den objektiven historischen Aufgaben und Zielsetzungen, die
von der Partei ausgearbeitet und von ihr durchgesetzt werden."[37]
Erwin Pracht, the prominent literary critic of the GDR, shares
the view expressed by Jehser when he writes that socialist
partiality is in "...qualitativem Unterschied zu allen bisheri-
gen humanistischen Inhalten des Parteiergreifens... die offene
und direkte Übereinstimmung mit den Zielen und Aufgaben der
marxistisch-leninistischen Partei."[38] Accordingly, every
author in the GDR is expected to produce works of literature
from which emanate his "ehrliche" and "bewußte" support of the

"Gesamtwillen und Gesamtplan"[39] of the SED. This view is
shared by Klaus Träger who states: "An die Stelle der
'Unabhängigkeit' ...tritt die bewußte Klassenverbundenheit,
an die Stelle der 'Freiheit' die sozialistische Parteilichkeit."[40] Far from bemoaning the restrictions imposed by the
concept of partiality as the confiscation of inherent rights
of an author to practice his craft as he sees fit, Träger en-
dorses the adherence to this concept as a beneficial guideline
to GDR authors in that it makes them "frei vom Kapital und damit
vom bürgerlichen Individualismus."[41] Erwin Pracht goes so far
as to ridicule the independence of Western writers as mere
illusion of "künstlerischen Hofnarren" which is nothing more
than "Narrenfreiheit."[42]

Socialist realism literature, therefore, as an essential
component of the overall super structure of the socialist state,
must necessarily be in harmony with the fundamental framework
of that entity. The overall accord of literature with the principles of Marxist ideology and Party dictates, however, does
not forbid the authors of socialist realism to criticize peri-
pheral elements within the socialist society. In fact, it is
the duty and obligation of every GDR author to expose potential
or actual impediments to the fulfillment of the socialist society. Consequently, many literary works deal with such problems as the "Außenseiter" who must be "reborn" politically
before he recognizes the virtues and benefits of socialism;
problems experienced in the work place that detract from harmonious working relationships between members of a brigade in
meeting assigned quotas; the hardships endured by the members
of a community as a result of temporary shortages of certain
consumer goods or industrial productivity. Such problems are
offered as evidence of minor obstacles that must be overcome
by a common zeal of the populace before the fruits of socialism can be enjoyed by all.

Consequently, the role of a writer of socialist realism
works is that of a creator within specified boundaries. When
planning or writing a literary work, the interests of socialism must always supersede private concerns. Every writer must

constantly be cognizant of the "inner censor" or else suffer
the consequences of its governmental counterpart. His work will
be censored. His professional reputation will be maligned.
Worst of all, he will not be published in the GDR and become a
non-entity.

Socialist partiality, therefore, serves as an extremely
useful yard stick for the political hierarchy in measuring the
loyalty of its writers. By examining the works of literature
according to this precept, the Party functionaries can easily
determine which writers they can trust and subsequently rec-
ommend for leadership positions in such organizations as the
"Schriftstellerverband" or even the Central Committee of the
SED. At the same time, deviation from this principle is clear
cause for punitive action. Indeed, the very existence of this
term as a criterion for socialist realism literature serves as
a constant reminder to every GDR writer to consider carefully
what he writes.

3. National Orientation

The third component comprising the concept of socialist
realism is "Volkstümlichkeit" or the element of a national orientation. As was the case for the categories of objective reflection of reality and socialist partiality, the call for a national orientation in socialist realism literature had its beginning in the Soviet Union. The genesis of this term may be
traced back to the 19th century when Prince A. Vjazemskij trans-
lated the French "nationalité" into the Russian "narodnostj."[43]
At first, there existed considerable perplexity and bewilderment among writers concerning the precise meaning of this term.
Even A. Puskin expressed a sense of consternation concerning
the essence of "narodnostj" as an element of literature that
was suddenly in vogue in Russia but whose precise characteristics no one had defined.[44] However, by the middle of the 19th
century there had emerged three interpretations of this term.
The first characterization of "narodnostj" encompassed Russian
folklore in the broad sense that included such elements as
customs and traditions which exhibited a uniquely Russian flavor.
The second interpretation of "narodnostj" focused more on the

55

unique socio-political makeup of the Russian society that included the Russian Orthodox Church, the ruling monopoly of the
Czar and the ethnic composition of the people. The third interpretation of "narodnostj" was provided by V. Belinskij who defined this term as literature that depicts the totality of life
and spirit of a people or country, thereby offering fundamental
insights into the essence of a particular nation or people.[45]

The key factor in fulfilling the prerequisite of "narodnostj"
in socialist realism today is perceived to be the presentation
of a problem or concern that has "nation-wide" implications.
The issue raised must be of concern to the great majority of
inhabitants of a specific nation or ethnic group instead of a
small interest group or individuals. Furthermore, the problem
must be addressed and solved in a manner consistent with the best
interest of the entire nation. Finally, the work of literature
must portray this national concern in a manner that is readily
understood by and is relevant to the broad spectrum of people
comprising the particular nationality.[46] Thus, "narodnostj"
is closely tied to "socialist partiality" in that both concepts
require the resolution of problems in favor of their respective
national entities. Indeed, one may observe a hierarchical relationship between these two terms that serve the same end.
While socialist partiality may be defined as the depiction of
problems in accordance with Party guidelines, these same Party
guidelines, at least in theory, must reflect the wishes of the
population as a whole. Consequently, adherence to the principle
of "narodnostj" may be characterized as the highest form of socialist partiality.

This concept of "narodnostj" was again transplanted to the
GDR and incorporated into socialist realism under the term
"Volkstümlichkeit." As had been the case in the Soviet Union,
there arose a demand in the GDR for literature that bridged
the remaining gaps between the upper and lower classes. Indeed,
it was fitting for the newly instituted "Arbeiter- und Bauern-
staat" to adopt the principle of "Volkstümlichkeit" as an integral part of socialist realism literature to eliminate the gap
between artists and readers while at the same time disseminating

issues of national concern to the broad spectrum of people
under the guise of a "direkter Ausdruck der Volksinteressen."[47]
As early as 1938 Bertolt Brecht had defined the concept of
"Volkstümlichkeit" as:

> ...den breiten Massen verständlich, ihre Aus-
> drucksform aufnehmend und bereichernd/ihren
> Standpunkt einnehmend, befestigend und korri-
> gierend/den fortschrittlichsten Teil des Volkes
> so vertretend, daB er die Führung übernehmen
> kann, also auch den andern Teilen des Volkes
> verständlich/anknüpfend an die Traditionen,
> sie weiterführend/dem zur Führung strebenden
> Teil des Volkes Errungenschaften des jetzt
> führenden Teils übermittelnd.[48]

The experimentation during the Bitterfelder Weg," therefore,
may be viewed as a direct response on the part of the political
hierarchy and the professional writers to put into practice the
concept of "Volkstümlichkeit" in full measure: "Es kommt jetzt
vor allem darauf an, die noch vorhandene Trennung von Kunst
und Leben, die Entfremdung zwischen Künstler und Volk zu überwinden."[49] Although this experiment in broadening the parameters of professional and lay writers produced no works of any
literary consequence, it must be viewed with a degree of admiration and respect for the willingness of the politicians to put
this theoretical principle into practice as a means of bridging
the gap between the elite and the great masses. Indeed, this
experiment if seen from the vantage point of infusing a greater
degree of "Volkstümlichkeit" into the literature of the GDR,
must be credited with considerable success in that it produced
a number of "Ankunftsromane" in which the interests of the
masses and their concerns were paramount, causing the Central
Committee of the SED to proclaim proudly: "Die Kultur der
Deutschen Demokratischen Republik ist eine wahrhafte Volks-
kultur. ...Überwunden ist in unserem Kulturleben das Gegen-
einander einer gehobenen Kultur für eine kleine Elite und der
billigsten Pseudokunst für die Massen."[50]

The incorporation of the element of "Volkstümlichkeit" served

a second purpose. It functioned as an ideal means of dissuading
GDR authors from dabbling in the odious practice of formalism
under the guise of serving an urgent national need for a literature characterized by elegant simplicity that was understood
and enjoyed by the great masses:

> Das Verständliche ist in keiner Weise identisch
> mit dem Simplifizierten, und das Banale geht
> durchaus nicht gesetzmäßig mit dem Klaren und·
> Zugänglichen konform. Sehr häufig tritt die
> Banalität gerade in der Form komplizierter
> 'Strukturen' zutage. Hingegen fesseln uns
> viele klassische Kunstwerke durch die Verbindung
> von durchgeistigter Klarheit und inhaltlicher
> Tiefe und Verdichtung.[51]

Literary critics of the GDR are emphatic in their contention
that adherence to "Volkstümlichkeit" in literary works in no
way connotes a lowering of the artistic mode of expression. Instead, these critics perceive the simplicity of form in socialist realism works to be a far superior form of communication
between the author and reader than the incomprehensible literary
maze of narrative styles and techniques exhibited in Western
literature. Therefore, GDR critics reject negative reviews of
socialist realism works by Western critics as mere "haughty attacks" against a mode of expression that is specifically designed
for mass appeal:

> Es muß noch einmal nachdrücklich darauf hin-
> gewiesen werden, daß die marxistisch-lenini-
> stische Ästhetik wie die sozialistische Kunst-
> politik die Grundaufgabe des Bitterfelder Weges,
> immer breitere Kreise des Volkes für die Kunst
> und für das immer tiefere Eindringen in ihre
> 'Geheimnisse' zu gewinnen, niemals als Herab-
> setzung, als Senkung des Niveaus der Kunst miß-
> verstanden hat. Wir haben uns und werden uns
> auch weiterhin energisch gegen jede Art von
> 'Einfachheit' verwahren, die in Wirklichkeit
> simplifizierend und im Grunde abschätzig - her-

ablassend im Sinne der imperialistischen Massen-
kultur ist.[52]

Far from perceiving "Volkstümlichkeit" as a weakness in socialist realism literature, the proponents of this concept deem
it to be a highly effective method for achieving the primary
goal of GDR literature, which is "den 'kleinen Kreis der Kenner'
zu einem großen Kreis der Kenner zu machen." By means of this
literary element, socialist realism writers hope to broaden the
awareness of the great masses to enable them to partake fully
of all aspects of GDR life and culture: "Das Volk versteht
kühne Ausdrucksweise, billigt neue Standpunkte, überwindet
formale Schwierigkeiten, wenn seine Interessen sprechen. Es
versteht Marx besser als Hegel, es versteht Hegel, wenn es
marxistisch geschult ist."[53] What Western nation, ask the proponents of socialist realism, pays a similar tribute to its
working class that it caters specifically to the cultural needs
of this segment of the population as does the German Democratic
Republic?

4. The Typical

The fourth essential component of socialist realism literature is the element of the typical. The justification for the
incorporation of the typical in socialist realism works is
based upon the positive assessment of this characteristic by
such venerated figures as Friedrich Engels and W.I. Lenin.
Even though Engel's pronouncements concerning the nature of the
typical are limited to two remarks, these statements, nevertheless, serve as the standard reference for socialist literary
critics in legitimizing this concept in socialist realism literature. Engel's first remark on this topic is found in his
letter to Margaret Harkness dated April 1, 1888 in which he
offers the less than profound statement: "Realismus bedeutet,
meines Erachtens, außer der Treue des Details die getreue
Wiedergabe typischer Charaktere unter typischen Umständen."[54]
In another letter to Minna Kautsky of November 1885, Engels
provides greater insight into his expectations of the typical
in literature. Here he praises Minna Kautsky's novel "Die
Alten und die Neuen," for the "scharfe Individualisierung der

Charaktere" who at the same time represent much more, "jeder
ist ein Typus, aber auch zugleich ein bestimmter Einzelmensch,
ein 'Dieser,' wie der alte Hegel sich ausdrückt, und so muß
es sein."[55] Engels, thus, advocated a literature that illustrates the essential characteristics of an individual or
event in such a precise and distinctive manner that it success-
fully conveys an accurate image to the reader that is representative both of an individual person or occurance and characterizes typical human nature or socio-political phenomena.

In his essay "Graf Heyden zum Gedächtnis" Lenin expounded
further on the nature of the typical that was begun by Engels.
He addresses the issue of the typical directly with the question: "Was ist characteristisch, was ist typisch für die politische Tätigkeit Heydens?" What are the elements that attri-
bute to Heyden the characteristics of a "typisch konterrevo-
lutionären Gutsbesitzers?" In order to succeed in portraying
characteristics of an individual as typical of an entire group
or class of people, Lenin advocates a portrayal of the dialectical relationship between the general and the specific and
the necessary and the coincidental that occurs in real life.[56]
By concentrating on the "Angelpunkt der individuellen Umstände,
die Analyse der Charaktere und der seelischen Verfassung der
betreffenden Typen,"[57] concludes Lenin, an author is able to
portray characteristics that are reflective both of individual
and typical behavior. Thus, by unmasking Count Heyden's sinister
personal traits behind a "Schleier edelmütiger Worte und
äußerlicher Gentlemanmanieren," asserts Lenin, the reader
recognizes in Heyden not only the characteristics of an individual but also the valid representation of the "räuberischen
Appetit der Fronherren"[58] against which the reader must be
warned.

In response to the positive pronouncements of Friedrich
Engels and W.I. Lenin concerning the function and nature of
the typical, this concept was adopted as a key element of socialist realism in the Soviet Union during the 1930's.[59] While
Soviet writers were encouraged to incorporate this principle
into their works, few if any authors had a clear understanding

of the specific nature of the typical. As in the case of the
other characteristics of socialist realism, a period of adjustment and experimentation was required before a workable definition of the typical emerged. Makcim Gorki, one of the first
Soviet writers to address the problem, offered the following
definition of the typical: "Eine Gestalt oder eine Situation
in einem literarischen Werk seien dann typisch, wenn sie ein
Extrakt aus den vielen gleichartigen, sich wiederholenden
Momenten der gesellschaftlichen Wirklichkeit darstellten."[60]
To convey the element of the typical, Gorki also advocated the
incorporation of a multitude of characteristics into a single
significant individual or event, thereby evoking in Belinski's
terminology the image of "der bekannte Unbekannte" in the eyes
and minds of the reader.

Following World War II the concept of the typical was expanded to include both the depiction of past orderly progress
of historical evolution as well as the projection of achievements of entire nations or political systems that as yet were
evident only in individuals. Thus, Pavel Vlasov from Gorki's
novel "Die Mutter" is cited repeatedly as the manifestation of
an individual who already embodies the true socialist characteristics that will be "typical" of entire nations and societies
in the future. L. Timofeew, the leading Soviet literary critic
of the 1950's, perceived the element of the typical to lie in
the depiction of realistic occurances which reflect typical
life in form and content.[61] Timofeew's rather vague characterization of the typical is still regarded as the official definition of this concept in the Soviet Union.

This imprecise definition of the typical was subsequently
incorporated into the framework of socialist realism literature of the GDR where it functions as a fundamental aspect of
artistic generalization:

> Die Typisierung ist diejenige Form der künst-
> lerischen Verallgemeinerung, die die Methode
> des sozialistischen Realismus kennzeichnet.
> In ihr sind wesentliche allgemeingültige Po-
> sitionen aus der Geschichte des Realismus aufge-

hoben. Ihr oberstes Prinzip ist die Wahrheits-
treue. Wir betrachten die Typisierung als eine
auf objektive Wahrheit zielende künstlerische
Verallgemeinerungsweise, die das Gesellschaftliche im Individuellen, das Allgemeine im Be-
sonderen, das Gesetzmäßige im Zufälligen, das
Ganze (oder die Beziehung zum gesellschaftlich
Ganzen) im Partikularen, das (historisch und
sozial für den Menschen) Wesentliche in den
konkreten Erscheinungen aufspürt, heraushebt
und künstlerisch überzeugend ausdrückt.[62]

By adhering to these principles, GDR writers of socialist
realism literature strive toward a presentation of "types" who
connote universal truths. In practice, more often than not,
this effort results in the creation of stereotypes whose one-
sidedness detracts from their credibility as representatives
of real life. Nevertheless, these "types" serve the specific
purpose of inspiring the reader to follow the example of the
depicted heroes who strive valiantly to build a better world
for all:

Durch den Typisierungsprozeß und in ihm wird das
angeführte Bezugsgefüge in den zur Darstellung
gebrachten Lebenserscheinungen aufgedeckt, gedank-
lich-anschaulich verdichtet und auf das ästhetisch-
gesellschaftliche Ideal in einer individuell bestimmten Weise bezogen, wobei der ganze Vorgang
stets einen Vorgriff und Impuls zur wirklichen
Lösung der gestalteten Probleme einschließt.
Sozialistisch-realistische Kunstwerke beschränken
sich durch eine so verstandene Typisierung nicht
darauf, bloß einzelne Fakten zu 'beschreiben',
sondern machen Aussagen über gesellschaftlich
Wesentliches. Sie sind das Ergebnis einer 'ver-
dichtenden', schöpferisch-umbildenden Widerspiegelung und einer ihr entsprechenden ästhetischen Wertung.[63]

5. The Positive Hero

Perhaps the most distinguishing characteristic of socialist realism literature is its continued adherence to and glorification of the positive hero in its works. While literatures of the world in general and Western literature in particular are characterized by an increasing trend toward abandoning the concept of the positive hero that began in the second half of the 19th century and accelerated in the 20th century to the point of developing its antithesis in the form of the antihero, socialist realism literature staunchly rejects this trend and maintains a positivist outlook that finds its purest expression in its unaltered faith in the positive hero. As R.W. Mathewson[64] notes, Russian literature has a rich tradition in which the positive hero is celebrated. Its origin may be traced through folklore to the beginnings of Russian literature where this concept was well established in both the oral and written tradition of the Russian culture. Consequently, the concept of the positive hero finds broad acceptance as a centerpiece for socialist realism literature.

The socialist realism version of the positive hero was molded to a large extent by M. Gorki who advocated the creation of a new hero who actively strives for the establishment of the socialist society. This new HUMAN BEING was to serve as the prototype of the modern version of the Russian hero per se and was not to be perceived merely as a mouthpiece of political functionaries. The new hero, as proposed by Gorki, exhibits all of the positive characteristics of traditional heroes. He fights for truth and justice. He liberates the proletariat from the exploitation of the upper classes. Most of all he is a tireless, effective proponent of the new socialist society in which the elements of truth, justice, freedom and equality will be realized.[65] The mission of the positive hero, therefore, is to serve as a role model to the reader for emulation by word and deed.

A similar formula of the positive hero was advocated by Belinski who also saw the primary function of the modern Russian hero in the establishment of the new socialist society. Conse-

quently, the new positive hero emerged in an abundance of literary works in which he performs herculean deeds for the benefit
of mankind. During the 1930's the positive hero played a key
role in espousing the wisdom of the collectivization process of
Russian agriculture. In World War II, the heroics of the positive hero were instrumental in the successful defense of the
Soviet Union against the invasion of the Germans and in securing
ultimate victory for Mother Russia. Today the positive hero is
above all an exemplary citizen of the Soviet Union and a staunch
supporter of the Communist Party. He is totally dedicated to
the realization of the socialist ideals and enjoys the utmost
of personal fulfillment from these noble tasks.

In general, the Soviet concept of the positive hero was subsequently adopted by the GDR and incorporated into its socialist realism framework. As in the Soviet Union, GDR socialist
realism literature is generally characterized by an upbeat, positivist "Weltanschauung" that reflects both the Soviet influence
and the continuation of the "klassische Erbe" to which socialist
realism critics point with particular pride. While Western
literature as a whole flounders in a quagmire of negativism,
estrangement, isolation, despair and anti-social tendencies,
socialist realism literature in the GDR is dedicated to the
exaltation of the noblest qualities of the human being.

The establishment of a new harmony of the individual with
himself and the socialist society in the contemporary GDR is the
central goal of GDR socialist realism works. Indeed, socialist
realism literature is dedicated to the celebration of the no-
bility of the human spirit with all its potential: "Der Mensch
in seiner Möglichkeit, in der Unendlichkeit seiner Möglichkeit,
herausgehoben durch die Arbeit an sich selbst aus jeder individuellen Enge und Bedrängnis."[66] Socialist realism literature
strives to "educate" its audience to "das Vergnügen an der
Meisterungsmöglichkeit des menschlichen Schicksals durch die
Gesellschaft."[67] It exalts in the promotion of the new socialist personality as the most progressive element of contemporary
society. This new socialist personality or positive hero exhibits genuine concern for the common good within the new social

order as opposed to the egocentric tendencies exhibited by
Western literary characters. Above all, the new positive hero
is unalterably convinced of the righteousness of his cause and
subsequently pursues his mission with a messianic fervor without regard to personal sacrifice.

The new positive hero in socialist realism literature, therefore, serves as a role model and "Wegweiser" for the populace
of the GDR as a whole. He has already undergone the transformation into the new socialist personality that the great majority
of the GDR citizens is yet to experience. He is the "anticipa-
tion" of the regeneration that will occur among the populace
as a whole. In the meantime, it is the function of the positive
hero to accelerate that transformation among his fellow citizens:

> Im Mittelpunkt des künstlerischen Schaffens muß
> der neue Mensch stehen, der Kämpfer für ein ein-
> heitliches, demokratisches Deutschland, der Akti-
> vist, der Held des sozialistischen Aufbaus. In-
> dem der Künstler dieses Neue, dieses Fortschritt-
> liche in der Zeit gestaltet, hilft er mit, Millio-
> nen fortschrittliche Menschen zu erziehen.[68]

The new positive hero of socialist realism literature is no
longer a figure found only in folklore or legends. As depicted
in socialist realism works, he is alive and at work today. He
is found in a multitude of settings and job descriptions. Wherever he appears, he is characterized by a genuine devotion to
promote the best interests of his fellow man, his community
and nation. He is totally dedicated to fulfilling the promise
of the new socialist society in which mankind is offered fulfillment of the elusive dream to live in a state of universal peace
and harmony free from physical and spiritual want.

Chapter III

"Moskauer Novelle:" A Model of Socialist Realism

If one were to compile a list of the five to ten most eminent
contemporary GDR writers to include such names as Günter Kunert,
Volker Braun, Reiner Kunze, Peter Hacks, Heiner Müller, Anna
Seghers, Günter de Bruyn and Fritz Rudolph Fries, the name of
Christa Wolf would surely be at the very top of such a select
group. Indeed, the more recent works have won Christa Wolf
such universal literary acclaim that she is generally regarded
as one of the world's major contemporary authors. Ironically,
however, it is precisely this world-wide accolade for producing
first-rate literature according to commonly accepted standards,
instead of the principles of socialist realism, that has made
Christa Wolf the object of a love-hate relationship in her
homeland. Who, then, is this person who on the one hand curries
the favor of the political hierarchy with such statements as:
"Der Kampf für den Sozialismus ist immer mehr zur einzigen
Möglichkeit geworden, sich konsequent menschliches Handeln und
Denken zu bewahren - schon heute..."[1] and on the other hand
incurs its wrath and consternation prompting even the president
of the German Writers' Union to implore the prodigal daughter
to come to her senses and to return to the camp of socialist
realism writers:

> Wir wären Prügel wert, wenn wir die diversante
> Absicht nicht durchschauten. Wo es die subjek-
> tiv ehrliche Absicht zu schützen gilt, werden
> wir sie lieber schützen. Unter uns brauchte es
> allerdings dazu einiges mehr an Offenheit und
> wechselseitiger Bereitschaft zu prinzipieller
> kameradschaftlicher Kritik. In dieser Verant-
> wortung rufen wir Christa Wolf zu: Besinn dich
> auf dein Herkommen, besinn dich auf unser Fort-
> kommen, wenn du mit deiner klugen Feder der
> deutschen Arbeiterklasse, ihrer Partei und der
> Sache des Sozialismus dienen willst.[2]

A brief account of Christa Wolf's biography may be helpful in shedding some light on the contradictory nature of the above statements and in providing some insight into the factors behind her beginnings as a writer totally devoted to the principles of socialist realism, her subsequent gradual abandonment of these characteristics, and her eventual total rejection of socialist realism as a literary method.

Christa Wolf was born in 1929 in Landsberg, a community that is now situated in Poland. In 1945, she and her parents fled to Mecklenburg in the midst of the final onslaught on Germany by the Allies from the Eastern and Western Front and the subsequent surrender of Germany. Thus, the sixteen-year-old daughter of a businessman had seen and experienced first-hand the horror of war. In 1949, during the year of her graduation from a "Gymnasium" in Bad Frankenhausen, Christa Wolf became a member of the Socialist Unity Party (SED), motivated in part by a fervent desire to prevent a recurrence of the National Socialist trauma of 1933-1945. From 1945 to 1953 she continued her education at the universities of Jena and Leipzig as a student of German literature under the tutelage of the highly controversial German professor Hans Mayer. In 1951, she married Gerhard Wolf, a fellow student. One year later she became the mother of the first of her two children. During the same year, the unusually ambitious student published her first review in the SED-controlled newspaper "Neues Deutschland."[3] Shortly thereafter Christa Wolf embarked fully upon a literary career when she accepted a position with the German Writers' Union which publishes one of the most highly regarded GDR literary journals "Neue deutsche Literatur." She performed her tasks as reviewer of books in such a highly satisfactory manner that she was accorded the distinct honor of being selected as editor of this prestigious journal from May 1958 to November 1959. Thus, within the short span of ten years, from 1952-1962, Christa Wolf made a name for herself in literary circles through the publication of nearly three dozen reviews in such governmentally approved places as "Neue deutsche Literatur," "Neues Deutschland," "Sonntag," and the "Berliner Zeitung." In general, these early publications

by Christa Wolf are characterized by a strict adherence to the
principles of socialist realism, advocacy of SED policies and
ceaseless exhortation of GDR writers to illustrate more enthusiastically the promises and virtues of the impending socialist
society in their works.

Despite the obvious success that Christa Wolf had attained
in her role as critic of the literary output of her contemporaries, she harbored a longing to try her own hand as a writer
of original literature. As early as 1956, she sought the ad-
vice of Louis Fürnberg as to the wisdom of her inclination to
become a writer and received his blessing in this endeavor:
"Selber schreiben möchtest Du können und wüßtest vielleicht
sogar, was? Christa!! Ja, wer soll denn schreiben können,
wenn nicht Du? So schreib doch!! So versuch's doch einmal!"[4]
And so Christa Wolf began the bittersweet transition from in-
terpretor to creator of literature:

> Manche meinen, von der Germanistik und der Li-
> teraturkritik führe ein direkter Weg zur 'richti-
> gen' Literatur. Ich will nicht bestreiten, daß
> die Kenntnis der literarischen Entwicklung und
> der genaue Einblick in Probleme angehender Schrift-
> steller mir nützlich sind, mir vielleicht Umwege
> ersparen. Andererseits wird es einem, je länger
> man sich mit Literatur beschäftigt, immer schwerer,
> selbst etwas zu veröffentlichen.[5]

From this date forward, Christa Wolf wrote a number of unpublished literary efforts representing different approaches
and genres until her "first" prose work, "Moskauer Novelle,"
appeared in 1961:

> 'Erstlingswerk'! - Übrigens gibt es das über-
> haupt nicht. Immer noch frühere Versuche in
> immer noch jüngeren Jahren fallen einem ein,
> von halb und dreiviertel ausgeführten Roman-
> und Dramenplänen über Tagebücher, politische
> und private Gelegenheitsdichtungen, gefühls-
> gesättigte Briefwechsel mit Freundinnen bis
> hin zu den kindlichen Märchenerfindungen...

jene lebenswichtigen Vorformen naiver Kunst-
ausübung.[6]

Thus, the formal debut of Christa Wolf as an author of
original literature had taken place. It will be the task of
this chapter to place this work in its historical perspective
within the context of GDR literature and to offer an analysis
of its subject matter to determine the degree of its adherence
to the prerequisites of socialist realism.

The regeneration of human beings from National Socialist
tendencies to ardent supporters of socialism, the main theme
of Christa Wolf's "Moskauer Novelle," is by no means an isolated literary occurance in the GDR. Following the end of World
War II, a seemingly endless series of literary works by a host
of former external and internal exiles came to grips with the
painful issue of the immediate German past. Work after work,
consisting of a healthy mixture of "Dichtung und Wahrheit,"
offered its version of the reprehensible events of the Nazi
past coupled with the heroic efforts of dedicated communists
to transform the inhumanity and brutality of man into an era
of brotherhood and benevolence in the emerging socialist society.

For the most part, the authors of these works were motivated
by two objectives in dealing with this particular subject matter.
First, there was a genuine desire on the part of many writers
to face up to the past. As Germans, they felt an urgent need
to admit, to confess, to atone for the horrors of the Nazi era.
Thus, the very act of recounting, reviving, and reliving, what
most were eager to forget, to bury and to blot from their minds
offered these writers a "liberating" experience, a catharsis,
which enabled them to continue to live as human beings. Second,
the atrocities of the immediate past, which were committed under
the worst form of a capitalist society, offered these communist
writers an unparalleled opportunity to illustrate the urgent
need for the dismantling of this political system and to promote
its replacement with socialism.

The parade of works exemplifying the regeneration of individuals from inhumane, bourgeois and fascist outlooks to proponents

of a new humanity emerging under the banner of socialism was
led by Hans Marchwitza's "Kumiak" trilogy, "Die Kumiaks," "Die
Heimkehr der Kumiaks," in which a family of miners is converted
to communism and subsequently spares no sacrifice in the service
of the Party. Theodor Plivier's novel "Stalingrad" provided a
penetrating insight into the horror of war perpetrated upon the
Russians by the Nazis and the subsequent heroic resistance
offered by the Soviets against the German onslaught. Anna
Seghers, one of the most dominant literary figures in the GDR
following her return from exile in Mexico, provided a number of
works that celebrated the conversion of individuals and entire
societies to Marxism. Among these works are "Der Aufstand der
Fischer von St. Barbara," "Die Toten bleiben jung," "Der erste
Schritt," "Der Mann und sein Name," "Transit," "Die Entscheidung"
and "Das Vertrauen."

Other works dealing with the growing awakening to the virtues
of socialism and their subsequent exemplary devotion to this
cause are Bodo Uhse's "Leutnant Bertram," and "Die Patrioten,"
Harold Hauser's "Wo Deutschland lag," Wolfgang Joho's "Die
Hirtenflöte," Elfriede Brüning's "...damit du weiterlebst,"
Stephan Hermlin's "Die erste Reihe," Otto Gotsche's "Zwischen
Nacht und Morgen," Ludwigs Renn's "Der spanische Krieg,"·
Franz Fühmann's "Drei Kameraden," Karl Mundstock's "Bis zum
letzten Mann," Harry Thürk's "Die Stunde der toten Augen" and
Bruno Apitz' "Nackt unter den Wölfen."

Despite this overwhelming display of literature proclaiming
the inevitable victory of socialism over capitalism, Alfred
Kurella, the man responsible for the implementation of the
"Bitterfelder Weg," chastised GDR writers for "die Unfähigkeit
einiger älterer Schriftsteller, über die antifaschistisch-
demokratische Kampflinie hinauszugehen und sich rückhaltlos
auf den Boden des Sozialismus, wie er sich nun einmal entwickelt,
zu stellen."[7]

The thirty-year old Christa Wolf was in complete accord
with the sentiment expressed by Kurella. In the foreword to
the anthology, "Proben junger Erzähler" which she edited in
1959, Christa Wolf boldly proclaimed: "Der groβe Stoff unserer

Zeit... ist das Werden des neuen Menschen."[8] She called for
an unabated flow of literary works in which the advancement
of the new age of socialism is illustrated. Both professional
and lay writers are urged by her to bear witness through their
works to their commitment and dedication to the socialist
cause. Finally, Christa Wolf reminded every aspiring GDR
writer that the fate of millions of people for a successful
realization of socialism had been placed "in jene Gruppe
jüngerer Autoren, die den Aufbau des Sozialismus an seinen
Zentren als Arbeiter miterlebt haben, denen unsere Gegenwart,
diese Übergangszeit mit ihrer Größe und ihren Widersprüchen,
zum Grunderlebnis und zum natürlichen Stoff für die Gestaltung
geworden ist."[9]

Christa Wolf even ascribed near supernatural powers to
the writers of socialist realism who through their works have
the means to affect regenerative changes in human beings. By
illustrating the new age of socialism as one of peace, harmony,
equality and humanity that can be realized only through the
active commitment and contribution of the masses, she asserts
that many former skeptics will be inspired to join this noble
effort, motivated by the conviction that

> der Einsatz für die Ideen des Sozialismus gleich-
> zeitig die erste konkrete Möglichkeit in ihrem
> Leben bedeutet, sich als Menschen zu beweisen und
> zu verwirklichen. Auf die Tatsache, daß die Men-
> schen sich unter dem Einfluß dieser Ideen und neuer
> gesellschaftlicher Verhältnisse zu verändern be-
> ginnen, gründet sich ja gerade unser Optimismus.
> Gleichzeitig ist diese Tatsache die Voraussetzung
> für weitere Fortschritte; denn von Fortschritt setzt
> sich immer nur so viel durch, wie wir durchsetzen,
> läßt Brecht seinen Galilei sagen. Hier liegen die
> großen Ideen, hier liegen die Fabeln für soziali-
> stische Schriftsteller unserer Zeit.[10]

Thus, Christa Wolf at the onset of her literary career
was filled with a messianic fervor for the advancement of
socialism by means of socialist realism literature. She is

dedicated to a total glorification of this political end. She castigates any work of literature that falls short of this prerequisite in her reviews for failing to comply with the fundamental function of literature as prescribed by GDR authorities. Accordingly, she bemoaned the lack of a convincing "Parteilichkeit" in Ehm Welk's novel "Im Morgennebel" and provided him and all GDR writers with her formula for socialist realism literature:

> Die Parteilichkeit des Autors erschöpft sich nicht
> in der ideologisch richtigen Aussage, in der in-
> tellektuellen Erkenntnis, sondern verlangt gerade
> vom Künstler, daB er auch gefühlsmäBig, mit seinem
> ganzen Wesen, in Sympathie und Abneigung auf der
> richtigen Seite steht. (...) GroBe realistische Li-
> teratur entsteht, wenn Gefühl und Verstand des
> Schriftstellers fähig sind, tief und richtig seine
> Zeit zu erfassen und sich aus der Wirklichkeit
> die MaBstäbe für sein künstlerisches Schaffen zu
> nehmen.[11]

This conviction was subsequently put into practice with the publication of her first work "Moskauer Novelle," a model of socialist realism literature, that incorporates all the essential prerequisites of that literary method.

1. Objective Reflection of Reality

Rarely, if ever, in the annals of GDR literature has a work of literature embodied so completely the principle of objective reflection of reality as is the case in "Moskauer Novelle." From the first page to the last, the theme and content of this work is dedicated to illustrating one fundamental objective: the conscious conversion of Vera Brauer, the members of the German medical delegation to Moscow and by extension the reader, i.e. the inhabitants of the GDR and the world at large to the reality of the Soviet model of socialism. More specifically, Christa Wolf in this "Novelle" has depicted the triumph of good over evil, socialism over capitalism and humanity over inhumanity from a socialist perspective. As a direct consequence of this evolution, former

mortal enemies on the battlefields of World War II stretching
from Stalingrad to Siberia, from Berlin to the Elbe, have become friends and allies. Even more remarkable is the total
reversal in attitude of the Germans toward the Russians. Whereas
the Germans until the end of World War II had always despised
the Russians as subhuman hordes, an abundance of favorable
experiences with their "liberators" in the GDR and in the Soviet
Union transformed the former hostile relationship into friendship with the Soviets.

What, then, are the specific elements of objective reflection of reality in this work that serve to illustrate the
Saul to Paul conversion of Vera Brauer, her companions and
by implication the inhabitants of the GDR to devout believers
in socialism?

The essence of the "Moskauer Novelle" is built around the
visit of a GDR medical team to Moscow for the purpose of entering into an agreement with their Soviet counterparts to exchange vital medical information for the mutual benefit of the
inhabitants of both countries. Already this venture to Moscow
by the delegation from the GDR, formerly part of a hostile nation toward the Soviet Union and its Marxist ideology, serves
as an important symbol of the regenerative process that has
taken place. Whereas a mere dozen or so years earlier compatriots of this German medical team had attempted to bring
utter destruction upon the "Russian hordes," the purpose of
this current mission of reformed Germans is to bind up the
wounds of the past, to solidify the friendship between the two
nations and to emulate to an even greater degree the role model
of the most advanced socialist society. As a result of the
personal experiences, the sights and sounds, and the "objective
reflection of reality" encountered on this trip, this group of
Germans will leave the Soviet Union totally convinced of the
inherent goodness and superiority of socialism over all other
political systems and an unshakeable reaffirmation of their
personal commitment to Marxism.

The need for a deliberate recommitment to the principles of
socialism by the German delegation is evidenced by the lingering

doubts harbored by them concerning the appropriateness of their
conversion to Marxism. Even Vera Brauer, a young German pedia-
trician and avowed Marxist, subconsciously vents a certain doubt
and skepticism about the intellectual, social and scientific
qualifications of their hosts to act as leaders of the communist world. Her lack of confidence in the ability of the Soviets
to be entrusted with this monumental task is evidenced in her
preconceived image of Moscow as a drab, backward city typifying
an overall backward Russian society. It comes as a considerable surprise to her, therefore, that Moscow is the opposite of
what she anticipated: "Sie habe sich Moskau anders vorgestellt,
sagte sie. Enger. Und grau."[12] Far from being a dull, color-
less city, Vera is impressed by the bustling life and vibrant
activity of this metropolis that is symbolized by its bright
colors: "Aber er wollte von ihr die Farbe Moskaus wissen. Sie
überlegte und meinte dann: Lichter Ocker, fast gelb. Und rosa."
(MN, p.6) Within minutes of her arrival in Moscow, therefore,
visible proof of the Soviet Union's legitimate claim to lead
the communist world is presented to Vera and her companions by
the depiction of Moscow as a glittering city, a worthy capital
of the communist world.

Similar to the unexpectedly pleasant surprise regarding the
"color" of Moscow, Vera Brauer recognizes in Pawel Koschkin not
just an official interpreter who facilitates communication between the two nations, but also the long-time friend she met at
the end of World War II in Germany. Thus, in the course of this
"Novelle" the personal relationship between these two individuals that had begun as adversaries during the war years blossoms
into intense mutual admiration and love. This metamorphosis
from hate to love between a "Russian" and a "German" is of
course symbolic of the new relationship between these two socialist nations. This new affection for one another on a personal and national basis must be nourished and cultivated as
is apparent from the initial conversation between Vera and
Pawel: "Genosse Koschkin, denken Sie nicht, daB ich mich nicht
freue." "Noch freuen Sie sich nicht, Vera," sagte er. "Aber
Sie werden sich freuen. Sie werden auch wieder Pawel zu mir

sagen."(MN, p.8)

Pawel is confident that this business trip by the delegates from the GDR to the USSR will culminate in an even greater bond of friendship on a personal and national level. This confidence is based upon his pride in the accomplishments of the Soviet Union under the banner of socialism. Once the German skeptics observe and experience life first-hand in the Soviet Union, Pawel believes the Germans will be convinced that the Soviets are deserving of their claim to the leadership of the communist world and that communism is worthy of implementation in the GDR.

Tangible proof of the remarkable Soviet accomplishments under socialism is presented immediately to Vera Brauer during her first walk through the streets of Moscow. The Soviet capital is depicted as a vibrant, pulsating city that would rival any Western capital. The modern Soviet metropolis displays all the signs of a prosperous, financial and cultural center anywhere. The streets are filled with a steady stream of cars and pedestrians who pursue their business in an orderly fashion. Muscovites of all shapes and sizes, dressed in a multitude of attire and "Lederstifelchen" carrying "volle Einkaufsnetze" are obvious indicators of the prosperity enjoyed by the inhabitants of this city under socialism. Indeed, evidence of Russian opulence abounds. In Vera's hotel room "wuchtige Sessel mit weiBen Schutzüberzügen, dunkelblaue Plüschvorhänge, Spitzendecke auf dem Bett, eine lila Seidenschirmlampe, marmornes Schreibzeug und eine Kristallkaraffe für Wasser"(MN, p.10) are only a few examples of Russian affluence. On the outside, a multitude of taxis, private automobiles and trains transport an unending flow of people to their destinations. Innumerable Muscovites are leaving the city for their vacation destinations, while a corresponding influx of visitors from all over the Soviet Union is flocking to their capital for its holidays. Wherever one looks, Moscow is full of vigor and buzzing with activity. All of this activity is monitored by unusually kind policemen whose sole interest is the safety and welfare of the people. While bustling activity characterizes the main parts of this great city,

outlying sectors are enveloped in peace and tranquility that
is conducive to self-improvement and reflection as is illustrated in the scene witnessed by the strolling Vera Brauer:
"An einem niedrigen, von Pflanzen umrankten Fenster saB im
Licht einer grünen Glaslampe mit Perlenfransen ein junger Mann
über Bücher gebeugt, die Hände in den Haaren vergraben."
(MN, p.13)

Vera, of course, immediately falls in love with this pulsating city. During her frequent walks she is soon overcome
by a great desire to get to know all of this metropolis: "Alles
sehen, keinen Augenblick verlieren. Drei Wochen sind eine kurze
Zeit."(MN, p.12) The more she sees of the city, the more Vera
experiences a remarkable transformation in her own attitude:
"Plötzlich wuchs das Gefühl in ihr, auf das sie den ganzen Tag
gewartet hatte: Lebenslust, Neugier und eine starke Freude."
(MN, p.12) So strong is the influence of what she sees in
Moscow that she feels a great urge "das ganze Leben neu zu
machen. Vera sehnte sich auf einmal danach, und es kam ihr
unaufschiebbar vor."(MN, p.12)

It is quite clear that the former skepticism and doubt concerning the efficacy of the Soviets as leaders of the communist
world has vanished. Far from harboring any lingering doubts
as to the propriety of the Soviet model for socialism Vera now
is filled with admiration for this society: "Vera bekam nicht
genug von dieser Stadt. Sie lief durch die StraBen, setzte
sich in den Parks auf die Bänke, fuhr unter und über der Erde
kreuz und quer bis in die entlegendsten Stadtteile. Am meisten
erregten und fesselten sie die Menschen, zu jeder Stunde in
Massen auf der StraBe, und doch alles andere als Masse. Die
Gelassenheit, gepaart mit Energie, die von ihnen ausging, packte
Vera."(MN, p.20) Thus, the sights and sounds, the people and
the overall atmosphere of Moscow have elicited an immediate
bond between Vera and the Russians and established an affinity
to and longing for a similar life style in Vera as expressed in
the final image before Vera's eyes prior to falling asleep after
her first day in Moscow: "Sein Gesicht [Pawel's G.B.] war ihr
nahegekommen, sie wuBte nicht warum."(MN, p.17)

The reason for the magnetic attraction of the Soviet way of life to Vera soon becomes apparent as she and her colleagues begin to meet the Soviet people. The stage is set for the first person-to-person meeting between the Germans and the Russians while on an excursion to a country hospital on a day so beautiful that it fills Vera with utter joy: "Das ist Leben, dachte Vera sehnsüchtig. Diese Sonne und dieses Land und diese Menschen."(MN, p.21) Following a warm welcome and an inspection of the ultra-modern hospital, the hospital director calmly relates the fact that during World War II, German soldiers had come within one thousand meters of overrunning and destroying the hospital compound. Despite this heinous attempt by their countrymen to subjugate the Russian population and to destroy all that is dear to them, the Soviet hosts nevertheless graciously invite the descendents of these perpetrators into their midsts to share their food and friendship as though nothing had happened. This magnanimity on the part of the Soviet hosts further symbolizes the greatness of socialism to Vera. This goodness emanating from the people of the Soviet Union is the foundation of the new Soviet society. These people, who had every right to demand revenge for the wrongs committed against them by the countrymen of this delegation, instead welcome them with open arms. Inspired by socialism, the Russians are willing to forget and to forgive the past enmity between the two nations and to begin a new era of friendship with their former enemies. The generosity of the Soviet people even extends to the point that they are eager to share the secret of their new found peace and tranquility with their German friends: "Er fragte sie nach ihrem Vornamen. 'Vera...,' wiederholte er. 'Sie wissen, was das auf russisch heißt?' 'Ich weiß es. Vor langer Zeit hat man es mir schon einmal gesagt.' ...'Das heißt Glaube. Wußten Sie es?'"(MN, pp.23-24)

Thus, the key to the Soviet achievement lies in its faith in socialism. Acceptance of this creed can, therefore, lead to a similar transformation of the German society. This is the fundamental message of this work. It is to the fulfillment of this end that Russians and Germans raise their glasses in a

symbolic toast: "'Auf Vera!' forderte er. 'Auf Vera,' sagte
Pawel und trank aus. 'Danke, Direktor. Danke Pawel,' sagte
sie ernst. Dann lachten sie alle bis ihnen die Tränen kamen."
(MN, p.24) As evidence of the feasibility of attaining a new
fraternal relationship between former enemies, the hosts and
guests drink, eat and sing to their hearts' content until a
genuine bond of permanent trust and friendship has developed:
"Man schüttelte sich die Hände, umarmte, küßte sich."(MN, p.25)
The festivities conclude with a final toast as a somber reminder that the enmity of the past between these two nations shall
have been overcome forever: "Daß es nie mehr geschieht."(MN,
p.26)

It is only fitting, therefore, that Vera and Pawel come
upon a "Wegwarte, die blaue Blume des Märchens" near a birch
tree forest after this profound experience. This symbol for
the key to "die Schätze der Welt" is thus obviously found in
the socialist system that transformed former Russian peasants
into the noble representatives of mankind. Accordingly, Vera
hears again the voice from the fairy tale: "Vergiß das Beste
nicht!"(MN, p.27) This voice serves as a reminder for the
visitor from the GDR that the "blaue Blume," the hope of mankind for a world of peace and tranquility has been realized at
least in one nation: "'Von jetzt an,' sagte sie leise, 'wenn
ich an Rußland denke, werde ich dieses Birkenwäldchen sehen.'"
(MN, p.28)

Similar acts of hospitality, helpfulness and genuine human
kindness are accorded the visitors from the GDR by a multitude
of Russians as exhibited by the motherly concern of the hotel
maid for Vera's good health, the cheerful help offered to the
visitors by ordinary citizens in finding the proper means of
transportation, and the lavish banquet given in honor of the
medical team by the workers of a collective farm. While all
of these acts of friendship by the Russians serve to underscore
the benevolence extended to their socialist partners, the relationship between Pawel and Vera above all else symbolizes the
potential for mutual admiration and love between the people of
these two socialist nations.

The first meeting between Pawel and Vera had occurred at the
end of World War II, when Pawel was part of the Soviet occupation
forces in East Germany. Even then Pawel was instrumental in
transforming Vera from a BDM-member[13] to an active collaborator
of the Soviet occupation forces and in kindling her thoughts pertaining to her future profession: "Jürgen schwärmte für die
Technik, aber Pawel schnitt ihm nach einer Weile das Wort ab.
Wie zu einem Erwachsenen sagte er mit vollem Ernst, es gäbe
nur einen wirklichen Beruf auf der Welt. 'Für mich gibt es
nur einen: Arzt.' So hatte Pawel dazu beigetragen, daß Vera
Ärztin geworden war."(MN, p.22) Thus, already during their
first meeting Pawel has sown the seeds of regeneration in Vera
by contributing to her transformation from an adherent to a
policy of nationalism and destruction to an individual dedicated to a healing process in mankind.

The unexpected reunion of Pawel and Vera fourteen years after
their first meeting is testimony to the fact that those early
seeds of kindness and affection by Pawel toward Vera have borne
fruit. Vera has indeed become a doctor as a result of that
statement by Pawel. Even more important is the fact that she
has become an ardent socialist and admirer of the Soviet Union.
It is only fitting, therefore, that these ideological partners
should renew their love for each other. This love, however,
can not come to full fruition in that both Pawel and Vera are
already married. Therefore, they must comply with the prevailing socialist realism code and remain loyal to their spouses.
Indeed, it is clear from the start that this love relationship
between a "Russian" and a "German" serves primarily a symbolic
function. It enables the author to portray Pawel beyond the
propaganda stereotype of soldier, citizen and socialist hero by
presenting him as a human being. While Pawel is a soldier and
hero in every sense of the word, these characteristics are depicted in such an expected, prefabricated fashion that they lose
all credibility. Pawel only comes alive as a human being when
depicted as an emotional, caring, loving, flawed human being.
Although he is married, he begins every day by phoning Vera.
His love for the German visitor is shown by his nervous, irri-

tated and moody behavior whenever they are together. His lips quiver so much with emotion when he holds Vera that he is unable to speak. He chastises Vera for smoking too much. He can neither eat nor sleep normally. The thought of her impending departure puts him into a state of melancholy and utter consternation.

This is not the normal German stereotype of a "Russian." Rather, it is the depiction of a "human being" in love. The message to the German reader is quite clear. Russians are not to be feared as subhuman creatures bent on looting and raping German women as had been instilled in the minds of the German populace by Nazi propaganda. Russians are people with feelings and emotions like all human beings. Indeed, the Russians, in many ways are more compassionate, considerate, forgiving people than Germans as evidenced by the kindness, courtesy and friendship extended to the German delegation. Is it not proper for us Germans, therefore, to reciprocate openly with similar friendship, gratitude and perhaps even love, thereby acknowledging our special relationship to begin to live "'mit offenem Visier,' arglos, ohne Hinterhalt"(MN, p.54) as Pawel and Vera have done?

Thus, this relationship between Pawel and Vera is not really a true physical or emotional entanglement between these two individuals. More than anything else, it is a symbol of a platonic love--an "affair of ideas" between two socialist nations. It is a symbol of the new relationship between two nations that have overcome the enmity of the past and henceforth will be united in permanent friendship. This new relationship is subsequently sealed in an appropriate manner, not with a kiss of passion but with a symbol of deep affection and respect: "Sie [Vera] zog seinen [Pawel's] Kopf zu sich herunter und küßte ihn auf die Stirn."(MN, p.105)

2. Partiality

The primary purpose for the existence of the "Moskauer Novelle" is the promotion of a stronger, permanent bond of friendship between the people of the Soviet Union and the German Democratic Republic. In particular, the "Novelle" attempts to

persuade recalcitrant elements within the population of the
GDR that such a relationship with the Soviet Union is a natural
and proper extension of postwar reality. Moreover, the Soviet
Union is depicted from a national and individual standpoint
as totally deserving of the leadership role in this partnership. Indeed, this work by and large consists of the depiction of a series of events whose sole purpose is designed to
enhance the image of the Soviet Union and its inhabitants in
order to inspire the German readers to become equally fervent
supporters of the "Soviet way" as have the members of the medical team to the Soviet Union.

The vital need for works of literature to depict a new
"partiality" toward the Soviet Union in order to counteract
the effects of hundreds of years of vilification of the Russians
by the Germans is expressed by Christa Wolf in her interview
with the Soviet writer Konstantin Simonow:

> C.W.: Für uns, für meine Generation fingen ja die
> Beziehungen zu den Russen viel später an als für
> Sie die Beziehungen zu den Deutschen – nicht nur,
> weil Sie älter sind als ich, sondern auch aus an-
> deren Gründen. Das Wort 'Russe' ist, soviel ich
> mich erinnere, in meinem Kopf erst seit Beginn des
> Krieges gegen die Sowjetunion, und zwar als ein
> Signal für Angst. Der Russe war eine schreck-
> liche Karikatur in Zeitungen und auf Plakaten, ein
> gefährlicher, dabei weit unter den Deutschen ste-
> hender Menschenschlag. Die ersten wirklichen
> Russen, die ich sah, waren Kriegsgefangene und
> Verschleppte, Männer und Frauen. Erst nach dem
> Krieg, als ich auf einem kleinen mecklenburgischen
> Dorf lebte und als Schreibhilfe des Bürgermeisters
> viel mit Offizieren und Soldaten der sowjetischen
> Besatzungsmacht zu tun hatte – erst da wurden Rus-
> sen für mich konkrete Menschen. Doch glaubt man
> nicht, wie lange es dauern kann, bis eine abstrakte
> Vorstellung von einem anderen Volk – sei es als
> Gespenst, sei es, später, als Ideal – sich mit Leben

füllt, mit einer Menge unterschiedlicher Gesichter,
mit Beziehungen, die einem viel bedeuten. Dieser
langwierige, wechselhafte Prozeß, in dem sich mir
aus einer großen Zahl von Begegnungen verschiedenster
Art ein neues, wie ich heute glaube, der Wirklichkeit
nahekommendes Verhältnis zu Russen, zum russischen
Volk, zur Sowjetunion, bildete, war eine der wich-
tigsten Erfahrungen in meinem Leben überhaupt, die -
wenn auch nicht unbedingt als 'Stoff' - für meine
Arbeit eine sehr große Rolle spielt.[14]

This Russo-phobia reached crisis proportions among the Germans
during the early days of the Soviet occupation of the Eastern
Zone. Everyone, who could, fled to the West. Those unlucky
enough to stay behind locked their doors and barred their windows in a desperate effort to protect themselves against the
"subhuman hordes from the steppes of Russia." This uncomfortable fact had to be brought into the open before a reconciliation between the Germans and Russians could take place. Accordingly, it was absolutely necessary to confront the inhabitants
of the GDR with their past inhumanity toward the Soviets before
a new relationship with the Russians could emerge.

Thus, historical fact and intellectual honesty compelled
Christa Wolf to address this uncomfortable issue in the "Moskauer
Novelle." The enormous difficulty encountered by the Germans
as a whole in overcoming their Russo-phobia is illustrated by
the action of the then sixteen-year-old Vera Brauer when she
came face to face with Pawel during the last days of the war:
"...und ich bin vor ihm ausgerückt. Kopflos geworden vor
seiner grünbraunen Uniform, setzte ich durch die Küche aus dem
Haus, vom Bürgermeistergarten aus schnurstracks über die Wiesen
und Koppelzäune hinter dem Dorf, alles in strömendem Regen."
(MN, p.11) Pawel, the young Soviet lieutenant, aware of the
prejudice harbored toward him, pursues Vera and confronts her
with her bigotry: "Guten Tag, Fräulein. Nicht wieder weglaufen,
hat keinen Zweck. Ich fresse nicht Kinder.'"(MN, p.11) This
forthright statement by Pawel has a sobering impact on Vera in
that it sensitizes her to the inhumane manner in which she

treated another human being. This realization results in a
transformation of Vera. She not only sheds her fear of the
"Russian" but even assists him in announcing the new Soviet
ordinances to the petrified German populace:

> Schon fünf Minuten später ging ich an seiner Seite
> durch das halbe Dorf, rüttelte an den fest ver-
> schlossenen Türen, sah, als Flüchtling an Scheunen
> und Bodenkammern gewöhnt, zum ersten Mal die Bauern-
> stuben von innen, jetzt, als ich sie räumen muBte,
> für Pawels Kompanie. Dem Bürgermeister war der
> Russenschreck in den Magen gefahren, er lag im Bett,
> lieB seine eisgrauen Schnurrbartspitzen vor Angst
> und unterdrücktem Groll zittern und sich warme
> Ziegelsteine auf den Bauch packen. 'Bürgermeister
> krank,' sagte Pawel mit einem unnachahmlichen Aus-
> druck von Ehrerbietung und Spott.(MN, pp.11-12)

It is obvious that the "Bürgermeister" and the rest of the
villagers are in need of a similar "healing" experience as that
encountered by Vera. Indeed, a gradual reconciliation between
the former enemies does take place. Slowly fear of the Russians
changes to tolerance; tolerance gives way to curiosity; curiosity leads to interest, and interest eventually culminates in
conversion and dedication to socialism as prescribed by the
Soviet model.

While this process of conversion to socialism began only
after World War II for the great majority of people residing
in the Soviet Occupied Zone, a few had embraced this political
ideology much earlier. One such person is Walter Kernten who
joined the "Spartakusbund" in the 1920's and has been an avid
supporter of communism ever since. As one of the first converts to Marxism, he endured unabated persecution for his political beliefs. He was imprisoned and sentenced to forced
labor for spreading the hated communist ideology. Despite these
hardships he remained true to his convictions.

The trip to Moscow, therefore, represents the high point in
the lives of each participant of the delegation from the GDR,
because each member of this team had undergone a metamorphosis

similar to that of Vera or Walter and now experiences the
crowning achievement of that long struggle. Understandably,
therefore, Vera, despite travel fatigue and the late evening
hour, yields to an uncontrollable desire to seek out the main
attraction to every communist: "Am ersten Abend muß man auf
dem Roten Platz gewesen sein."(MN, p.11) Even though she is
unsuccessful in locating this inner sanctum of Moscow on this
night, the full impact of this experience is related later
when Pawel remarks: "Da sagte er, auf den Weg weisend, den
sie gekommen waren: 'Hier ist Lenin gegangen.' 'Hier?'
fragte Vera. Dann sprachen sie nicht mehr bis zum Hotel."
(MN, p.34) So moving is the experience of treading on the
same path as one of the high priests of communism that silence
is the only fitting response. In a similar manner, Walter
Kernten, the symbolic patriarch of the German delegation, is
rewarded for his steadfastness and strength of conviction. As
Vera observes Walter Kernten strolling along Red Square, she
knows that this early apostle of Marxism at that moment is am-
ply rewarded for the many years of suffering for his political
beliefs: "Ihr Blick fiel auf Walter. Er stand allein, gebückt,
alt geworden und blickte auf den roten Stern am Spaßkiturm.
Vera kannte das Leben dieses Mannes und begriff: Das war sein
Tag."(MN, p.18)

It is clear, therefore, that the members of the GDR delegation are fervent adherents to socialism. They have been chosen
both for their medical expertise and political convictions to
forge an even stronger bond of scientific and political cooperation between the GDR and the Soviet Union. As representatives
of their respective nations, the Russians and Germans in this
"Novelle" pledge their lives to the pursuit of the ultimate
New Year's resolution: "'Lange und sinnvoll leben,' sagte
Walter. 'Das ist der Grund für alles, was wir tun!'"(MN, p.50)
More specifically, the representatives of these two nations
resolve to bring about the conversion of all people to the
principles of socialism: "'Eines Tages wachen wir auf,' sagte
sie leise, 'und die Welt ist sozialistisch. Die Atombomben
sind im Meer versenkt, und der letzte Kapitalist hat freiwillig

auf sein Aktienpaket verzichtet!'"(MN, p.51)

This dream of a world-wide utopian society under the banner of socialism is subsequently acted out in miniature form during a banquet at a Russian collective farm. Here Russians and Germans have shed all former animosity toward one another and have united in an unparalleled display of friendship and brotherhood that concludes appropriately enough with the singing of "Brüder, zur Sonne, zur Freiheit!" as an unmistakeable symbol of the new solidarity established between these two nations in their effort to promote the course of socialism.

3. National Orientation

It is clear from the outset that the "Moskauer Novelle" fully complies with the prerequisites of the concept of national orientation in that this work does not deal with personal idiosyncrasies or private relationships between individuals. Instead, it focuses on the changing relationship between two nations. Thus, in large measure the main characters of this "Novelle" are not "flesh and blood" individuals but mere types acting out the expected mode of behavior within the all-encompassing super structure of the post-war reality as prescribed by the tenets of socialist realism.

The "Moskauer Novelle," therefore, may be seen as a didactic effort and an act of atonement for the individual and collective guilt borne by the Germans as a result of the atrocities committed against their newfound friend and ally. Thus, Vera Brauer's personal "Verschuldung" in protecting the identity of former Nazi sympathizers who terrorized the neighborhoods of the German village and set fire to a barn in which Pawel Koschkin was permanently injured while risking his life to save Vera's brother is an event "typical" of hostile German behavior following the war toward the Russians and not an important reference to Vera's character development. The underlying message of this incident is that most, if not all, Germans are guilty in one way or another of wrongs committed against the Russians.

The propriety for German atonement on a personal and national level for their "Verschuldung" against the Russians is underscored by the magnanimous treatment the visitors receive in the

USSR. This point is illustrated in the changing relationship between Vera and Pawel. Following their initial meeting at the end of the War, Vera repeatedly lies to the Soviet authorities in order to protect Nazi sympathizers who terrorize the community, thereby greatly endangering the lives of the Soviet troops. Indeed, Vera's "Verschuldung" leads to physical harm both to Germans and Russians. Despite these acts of hostility toward the Russian soldiers, Pawel risks his life to save Vera's brother from certain death by carrying him out of a burning barn. This act of heroism and good will on the part of Pawel in return for the ill will accorded him and his fellow countrymen forms the basis for a transformation in Vera. She is among the first to see the Russians, not as conquering hordes from the East, but as rescuers of the Germans from their own depravity. Pawel, thus, becomes the symbol for the Soviet benefactors who have come, not to return evil for evil, but to point the "prodigal Germans" to the road of salvation--the establishment of a socialist society.

This promise of a new humanity is the underlying motivation for Vera Brauer, and subsequently the people of the GDR, for embracing the tenets of socialism. Vera Brauer, in her role as the "positive hero" of this work, serves primarily as a means of illustrating the regenerative process that has taken place in the GDR as a whole. Thus, the trip to the Soviet Union represents Vera's ultimate confirmation of her conversion to and wholehearted acceptance of the Soviet way of life and political system. The conversion of Vera from a former BDM member to an ardent supporter of Marxism, therefore, symbolizes a similar transformation of actual or hoped for acceptance of Marxism by the population of the GDR as a whole. The rationale for such a regeneration is illustrated in the multitude of positive experiences in Moscow, Kiev and the Soviet Union as a whole encountered by Vera and the entire GDR delegation.

In accordance with the principle of national orientation, a primary function of socialist realism literature is the bridging of the gap between artists and the great masses of the people with easily understandable literature of great interest to the

great majority of the people. The subject matter of this
"Novelle" fulfills this criterion in that it illustrates the
process of regeneration from Nazism to socialism of key individuals who are representative for the conversion of an entire
nation. The format of this work also abides by the prerequisite stipulated by this principle through its adherence to an
extremely simple style and form. The sentence structure and
vocabulary employed in this work are rudimentary to the degree
that they seem to be tailored to an audience consisting primarily of the working class.

The elementary sentence structure is complemented by a corresponding simplicity in form. Present tense authorial narration is the primary mode of conveying the action of the "Novelle"
during the trip to the Soviet Union while periodic flashbacks
by various characters serve to underscore the significance of
the experiences in the USSR for the delegation members. Thus,
the flashbacks, narrated in the past tense, allude to the past
animosity between the Russians and the Germans while present
tense narration by contrast is used to emphasize the new, present
relationship of friendship and cooperation between the two
countries. This interplay of present achievements over past
difficulties underscores the great changes that have taken place
among the German people. By apportioning by far the greatest
part of the "Novelle" to displaying the "present" prosperity
in the Soviet Union and the willingness of the Soviet mentors
to share their good fortune with the visiting delegation, and
therefore by implication with the GDR, the wisdom of a close
alliance with the Soviet Union becomes self-apparent.

Christa Wolf has offered her personal testimonial in this
work to the continued enhancement and cultivation of the closest
possible ties between the people of the GDR and the Soviet Union.
At this early stage in her career Christa Wolf is totally committed to the principles of socialism and has used her first
work to proclaiming that committment.

4. The Typical

It becomes immediately apparent to the reader that except
for the crimes committed by Nazi sympathizers after the war,

the entire "Novelle" is primarily dedicated to a depiction of
life in a near utopian society in the Soviet Union. In this
most advanced socialist society everyone seems to live a life
of contentment, free from the worries that beset individuals
of other nations. In this land of Oz, there is no crime, no
shortages, no personal strife, no personal failure. Instead,
the people of the USSR exude an abundance of goodwill, kindness,
love, hospitality, compassion, peace and overall contentment.
Life in this "paradise" is, appropriately enough, acted out by
characters who fit the mold of the "Antizipation" of all advanced states of socialism. Such projections must necessarily
focus on near utopian ideals which in turn are advanced by
equally flawless personalities. It should come as no great
surprise, therefore, that every character in this work exhibits
the noble characteristics expected from a populace residing
in an advanced state of socialism. Furthermore, it is in keeping with the reality of the USSR-GDR relationship that the
Russian characters have already achieved the ultimate degree
of the anticipated socialist "type" while the Germans for the
most part are still in the process of perfecting this hoped for
personality.

Thus, the entire cast of characters consisting of Pawel
Koschkin, Walter Kernten, Professor Lidia Worochinowa, Sergeant
Jakow Maximovitsch, the maid Deschurnaja, Pawel's wife Sina,
Vera's husband and even the general citizenry of the Soviet
Union residing in the cities and in the country-side serve
merely as distinct entities which together form a mosaic that
depicts a state of contentment and bliss experienced in an advanced socialist society. Each character, therefore, is endow-
ed with a special trait that contributes to the overall portrait
depicting life in an advanced socialist state. As a result,
none of these characters is a fully developed individual.

Thus, Vera Brauer fulfills her primary function in this
"Novelle" by serving as the role model for the process of regeneration for the inhabitants of the GDR from fascism to socialism. Only this aspect of Vera's life seems important to
the author. Subsequently, only those personal characteristics

and events in Vera's life relating directly to this transformation are depicted. Accordingly, only the confession by her father "falsch gelebt zu haben" is offered from Vera's formative years. Beyond this "pertinent" episode, Vera's past remains a mystery. Even her instant reversal from utmost hatred and fear of all Russians to the miraculous trust and friendship she develops toward Pawel is presented only as a de facto event without further explanation. Her subsequent relationship with Pawel after World War II and during her visit to the Soviet Union focuses only on those aspects which serve to confirm her decision to become a socialist. Fleeting references to the current family serve primarily as a means of underscoring her closeness to Soviet life. Thus, the letters she writes to her husband illustrate the torment of her struggle to remain true to him in light of the advances of her Soviet suitor. Even the allusion to her son seems to be included only to reinforce her political convictions in that he has been told the fairy tale in which the "blaue Blume" serves as a symbol for socialism as the key to "das Beste" in life, thereby ensuring the continuity of socialism in future generations.

In a similar manner, Pawel Koschkin serves the function of representing the goodness of the Russian character. He is a loyal soldier and citizen who did his duty in defending his native country and in contributing significantly to the downfall of the Third Reich. As a member of the Soviet occupation forces, he returns the evil perpetrated against him with kindness. He saves the life of an enemy and contributes to the mental and spiritual cleansing of the East German people. He bears the physical handicap he obtained while saving Vera's brother with grace and forgives those responsible for this mishap. Thus, Pawel also serves as the "Antizipation" of the socialist personality with whom a close association and friendship is highly desirable and appropriate. As in the case of Vera Brauer, little else is known of Pawel's personal life or background, because such information is not essential to the essence of depicting a role model of the socialist personality.

Walter Kernten represents the "typical" German who embraced

the precepts of communism during the 1920's, the formative
years of that ideology in Germany. He is depicted as a dedicated socialist who remained true to his convictions despite
the persecution and suffering inflicted upon him for his political beliefs. Following World War II, this kind and
generous man became Vera's formal political mentor and "adopted"
father following the death of her parents. He continues this
role even during Vera's adult years and looks after her during
the trip to the Soviet Union. Walter Kernten, therefore, represents another piece of the puzzle that depicts socialists in
a very favorable light. As in the previous cases, nothing is
known about Walter outside of this specific function assigned
to him.

In a similar manner, Professor Worochinowa, Sergeant
Maximovitsch, the Deschrunaja, Pawel's wife Sina, Vera's husband and the supporting cast of the Russian populace serve the
function of adding certain specific positive characteristics
to the portrait of socialist life. Professor Worochinowa is
depicted as the highly professional physician who at the same
time finds time to intervene personally on behalf of Pawel to
procure a "cure" for his temporary professional stagnation.
Sergeant Maximovitsch provides further evidence of the inherent
goodness of the Russian citizen-soldier. The former war hero
is now a productive member of society who has cast aside all
hostility toward his former enemies as shown by his invitation
of the entire German delegation to a grand celebration of
Russian hospitality toward their guests. Equal loving concern
is shown for Vera's well-being, the visitor from Germany, by
Deschurnaja, the hotel maid. Indeed, Deschurnaja shows Vera
such affection that she assumes the role of the Russian "mother"
to Vera as a complement to the role assumed by Walter, the
German "father," thereby symbolizing the loving care extended
to socialists in both nations by these binational parent figures.
Pawel's wife and Vera's husband perform the function of depicting faithful, supporting partners of their spouses in time of
conflict. They are evidence of solid marital realtionships in
each socialist nation that serve as solid foundations for the

stability of the personal and national well-being. The benefits
of life in such a socialist society are shared by all as evidenced by the happy, healthy robust inhabitants of the Soviet
Union both in the big cities and on the collective farms. Thus,
the composite of the various character types adds up to an idyllic portrait of life in a socialist society.

5. The Positive Hero

In faithful compliance with the prerequisites of socialist
realism, the "Moskauer Novelle" deals directly with the final
and most important component of this literary method, the issue
of the positive hero, during a train ride to Kiev: "...und
wie selbstverständlich ergab sich dann eine neue Frage: Wie
er denn aussehen werde, der Mensch der Zukunft."(MN, p.52)
The answer to this question focuses on the fundamental issue
debated endlessly in literary, sociological and political
spheres in that it provides the justification for the very
existence and labors of the socialist societies. Thus, the
answers provided to this question in this work must be viewed
as representing Christa Wolf's ultimate hopes and dreams for
socialism.

It is no coincidence that Pawel Koschkin, Vera Brauer's
earliest political mentor and representative of the Soviet viewpoint, should speak first in providing his vision of the future
human being, i.e. positive hero:

'Sicher,' sagte er, 'wird er seine Schwächen haben,
unser hochgebildeter, vielseitiger Herr Enkel.
Eine seiner Schwächen wird übrigens sein, daß er
über unsere Debatten erhaben lächelt, wenn er sie
zufällig in alten Büchern aufgezeichnet findet. Na
ja, er wird alles besser wissen. Er wird das Problem der Raumschiffahrt ebensogut gelöst haben wie
das der Verkehrsdichte auf der Erde. Er wird es
fertigbringen, die doppelte Menge von Menschen zu
ernähren. Er wird Leben erzeugen und es--viel-
leicht--auf anderen Planeten entdecken. Er wird
vergessen haben, was uns noch so drückt, und sich
mit Problemen herumschlagen, die wir nicht einmal

ahnen. Bei alldem aber wird er--und das wird seine
größte Leistung sein--kein Roboter werden, kein
perfektioniertes Ungetüm, sondern endlich: Mensch.
Er wird aufrecht über die Erde gehen, lange und
intensiv leben, glücklich sein und wird wissen,
daß dies seine Bestimmung ist.' Verlegen brach
er ab. 'Nun habe ich euch eine Rede gehalten...'
Einen Augenblick lang sahen sie diesen Menschen vor
sich, um dessentwillen alles sich verlohnte. Dann
fragte Vera gespannt: 'Pawel, was ist die wichtigste Eigenschaft Ihres Zukunftsmenschen?'
'Brüderlichkeit,' antwortete er, ohne zu über-
legen. 'Mit offenem Visier leben können. Dem
anderen nicht mißtrauen müssen. Ihm den Erfolg
nicht neiden, den Mißerfolg tragen helfen. Seine
Schwächen nicht verstecken müssen. Die Wahrheit
sagen können. Arglosigkeit, Naivität, Weichheit
sind keine Schimpfwörter mehr. Lebenstüchtigkeit
heißt nicht mehr: heucheln können.'(MN, pp.52-53)
The incarnation of this ideal human being is the supreme
goal of all socialist activity. The realization of this dream
serves as the prime mover in the lifelong struggle to expand
the frontiers of socialism. The solidarity of international
socialism in working toward the attainment of this goal is
indicated by Vera's reaction following Pawel's emotional testimonial: "Vera gab ihm impulsiv ihre Hand. Er drückte sie
heftig und hielt sie fest."(MN, p.53)
Following Pawel's declaration concerning the nature of the
new positive hero, it is Vera's turn to offer her projection
of this personality as the representative of the German socialist viewpoint: "'Und Sie, Vera?' fragte Pawel. 'Charakterstärke, Kraft zur Selbstüberwindung,' sagte sie."(MN, p.53)
Vera's response to this question is obviously directed for
present and future consumption. Her call for "Charakterstärke"
and "Selbstüberwindung" is a pointed reference to Pawel for the
immediate need of these traits in order to conquer their mutual
inclination toward infidelity and as a general appeal for a

universal adherence to a code of ethics and morality.

It is evident that the main characters in this work have
already achieved the standards set forth for the positive hero.
Pawel in particular exhibits all of the prerequisites for such
an honor in that he is by no means an unfeeling robot, but
rather an emotional, sensitive human being. Most of all, he is
the personification of the principle of "brotherhood." He has
extended a helping hand to undeserving individuals. He has contributed to the metamorphosis of human beings from an ignoble
past to a noble present. In the end, he has learned to accept
his handicap and how to overcome it. He has opened his inner
self to another person by declaring openly his love for that
person in a gesture of complete trust--the ability "mit offenem
Visier leben zu können." Pawel Koschkin has built lasting
bonds of friendship on a personal and national level. Most
important of all, he is a credible witness for the realization
of the new socialist society. Here, then, is the representative
of the new positive hero of the first magnitude.

Vera Brauer is the second person to qualify for the status
of the positive hero. She is the primary symbol in this work
for one who has undergone the successful conversion from fascism
to socialism. She has exhibited the strength of character to
admit the error of her past and to embrace the promise of a new,
antithetical "Weltanschauung." Under the early tutorship of
Pawel Koschkin and Walter Kernten in later years, Vera has
evolved into an ardent socialist who contributes to the well-
being of her fellow citizens on the political and professional
level. Vera is the epitomy of the continuously evolving, growing individual in a professional and personal sense. It is this
quality that makes her so attractive to Pawel and ultimately
serves as a catalyst for his future self improvement in professional life. Vera, in the truest tradition of a friend, recognizes Pawel's problem and helps him to overcome his handicap.
Finally, it is Vera who through her "Charakterstärke" and
"Selbstüberwindung" contributes to the proper resolution of
her emotional involvement with Pawel while parting as eternal
friends. Vera, who has been the recipient of so many benefits

from Pawel, is finally able to reciprocate in kind. It would
be difficult to find a more deserving candidate for positive
hero status.

The third positive hero is found in Walter Kernten. This
quiet, elderly man functions to a large extent as the chaperone
of the delegation from the GDR to the Soviet Union. He is the
spiritual father of this group both in age and in the length
of his devotion to socialism. He has helped lay the ground-
work for the new socialist society. To a large extent, therefore, he deserves the credit for the new age of socialism that
is unfolding. While Walter Kernten does not play a highly
visible role in this work, all know that he is the "rock" upon
which their present and future is built. Perhaps Walter
Kernten's own statement summarizes most aptly his qualifica-
tion for the new, positive hero status: "'Lange und sinnvoll
leben,' sagte Walter. 'Das ist der Grund für alles, was wir
tun.'"(MN, p.50) Walter Kernten had lived his long life according to this principle.

These are the unquestionable representatives of the positive
hero in this work. One could even include Professor Worochinowa,
Sergeant Maximovitsch, the Deschurnaja, Pawel's wife and Vera's
husband in this category. All of these characters exhibit
enough positive qualities to be worthy of this title. Indeed,
the entire "Novelle" exudes such an abundance of good will,
compassion, friendship, love and brotherhood that the reader
on occasion must remind himself that he is not confronted by a
fairy tale. It is no wonder, then, that all of these positive
heroes appropriately seem to live in a land reminiscent of
Shangri-La.

How does one respond to this first work of literature produced
by Christa Wolf? What are the literary merits and shortcomings
of the "Moskauer Novelle" that characterize it as a work of socialist realism and as a work of literature per se? Perhaps
Christa Wolf provided the most accurate and credible analysis
of the first work of literature in the essay "Über Sinn und
Unsinn von Naivität" written in 1973.[15] The fourteen year time
span following the actual writing of the "Novelle" provided her

with the necessary distance and cooling off period to enable
her to react in an unemotional and objective manner to her first
published work.

It is clear from the very beginning of this essay that Christa
Wolf experiences great difficulty in confronting her first literary product. She has "keine Lust" to face this task and has
to "force" herself to fulfill her promise to write the essay
about her first literary work. So odious is this task, "daß
mir tagelang gar nichts einfiel und ich die Angelegenheit für
erledigt erklären wollte, bis mir die unselige Idee kam, jenes
Produkt, von dem gegen meinen Willen noch einmal die Rede sein
sollte, nach vierzehn Jahren wieder zu lesen."[16] The act of
rereading the "Moskauer Novelle" proves to be extremely painful
to the author in that she is confronted by such literary flaws
as "ungeschickte Sätze," "verunglückte Bilder," "hölzerne
Dialoge," and "naturalistische Beschreibungen." Even more
embarrassing to her than these stylistic defects is the entire
structure and simplistic formulation of the action:

Mehr schon bestürzte mich ein Zug zu Geschlossen-
heit und Perfektion in der formalen Grundstruktur,
in der Verquickung der Charaktere mit einem Hand-
lungsablauf, der an das Abschnurren eines aufge-
zogenen Uhrwerks erinnert, obwohl doch, wie ich
ganz gut weiß, die Vorgänge und Gemütsbewegungen,
welche Teilen der Erzählung zugrunde liegen, an
Heftigkeit und Unübersichtlichkeit nichts zu
wünschen übriglieBen.[17]

The only explanation Christa Wolf offers in defense of this
example of literary ineptitude is found in her strict adherence
to socialist realism guidelines:

Da zeigt sich (beinahe hatte ich begonnen, es zu
vergessen), wie gut ich meine Lektion aus dem
germanistischen Seminar und aus vielen meist
ganzseitigen Artikeln über Nutzen und Schaden,
Realismus und Formalismus, Fortschritt und Dekadenz in Literatur und Kunst gelernt hatte--so
gut, daß ich mir unbemerkt meinen Blick durch

diese Artikel gärben lieB, mich also weit von
einer realistischen Seh- und Schreibweise ent-
fernte.[18]

In retrospect, the author of the "Moskauer Novelle" can not
fathom the degree of her naivité and overall gullability that
enabled her to write a work of such obvious incompatibility
with reality:

> Das beginnt mich nun doch zu interessieren, auBer-
> halb und jenseits Ihrer Fragestellung. Wie kann
> man mit fast dreiBig Jahren, neun Jahre nach der
> Mitte dieses Jahrhunderts und alles andere als un-
> berührt und ungerührt von dessen bewegten und be-
> wegenden Ereignissen, etwas derart Traktathaftes
> schreiben? (Traktat im Sinne der Verbreitung from-
> mer Ansichten, denn allerdings läBt sich dieser
> Liebesgeschichte zwischen einer Deutschen und einem
> Russen, wie sie da säuberlich in Grenzen gehalten
> und auf das Gebiet der seelischen Verwirrungen
> gewiesen wird, eine gewisse fromme Naivität nicht
> absprechen...[19]

Of central concern to Christa Wolf in coming to grips with
her first work is not only the obvious lack in literary quality,
but rather the false perception of reality that is conveyed
through the political lenses of socialist realism. Such a
compromise of truth, whether done intentionally or unintention-
ally, is indefensible on an ethical and moral basis:

> Nicht daB ich die eminenten Beziehungen zwischen
> Literatur und gesellschaftlicher Moral leugnen
> wollte; nur sollte die gesellschaftliche Moral
> eines Autors sich nicht darin erschöpfen, daB er
> seiner Gesellschaft möglichst vorenthält, was er
> von ihr weiB; obwohl es doch eine Zeit gab--man
> vergiBt zu schnell!--, da gewisse, nach vorgefer-
> tigten Rezepten hergestellte Abziehbilder unter
> dem Stempel 'Parteilichkeit' laufen konnten und
> wir, Anwesende immer eingeschlossen, uns an
> einen recht fahrlässigen Gebrauch dieses Stempels

gewöhnten.[20]

In general, therefore, Christa Wolf confesses that her first work was the result of youthful naivité. She takes great pain to distance herself from that first effort in terms of its political content and mode of expression. She seems to say that such mistakes are a necessary part of the human maturing process. The most important point in making these mistakes, she asserts, is to use them as a learning experience and thereby transform a loss into a potential gain.

Thus, Christa Wolf's own assessment of the "Moskauer Novelle" is that of a third-rate work of literature. Ironically, the reason for the literary deficiency is attributed to the strict adherence to socialist realism criteria. Therefore, the "Moskauer Novelle" can justifiably be labelled a first-rate work of socialist realism and a third-rate work of literature.

Chapter IV

"Der geteilte Himmel:" A Breakdown in Socialist Realism

The second decade in the existence of the German Democratic
Republic brought with it a sense of maturity as a state as
evidenced by the ever increasing number of Western and Third
World nations establishing formal or informal diplomatic relations with the GDR. As a result, official recognition of the
GDR as a separate, independent nation was no longer merely a
political strategem of the Eastern Block but a political reality recognized by all but the staunchest opponents of a divided
Germany. This international recognition of the fledgling nation
as a sovereign state coupled with the considerable advances
made in the economic, social, and political sectors injected
a new sense of optimism and accomplishment into the inhabitants
of the GDR. The young nation had come a long way from the near
total mental and physical devastation experienced in 1945 to
achieve the status of a major economic, military, and political
force within the Warsaw Pact and the world at large. In short,
the German Democratic Republic had "arrived" as a nation in
the world community.

The literature of the GDR reflected this new-found feeling
of legitimacy as a nation and the justified pride in the economic and social progress achieved in a plethora of works in
the early 1960's which were appropriately labeled as "Ankunftsliteratur." This term signified the maturing of the literary
process in the GDR commensurate with its socio-political achievements in which literature no longer focused on the depiction of
the early class struggle but instead turned to a more realistic
portrayal of life in the newly established socialist society.
As such, the "Ankunftsliteratur" had the specific function to
illustrate the significant progress achieved under socialism.
This self-examination was perceived by Walter Ulbricht to be
a legitimate means of extolling both the political virtues of
socialism in the GDR and an appropriate continuation of the
"klassische Erbe" that had been incorporated into socialist

realism literature:

> Goethes 'Faust' und Schillers Dramen zeigen in
> ihrem Inhalt die engen Beziehungen des Dichters
> zu seiner Gegenwart und zeugen von den tiefen
> historischen Kenntnissen, über die die beiden
> Größten unserer klassischen Literatur verfügten.
> Ist es nicht heute erst recht notwendig, daß die
> Schriftsteller in den vordersten Reihen derjeni-
> gen sind, die das Neue der Gesellschaft verkünden
> und den Kampf gegen das Alte, Überlebte, Verfaulte,
> Dekadente führen? In unserer Republik haben sich
> neue gesellschaftliche Beziehungen der Menschen
> entwickelt. Aber wo gibt es eine solche Darstellung
> dieser Entwicklung in künstlerischer Form, wie sie
> die Klassiker des Bürgertums über die Entwicklung
> ihrer Klasse im Kampf gegen die feudale Gesell-
> schaftsordnung gestaltet haben?[1]

As a result of this appeal by Ulbricht during the Bitterfeld Conference in 1959, there emerged in the first half of the
1960's a new literature that fused "Kunst und Leben, Kopfarbeit
und Handarbeit, materielle Bedürfnisse und moralische Maximen"
in a heretofore unparalleled fashion. This course for the new
literature had been charted by Regina Hastedt who had voluntarily worked in a coal mine in Oelsnitz where she had experienced first-hand the life and working conditions of the coal
miners, had befriended the workers, and had experienced a mental and spiritual renewal as a result of the association with
the great activist Sepp Zach. These experiences comprise the
essence of Hasted's subsequent work "Die Tage mit Sepp Zach"
(1959) which Ulbricht offered as a model worthy of emulation
by all GDR writers.

In an effort to gain a similar first-hand knowledge of life
"unter den Kumpeln" in a variety of settings, to carry on the
classical tradition exemplified by Goethe and Schiller in depicting accurately contemporary life, and to bridge the gap
between "Kopfarbeit and Handarbeit" a large number of GDR
writers such as Brigitte Reimann, Eduard Claudius, Franz Fühmann,

Erwin Strittmatter, Hans Marchwitza, Werner Reinowski, Helmut
Hauptmann, Herbert Nachbar and Christa Wolf served their time
in various coal mines, factories and construction sites. Among
the numerous works dealing with the general topic of the work-
ing place within contemporary GDR society are Herbert Nachbar's
"Die Hochzeit von Länneken"(1960), Werner Bräunig's "In diesem
Sommer"(1960), Bernhard Seeger's "Herbstrauch"(1961), Günter
und Johanna Braun's "Eva und der neue Adam"(1961), Brigitte
Reimann's "Ankunft im Alltag"(1961), Franz Fühmann's "Kabelkran
und blauer Peter"(1961), Karl-Heinz Jakobs' "Beschreibung eines
Sommers"(1961), Joachim Wohlgemuth's "Egon und das achte
Weltwunder"(1962), Brigitte Reimann's "Die Geschwister"(1963),
Herbert Nachbar's "Oben fährt der groBe Wagen"(1963), Erwin
Strittmatter's "Ole Bienkopp"(1963), and Christa Wolf's "Der
geteilte Himmel"(1963).

Despite this massive outpouring of literature concerning
the topic of the GDR "Alltag" an embarrassingly small number of
these works could claim any real literary merit. Even Eva
Strittmatter conceded during a "Konferenz junger Schriftsteller"
that until 1962 only one GDR work had achieved any literary significance: "Wenn wir von Claudius' Ähre, der viel mehr der
Garbe der Wirklichkeit als der selbstständige Held des Buches
war, absehen, findet sich nicht eine literarische Gestalt in
allen diesen Büchern, die für unsere Entwicklung Bedeutung
erlangt hätte.[2]

Although the Party functionaries sought a continuation of
literary works that conformed to the guidelines set forth by
the tenets of socialist realism, there emerged the first signs
of a movement away from these strict guidelines toward a more
realistic and truthful depiction of life in the GDR. While
several of the above mentioned works had included some negative
elements in their depiction of the GDR "Alltag," among the first
works to indicate an entirely new tone in GDR literature was
Günter Kunert's television drama "Monolog eines Taxifahrers"
which was scheduled to appear on GDR television on December 23,
1962. However, the program was cancelled prior to its showing
by the authorities due to its alleged anti-socialist realism

characteristics. Kurt Hager justified the cancellation on the
basis of the play's negativism as illustrated by his summary
of the play in which a taxi driver helps a girl,

> das kurz vor der Entbindung steht. Er bringt es
> ins Krankenhaus, nimmt aber keine Bezahlung dafür
> und versucht den ganzen Tag, den Vater des Kindes
> zu erreichen. Dabei stößt er dauernd auf Hinder-
> nisse. Obwohl das Stück in der DDR spielt, ist der
> Mensch auf sich gestellt... Die Diskreditierung und
> Verfälschung unserer Gesellschaft wird dadurch ver-
> stärkt, daß... der Taxifahrer... bei seinem Versuch,
> einem anderen Menschen zu helfen immer auf Unver-
> ständnis, Widerstand und Feindschaft stößt.[3]

The fact that Hager had totally misunderstood the point of
the play made no difference in denying the public access to the
work. The very fact that the work required some thought for a
proper interpretation seemed to be reason enough to remove it
from the public in order to guard the people from a possible
"misinterpretation." Kunert's television play was by no means
an isolated occurrence by GDR writers to buck socialist realism
guidelines. Already during the Fifth Writers' Conference in
1961, Paul Wiens had stated boldly that an accurate reflection
of reality could not always be achieved by means of socialist
realism tenets. Further evidence of a change in attitude
toward the narrow restrictions of socialist realism guidelines
was offered by Jean-Paul Sartre in his speech "Die Abrüstung
der Kultur" in Moscow in 1962 in which he pleaded for ideological coexistence between East and West. Ernst Fischer during
the same meeting revived and reinterpreted the formally despised
terms "formalism" and "decadence" in more moderate tones in his
address entitled "Entfremdung, Dekadenz, Realismus." Finally,
Louis Aragon upon receiving an honorary degree in Prague called
for an

> offenen Realismus einen nicht akademischen, nicht
> festgelegten Realismus, der sich auf neue Fakten
> besinnt und sich nicht an denen genügen läßt, die
> schon seit langem abgerichtet, politisch herge-

richtet sind, der sich auf seinem Wege modifiziert,
um imstande zu sein, die ungenormte Wirklichkeit
zu erkennen, der sich nicht damit zufrieden gibt,
alle Schwierigkeiten auf einen gemeinsamen Nenner
zu bringen, der nicht dazu da ist, das Geschehen
wieder zurückzuführen in die prästabilisierte Ord-
nung, sondern der den Nerv des Geschehens zu treffen
weiß.[4]

In light of these theoretical and actual deviations from the
established norm of socialist realism principles, Walter Ulbricht
deemed it necessary to set the parameters within which literature was to function in the GDR. While acknowledging a certain
loosening of the reins, Ulbricht reminded every writer in the
GDR in his speech of December 9, 1962 that the essential prerequisite for socialist realism had not changed:

Manche Leute meinen, da wir gegen den Stalinschen
Personenkult sind, müsse man jetzt Freiheit für
alles geben, auch für den westlichen Formalismus
und die abstrakte Kunst. Nein, haben wir gesagt,
das hat mit Stalin nichts zu tun. Daß Stalin
einen falschen Standpunkt in der Frage des sozialistischen Realismus hatte, das wissen wir. Darüber
gab es Auseinandersetzungen.[5]

This atmosphere of liberalization within strict parameters
serves as the background for the appearance of Christa Wolf's
second work "Der geteilte Himmel." As we shall see, "Der
geteilte Himmel" renders a much more realistic reflection of
life in the GDR during the early 1960's. This sober portrayal
of the daily concerns of GDR citizens on an individual and national level marks a breakthrough in the quality of GDR literature which is achieved by an adherence to and deviation from
the guidelines of socialist realism in form and content.

While the "Moskauer Novelle" had caused hardly a ripple among
literary and even political circles within and outside the borders of the GDR, the appearance of "Der geteilte Himmel" was
"the" literary event of 1963 in the GDR. Literary discussions
and debates over the subject matter and mode of presentation

of this novel gripped the entire country, ranging from the
ordinary citizen on the street and in the factory, to political
potentates and literary critics in the East and West. Such renowned critics and men of letters as Eduard Zak, Günther Wirth,
Hans Koch, Dieter Schlenstedt, Hans Jürgen Geerdts, lay writers
from the VEB Waggonwerk Ammendorf, the editorial staff and
readers of the journals "Freiheit" and "Forum," as well as the
political magnates Alfred Kurella and Walter Ulbricht provided
their respective favorable and/or unfavorable reactions to this
work.[6]

The central issues of these debates revolved around the
manner in which Christa Wolf had portrayed such aspects as
divided Germany, the flight of GDR citizens to the West, economic and political hardships experienced in the GDR, the role
of the outsider, and the depiction of the Party and its adherents in this novel. These topics of everyday concern to the
average citizen were presented in a refreshingly objective
manner and accounted for the sale of 160,000 volumes within a
few months. The demand for this book was equally great on the
international market which resulted in the translation of the
novel into Czech, Russian, Rumanian, Serbian, Croatian, Polish,
Hungarian, Bulgarian, Finnish, Japanese, French, Spanish and
English. As a crowning achievement, the novel was made into
a film by the GDR DEFA film company under the direction of
Konrad Wolf in 1964.

Thus, at the ripe-old age of thirty-four Christa Wolf had
taken a giant leap forward in her status as a writer and political figure in the GDR. As a result of her celebrated literary
success she was nominated for membership on the Central Committee of the SED. She was awarded a "Nationalpreis III.
Klasse" by the Academy of Arts of the GDR. During the Second
Bitterfeld Conference she was accorded the distinct honor of
addressing the professional and laywriters on the function and
nature of literature in the GDR. Finally, she was selected
to the prestigious P.E.N. society of the German Democratic
Republic. Christa Wolf suddenly had become one of the foremost
writers and celebrated personalities in the GDR. An analysis

of her second work will show that she had indeed progressed
dramatically as a writer and fully deserved the honors bestowed
upon her.

1. Objective Reflection of Reality

Whereas the "Moskauer Novelle" depicted an incredibly false
picture of reality in the Soviet Union which served as an en-
ticement to the members of the delegation from the GDR to embrace socialism as the wave of the future on the basis of those
fabricated achievements, "Der geteilte Himmel" offers a look
behind the façades and lofty Party slogans in an effort to
present an "honest" picture of life in the GDR at the beginning
of the 1960's. Gone is the distasteful sugar coating and over-
laden frosting of irreality of the "Moskauer Novelle." It is
replaced in "Der geteilte Himmel" by a major effort to impart
the truth concerning life in the GDR during the years 1960-1961.
This depiction of the actual state of socialism within the GDR
is testimony to the integrity of Christa Wolf as a writer and
human being. It is a commitment to truth conveyed in a remarkably sophisticated literary mode which earned Christa Wolf both
international literary acclaim and considerable criticism within
her own borders.

As had been the case for Vera Brauer in the "Moskauer
Novelle," it is the central purpose of "Der geteilte Himmel"
to promote the conscious awakening and subsequent commitment
of Rita Seidel, the main character in this novel, to socialism.
In sharp contrast to the "Moskauer Novelle," however, in which
this commitment to socialism by Vera Brauer was achieved on
the basis of a near utopian display of friendship, brotherhood
and the fulfillment of all material and spiritual needs within
the Soviet socialist society, Rita Seidel in "Der geteilte
Himmel" is "educated" to the virtues inherent in a total commitment to a noble cause despite the hardships and personal
sacrifices endured for that cause. While the overall purpose
of these two works is nearly identical, therefore, the means
of attaining this goal is marked by stark contrast.

From the onset, "Der geteilte Himmel" departs from the norm
of socialist realism works of its time that depicted the cus-

tomary picture of individual and collective contentment and
harmony expected within a socialist society by startling the
reader with the presentation of an ominous metaphor of gloom
and doom in the prologue of this novel:

> Die Leute, seit langem an diesen verschleierten
> Himmel gewöhnt, fanden ihn auf einmal ungewöhnlich
> und schwer zu ertragen, wie sie überhaupt ihre
> plötzliche Unrast zuerst an den entlegensten Dingen
> ausließen. Die Luft legte sich schwer auf sie, und
> das Wasser - dieses verfluchte Wasser, das nach
> Chemie stank, seit sie denken konnten - schmeckte
> ihnen bitter.[7]

What, then, was the reason for "den verschleierten Himmel"
and the "Schatten" that had fallen over the GDR? What was the
cause of the widespread "Unrast" among its inhabitants? What
"Gefahren, die alle tödlich sind" were threatening the very
lives of the populace of this socialist society? What terrible
calamity had happened to warrant the opening paragraph of the
main body of a socialist realist novel to depict "one of its
own" in a state of complete mental disorientation following a
suicide attempt?

> In jenen letzten Augusttagen des Jahres 1961 erwacht
> in einem kleinen Krankenhauszimmer das Mädchen Rita
> Seidel. Sie hat nicht geschlafen, sie war ohnmächtig.
> Wie sie die Augen aufschlägt, ist es Abend,... sie
> weiß gleich wieder, was mit ihr... geschehen ist...
> Sie hat noch undeutlich ein Gefühl von großer Weite,
> auch Tiefe... Ach ja, die Stadt. Enger noch: Das Werk,
> die Montagehalle. Jener Punkt auf den Schienen, wo
> ich umkippte. Also hat irgendeiner die beiden Waggons
> noch angehalten, die da von rechts und links auf mich
> zukamen. Die zielten genau auf mich. Das war das
> Letzte.(GH, p.9)

Whether in the country or the city, at the work place or in
the home, life in the GDR as depicted in this novel is far from
ideal. So it is with Rita Seidel, a nineteen-year-old insurance
employee who is mired in absolute boredom and frustration as a

result of the monotony of her life in an isolated village. A
romantic at heart, this highly sensitive and emotional girl
leads a totally apolitical existence and perceives life through
the eyes of a naive observer of the harmony in nature while her
own fate seems doomed to loneliness and despair:

> Oft dachte sie: Niemals krieg ich von diesem Fen-
> ster aus noch was Neues zu sehen. In zehn Jahren
> hält das Postauto auch noch hier, Punkt zwölf Uhr
> mittags, dann werden meine Fingerspitzen staub-
> trocken, ich wasche mir die Hände, noch ehe ich
> weiß, daß ich essen gehen muß.
> Tagsüber arbeitete Rita, abends las sie Romane,
> und ein Gefühl der Verlorenheit breitete sich in
> ihr aus.(GH, p.15)

This humdrum existence is unexpectedly interrupted by the appearance of Manfred Herrfurth, a 29-year-old Ph.D. student in
chemistry, with whom Rita immediately falls in love. Commensurate with his profession as a chemist, Manfred is an unemotional,
aloof individual whose primary concerns revolve around his profession. His characteristics as a "loner" or "outsider" are
evident even to the naive Rita when she asks him during a dance:
"'Ist das schwer, so zu werden, wie Sie sind?'"(GH, p.12) Despite these obvious reservations concerning Manfred's personal
characteristics, Rita responds affirmatively to the chemist's
casual question: "'Könnten Sie sich in einen wie mich ver-
lieben?'"(GH, p.12) And so a near perfect love relationship
evolves between Rita and Manfred. Rita "fühlte, daß sie lebte
wie nie vorher"(GH, p.18) while Manfred who had never been able
to commit himself to a lasting relationship realized: "An dieses
Mädchen band ihn das erste Wort, das sie zu ihm sagte. Er war
getroffen, auf unzulässige, fast unwürdige Art im Innersten
verwundet."(GH, p.19)

And so it seems at this point that this novel will serve as
yet another testimonial to the triumphant regeneration of
lonely, isolated individuals into active, inspired, well-adjust-
ed members of a socialist society. Ironically, however, it is
precisely the intrusion of politics into this apolitical rela-

tionship that is responsible for the disintegration of this
blissful state into estrangement, disharmony, and alienation
that leads first to the dissolution of the emotional bond between these two people and eventually to their permanent physical separation within two antithetical socio-political sys-
tems--Rita remains in the GDR while Manfred flees to the West.
The strain brought about by this emotional and physical separation leads to Rita's mental and physical breakdown and her subsequent suicide attempt. What were the underlying causes of
this traumatic experience? What aspects of the socialist society were so odious to Manfred that he abandoned his country
and the only person he loved for another political system?

Instead of depicting another "expected" picture of a utopian
order in the GDR that would be recognized by all as sheer propaganda and, therefore, would be an insult to their intelligence,
Christa Wolf has departed from the norm and written an unprece-
dentedly realistic account of the experiences of two ordinary
inhabitants in the GDR. The opposite reaction to similar
experiences by these individuals is equally realistic and can
be supported by ample evidence on both sides by those who chose
to remain in the GDR and those who fled to the West. Thus, the
concept of truth which plays a major role in this work is supported by ample evidence on both sides of the Iron Curtain.

Far from approaching the "Paradise" portrayed in the "Moskauer
Novelle," life in the GDR is beset by problems which cause it
to fall far short of the lofty goals espoused by Party guidelines and slogans. The simple fact is that it has proven to
be far more difficult to establish the socialist utopia than
the architects of that socio-political order had imagined. For
one thing, the GDR is inhabited by people who for the most part
were ardent or passive supporters of the Nazi past. While some
of the Nazi supporters truly converted to socialism, many have
adjusted to the new political order in the manner of the Herrfurth
family: "In irgendeiner der fünfundvierziger Aprilnächte hat
meine Mutter das Führerbild verbrannt. Seitdem hängt diese
Herbstlandschaft bei uns über dem Schreibtisch, du erinnerst
dich?"(GH, p.45)   PRAGMATIC.

It is no wonder, therefore, that Manfred Herrfurth can be
justifiably skeptical of all the political slogans proclaiming
the dawning of a new age of socialism. "Wir lachten laut, wenn
wir die Plakate lasen: Alles wird jetzt anders. Anders? Mit
wem denn? Mit diesen selben Leuten?"(GH, p.45) Indeed, wherever one looks the remnants of the Nazi era or at least anti-
socialist tendencies surface. The most graphic illustration
is depicted in the home life of the Herrfurth family. This
household is plagued by a generation gap in which Manfred loathes
his parents for their support of National Socialist ideas, their
mistreatment of him in his early childhood to impress their Nazi
superiors and their present cowardice in showing their real political convictions. In essence, they were in the past and are
in the present people devoid of any real convictions, "Mitläufer"
in the classical sense. It is less than surprising, then, that
these people make it a habit to listen to "eine freie Stimme
der freien Welt"(GH, p.149) and would readily flee to the West
if only they were younger.

The fact that the people of the "Herrfurth mentality" are
strewn throughout the GDR is evident in the railroad car factory in which Rita works during her vacation while studying to
become a teacher. While she is assigned to the famous "Brigade
Ermisch" she soon discovers that even these so-called "tüchtigen
Zwölf" are torn by internal strife and intentionally produce
far less than they are capable of producing in order to make
life as easy as possible for themselves. When production quotas
cannot be met, the plant manager escapes to the West leaving the
entire operation in the lurch. Consequently, productivity de-
clines daily until there is a standstill in the factory and murmurs of dissatisfaction and unrest are heard throughout the
plant until reality exposes as farcical the political banners
depicting enthusiastic workers performing their various tasks:

> Beklommen lauschte Rita auf das allmähliche Absinken
> der brüllenden, stampfenden, kreischenden Geräusche
> in den Hallen. Gespannt sah sie in die resignierten,
> abwartenden Gesichter ihrer Brigade, verglich diese
> Gesichter mit denen auf den Zeitungsbildern, die noch

heute an der Bretterwand der Frühstücksbude hingen
und fragte sich: Wer lügt hier? Auf einmal waren die
immer längeren Pausen ('Keine Arbeit! Kein Material!'
sagte Ermisch meistens schon früh bei Schichtbeginn)
angefüllt mit Gehässigkeiten und Gezänk.(GH, p.53)

The great majority of the populace exhibits similar apathy
and disinterest in the productivity and political goals with
which they are bombarded on a daily basis. In stark contrast
to the political rhetoric, the reality of the socialist society depicted here is one on the verge of complete collapse:

'Was ist los?' fragte sie Rolf Meternagel.

'Was los ist? Das Normale. Das, was kommen mußte.
Wenn keiner sich verantwortlich fühlt und jeder nur
in seinem kleinen Eckchen kramt, und das bis hoch
hinauf in die Leitung, dann muß aus vielen kleinen
Schweinereien eines Tages die ganz große Schweinerei
werden. Dann hat die Materialverwaltung keine Ahnung
von der neu anlaufenden Produktion, dann ist also das
Material nicht eingeplant, dann ist auch die Technolo-
gie nicht fertig und keiner weiß, was er machen soll.
Laß dann noch ein paar Zulieferbetriebe stocken,
wie es jetzt geschieht, und du hast alles, was du
brauchst.'(GH, pp.53-54)

Only Rolf Meternagel, a member of the "Brigade Ermisch,"
struggles relentlessly to increase the productivity of the
group. As a result of his efforts he is hated by the brigade
members and leads the life of an "outsider." Undaunted by the
hostile feelings of his comrades toward him, Meternagel pursues
his mission out of a sense of duty, morality, and political
conviction to socialism:

'Verpflichtung' lasen alle. Anstatt acht Rahmen
täglich, sollte jeder von ihnen zehn Fersterrahmen
pro Tag einbauen. 'Und erzählt mir nicht, daß das
nicht möglich ist.'
'Möglich ist vieles,' sagte Franz Melcher. 'Bloß
sein eigenes Nest bescheißen, das ist unmöglich für
einen normalen Menschen.'

'Was nennst du normal?' fragte Herbert Kuhl schnell.
Rita glaubte einen Funken von echtem Interesse in
seinen Augen zu sehen, der aber sofort wieder er-
losch.
'Was normal ist?' fragte Rolf Meternagel gefähr-
lich leise. Jetzt erst, da er sich der Lust hingab,
sich gehenzulassen, merkte man ihm die Anspannung der
Selbstbeherrschung an. 'Das werd ich dir sagen.
Normal ist, was uns nützt, was unsereinen zum Menschen
macht. Unnormal ist, was uns zu Arschkriechern, Betrügern und Marschierern macht, die wir lange genug gewesen sind. Aber das wirst du nie begreifen, du -
Leutnant.'(GH, p.74)
Despite this outburst, no one had signed Meternagel's
"Verpflichtung" calling for greater productivity. The reason
for this noncompliance on the part of the workers is their disinterest in working for some abstract political cause when they
are confronted with more concrete, personal issues:

Was war ihnen wichtig? Die Braut, das kleine ererbte
Grundstück, das Motorrad, der Garten, die Kinder, die
alte Mutter, die blind war und Pflege brauchte, die
neuen Arbeitsnormen, Schauspielerfotos. Vielerlei, was
an ihnen zerrte, verfluchte und doch gehätschelte Ver-
strickungen verschiedener Art. Anspruchslose Vergnügun-
gen, die man ihnen früher untergeschoben hatte für
das große Vergnügen, das man ihnen vorenthielt: aus
dem vollen zu leben. Nun klammerten sie sich an ihre
Gewohnheiten, nun hackten sie erbittert nach Meternagel.(GH, p.75)

Perhaps the most serious indictment of the socialist order
in the GDR during the early 1960's was its refusal to tolerate
constructive criticism that was offered by its citizens. Indeed, it was Manfred Herrfurth's betrayal by one of his "friends"
when Manfred attempted to improve the system by pointing out
"Fehler im Studienbetrieb," "den tollen Ballast," and "Heuchelei,
die mit guten Noten belohnt wurde"(GH, p.131) that turned him
forever against the socialist credo. Instead of examining this

criticism in an objective fashion, the political dogmatists
turned against him. His "friend" labelled him one of those
"'vom Leben abgekapselten, in bürgerlichen Irrmeinungen be-
fangenen Intellektuellen, die unsere Universitäten in den
ideologischen Sumpf zurückzerren wollen.'"(GH, p.132) This
myopia and intolerance of criticism by Party members transformed Manfred from a skeptical collaborator of socialism to
a defector: "Er, er ist es gewesen, der mich zwang, dem Bild
ähnlicher zu werden, das er da wider besseres Wissen von mir
entworfen hat."(GH, p.132)

Similarly dogmatic Party functionaries are still performing
their destructive work in the person of Mangold who constantly
intimidates both the professor and students in Rita's class
with his political outbursts, thereby threatening to alienate
one of the most recent converts to socialism: "Vor allem aber
fühlte sie, [Rita] daB Mangold, wenn er sich durchsetzen konnte,
ihr viel mehr zerstörte als die Möglichkeit, Lehrerin zu werden."
(GH, p.123) Indeed, Mangold's ideological tirades have a
similar effect on Rita that the betrayal of Manfred's "friend"
had on him: "Dieses AuBenseitergefühl hatte sie ja nicht das
erste Mal. Aber so schmerzlich und beschämend war es noch nie
gewesen. Das sonst schon vertraute Gesicht der Stadt war für
sie heute zu einer Grimasse umgestülpt."(GH, p.125)

In light of these and numerous other negative aspects of
life in the GDR, Manfred and Rita reach diametrically opposed
decisions concerning their response to this deplorable state
of affairs. Manfred decides to wash his hands of all the shenanigans during a party at his professor's home. At this party,
which was attended by less than avid socialists, Manfred is informed by his friend Martin Jung that their Spinn Jenny had
been rejected for production by the political authorities.
Manfred sees in this rejection the final proof of his expend-
ability: "Sie brauchten ihn nicht. Da gab es irgendwelche
Leute, die konnten groBe Hoffnungen eines Menschen mit einem
Federstrich vernichten. Dieses ganze Gerede von Gerechtigkeit
war nichts weiter als Gerede."(GH, p.110) This second rebuff
by the system at a time when "Er war drauf und dran gewesen,

sich einfangen zu lassen."(GH, p.111) finalizes his decision
to abandon this system forever. This step, however, has far
greater implications than a mere change in political outlook.
It means the severance of the bond of love with Rita:

> Sah sie ihn denn zum erstenmal? Das nicht. Doch
> wer kennt nicht die Schwierigkeit, den wirklich zu
> sehen, den man liebt? In diesen wenigen Sekunden
> rückte Manfred für sie aus der unscharfen Nähe in
> einen Abstand, der erlaubt, zu mustern, zu messen,
> zu beurteilen. Es heiBt, dieser unvermeidliche
> Augenblick sei das Ende der Liebe. Aber er ist nur
> das Ende der Verzauberung. Einer der vielen Augen-
> blicke, denen die Liebe standzuhalten hat.
> DaB beide es gleichzeitig wuBten, war viel. Es gab
> etwas wie eine stumme Verständigung. Jedes Wort
> hätte verletzen müssen, aber Blicke... In seinen Augen
> las sie den EntschluB: Auf nichts mehr bauen, in
> nichts mehr Hoffnung setzen. Und er las in ihrem
> Blick die Erwiderung: Nie und nimmer erkenn ich das
> an.(GH, p.112)

Consequently, the toast Manfred offers at the conclusion of
the party serves as ultimate proof of his change in attitude
toward the socialist ideology: "'Auf unsere verlorenen
Illusionen.'"(GH, p.116) Thus, it is only a matter of time
before Manfred's distancing from the political ideology of
the GDR takes on tangible form in his escape to the West.

Whereas the difficulties experienced in the GDR led to
Manfred's decision to leave the GDR, the same hardships awaken-
ed in Rita a sense of duty and moral obligation to contribute
to their elimination. Instead of abandoning her compatriots,
as so many did in the course of this work, Rita is prepared to
do whatever is necessary to reverse these undesirable conditions:

> Verwundert beobachtete Rita an sich, daB in den
> schwärzesten Tagen, als es fast keine Arbeit mehr
> gab und die Brigaden in bösem Schweigen in ihren
> Bretterverschlägen zusammenhockten, ihre eigene

Mutlosigkeit in Ungeduld umschlug und in die Bereit-
schaft, einen Umbruch, wenn er doch endlich kommen
sollte, mit aller Kraft zu unterstützen.(GH, p.54)

Thus, it is Rita who becomes the staunchest ally of Rolf
Meternagel. She is the first to supply him with the much needed
psychological support in his effort to convince the brigade members to abandon their work slowdown when she asks: "'Wie lange
wollen Sie das noch mitansehen?'"(GH, p.56) And so, little by
little, the conditions in the factory improve. In time, the
installation quota of the brigade is raised from eight to ten
windows per day. Several individuals have signed Meternagel's
"Verpflichtung," the animosity among brigade members abates and
a sense of camaraderie emerges. Ernst Wendland, the new plant
manager, while not "turning the country around" as his name
indicates, does improve the working atmosphere and productivity
record of the railroad car factory by means of a noticeable
coordination of effort "von oben und unten."

Most importantly, however, there is a real effort underway
to silence the "Mangolds" of the GDR. Rita is among the first
to recognize the pathetic nature of this Party functionary:

Mangold sprach lange. Rita wuBte, was er sagen
würde. Sie hörte kaum zu, aber sie sah ihn aufmerksam an. Er kam ihr wie entzaubert vor.
Merkte denn niemand sonst, wie hohl jedes Wort
aus seinem Munde klang? Wie lächerlich sein Pathos
war? Ihr war, als könne sie den Mechanismus sehen,
der diesen Menschen bewegte.
Sie schämte sich für alle, die vor ihm zu Boden
blickten.(GH, p.129) Erwin!

Subsequently, even Egon Schwarzenbach, a Communist Party
member, rises to silence the destructive, intimidating threats
of Mangold so that a new sense of freedom overtakes the class
members. Thus, the Communist Party is cleansing itself by unmasking the idle chatter of the politicians for what it is.
The message to the political tyrants is quite clear. The inhabitants of the GDR will no longer tolerate political dogmatists. The people have a right to expect truthful responses

from their political leaders pertaining to their actions. This
new relationship between the inhabitants of the GDR and its political leaders will not come about by itself, it must be won:
Es stimmt: Ohne Schwarzenbach hätte alles anders aus-
laufen können. Warum nur hatten sie allein kein Zu-
trauen zu sich? Was hinderte sie, einfache menschliche
Fragen zu stellen, wie Schwarzenbach es jetzt tat,
jemandem aufmerksam zuzuhören, ohne ihm zu mißtrauen?
Was hinderte sie, jeden Tag so frei zu atmen, wie jetzt?
Sich immer so offen anzublicken?(GH, p.130)
Slowly a new courage to criticize those aspects in the GDR
that are wrong takes hold. Inspired by Rita's zest for truth,
Schwarzenbach continues the struggle for reform in the university setting that was begun by Manfred. Although Schwarzenbach
too is afraid of the possible consequences of his action, he is
convinced that: "Wir brauchen keine Nachplapperer, sondern
Sozialisten."(GH, p.185) Thus, the change from the widespread
hypocrisy to a new forthrightness and truth which Manfred had
sought seems to be on the ascent. At least Schwarzenbach and
Rita are willing to risk any political repercussions for this
noble principle:
Die Leute, die ihn verdächtigen, haben mehr Macht
als er, denkt Rita. Und Schwarzenbach, als habe er
ihren Gedanken erraten, sagt: 'Sollen sie ruhig noch
ein paar Versammlungen machen und über mich schimpfen.
Ich werde daran denken, wie gierig sie nach Aufrich-
tigkeit sind. Ich werde sagen: Jawohl, wir haben
eine besondere Lage. Zum erstenmal sind wir reif,
der Wahrheit ins Gesicht zu sehen. Das Schwere nicht
in leicht umdeuten, das Dunkle nicht in hell. Vertrauen
nicht mißbrauchen. Es ist das Kostbarste, was wir uns
erworben haben. Taktik- gewiß. Aber doch nur Taktik,
die zur Wahrheit hinführt.
Sozialismus- das ist doch keine magische Zauberformel.
Manchmal glauben wir, etwas zu verändern, indem wir
es neu benennen. Sie haben mir heute bestätigt: die
reine nackte Wahrheit, und nur sie, ist auf die Dauer

der Schlüssel zum Menschen. Warum sollen wir unseren entscheidenden Vorteil freiwillig aus der Hand legen?'" (GH, p.185)

Perhaps the ultimate symbol for the dawning of a new era in the socialist world, the proof that "So wie es jetzt ist, bleibt es nicht..."(GH, p.39) is found in "die Nachricht" of the successful launch of the first man--a cosmonaut-- into space. The symbolism of this scientific achievement is obvious. As this "Bauernsohn" had become a cosmonaut, so too the burdensome life of the people living under socialism will reap the fruits of technology in a better world. With time, the present hardships will be overcome as man had conquered the forces of gravity that heretofore had bound him to the confines of this planet.

Despite the fact that Manfred and Rita have come to view life in the GDR from totally different perspectives, the couple makes one final effort for a reunion. Following his departure to West Berlin, Manfred invites Rita to visit him there. Although Manfred notices immediately that: "'Aber du hast dich verändert'"(GH, p.170), he nevertheless entices Rita to remain with him: "'Na,' sagte Manfred spöttisch. 'Nun sieh dich um. Die freie Welt liegt dir zu Füßen.'"(GH, p.171) This obvious allusion to Christ's temptation by the devil with its totally negative implications for Manfred is one of the few outright defamations of character in this work. Like Christ, Rita staunchly resists the temptations that the West has to offer and remains true to her political ideology:

Aber schließlich läuft alles das doch auf Essen und Trinken und Sichkleiden und Schlafen hinaus. Wozu aß man? fragte ich mich. Was tat man in seinen traumhaft schönen Wohnungen? Wohin fuhr man in diesen straßenbreiten Wagen? Und woran dachte man in dieser Stadt, ehe man einschlief bei Nacht?(GH, p.173)

In essence this final meeting between these two people who are still deeply in love confirms the fact that each person perceives life through a "politische Brille" that is so fundamentally different that it makes a reunion impossible. Despite Manfred's pleadings: "'Dich lieb ich, keine andere, und für

immer. Ich weiß, was ich sage. Vor dir hat das keine von mir
gehört. Ist es zuviel verlangt, dich zu bitten: Geh mit?...'"
(GH, p.179), Rita knows that she could not function in the West
to the same degree that Manfred was unable to tolerate life in
the GDR. Her entire being is dedicated to bringing "eine neue
Moral" into the world as evidenced by the fact that even in the
West she cannot forget the struggle of her comrades to advance
this new age. In an environment of plenty, her thoughts go
back to Rolf Meternagel who struggles valiantly to overcome the
deficiencies: "Er hat sich mehr vorgenommen, als er schaffen
kann. Aber gerade deshalb hätte sie nicht fertiggebracht, ihn
im Stich zu lassen. Auch mit Worten nicht."(GH, p.175)

While Manfred is convinced: "Der Mensch ist nicht dazu
gemacht, Sozialist zu sein"(GH, p.180), Rita is equally certain
that she is part of a "...Sog einer großen geschichtlichen
Bewegung..."(GH, p.181) For the sake of this mission, Rita
gives up the man she loves and returns to the GDR: "Wie viele
Nächte habe ich wach gelegen und versuchsweise 'dort' an seiner
Seite gelebt, wie viele Tage hab ich mich gequält. Aber die
Fremde ist mir fremd geblieben, und dies alles hier heiß und
nah."(GH, p.181) The price of this commitment to socialism
was very high for Rita. The anguish and grief endured by her
as a result of her separation from Manfred led to her mental
breakdown and suicide attempt.

Thus, there is indeed much cause for the "verschleierten
Himmel," the "Unrast" and "Schatten" that envelop life in the
GDR. Nevertheless, there is also reason for optimism in that
some of the impediments to a better, freer life have been overcome. The "Brigade Ermisch" has become more cooperative and
more productive. The entire factory now is meeting its production quota and is in the good hands of an understanding, compassionate manager. Truth is on the ascent. Mangold has lost
his influence while constructive criticism is on the increase.
Even the Spinn Jenny, Manfred's invention, is receiving a second
look for possible mass production. The orbiting cosmonaut is
proof of the potential of man to overcome any problem confronting
him. Finally, Rita has recuperated from her illness and has

become a stronger person as a result of her experiences and is
now ready to face life again: "Sie hat keine Angst, daB sie
leer ausgehen könnte beim Verteilen der Freundlichkeit. Sie
weiB, daB sie manchmal müde sein wird, manchmal zornig und
böse."(GH, p.199) Life will not be easy for anyone in the GDR.
However, there is the feeling that the worst is behind them.
The crisis has passed; a new calm is setting in that brings a
much deserved respite and hope to the weary: "DaB wir uns
gewöhnen, ruhig zu schlafen. DaB wir aus dem vollen leben, als
gäbe es übergenug von diesem seltsamen Stoff Leben."(GH, p.199)

2. Partiality

While Christa Wolf unquestionably wrote "Der geteilte Himmel"
from the perspective of socialist partiality, adherence to this
concept no longer implies unquestioned subservience to Party
doctrine but rather an individual commitment to work for the
establishment of a socialist society that is characterized
above all else by truth. In accordance with this definition
of partiality, Christa Wolf reserves the right to portray both
positive and negative elements within the socialist society of
the GDR. Indeed, with truth instead of political ideology
serving as the guiding light for this work, Christa Wolf has
deviated from the standard format of socialist realism and returned to a universally accepted function of literature.

In accordance with her search for truth, Christa Wolf has
depicted life in the GDR as she may have experienced it in the
factory, the university, in social gatherings and on a private
level. In general, the sum total of these experiences is negative with only an occasional glimmer of hope breaking through
the litany of trials and tribulations in all segments of life
in the GDR. It is not necessary to recount the problems encountered in the railroad car factory, the "Brigade Ermisch," the
poisonous atmosphere within the Herrfurth family and the university setting. While the unveiling of these problems contributes
to the shattering of the traditional concept of socialist partiality in which only the achievements of socialism were extolled, the most striking departure from traditional socialist
partiality lies in the negative depiction of Communist Party

Maugdd.

functionaries and the glaring absence of positive influences
emanating from the Party to those in need of regeneration.

The most glaring example of a negative Party functionary is
depicted in the person of Mangold. Mangold symbolizes all those
loud-mouthed, self-righteous, dogmatic Party members who use
their position in the SED to shout their slogans and commands
at their fellow citizens in order to enhance their own power
base by degrading others. Such Party officials who still attempt to "diktieren, anstatt zu überzeugen" are in effect no
less destructive to the cause of socialism than the most antagonistic segment of the population represented by Frau Herrfurth
with whom Mangold shares many traits: "Der gleiche blinde Eifer,
die gleiche MaBlosigkeit und Ich-Bezogenheit... Kann man denn
mit den gleichen Mitteln für entgegengesetzte Ziele kämpfen?"
(GH, pp.123-24)

While other works of literature in the GDR had dared to point
out minor flaws in Party officials, none had taken the drastic
step of labelling certain SED members as enemies of the state
in that their behavior was counterproductive to the goals of
the SED. It is only Christa Wolf's utmost commitment to truth
that enables her to make this assertion and then to illustrate
this point with the specific examples of unjust treatment accorded to Manfred Herrfurth, Martin Jung, and Sigrid as well
as the intimidation wrought upon untold observers of these
incidents.

Truth, not political ideology, again is uppermost in the
mind of Christa Wolf when she permits the enraged Martin Jung
and Manfred Herrfurth to attack the hypocrisy of the entire
system, to castigate the Party officials as "Nichtskönner" and
"Bremsklötze" who through their incompetence are an impediment
to the realization of socialist goals and a negative influence
on actual or potential converts to socialism. Indeed, it was
the combination of a dogmatic attack by a "Mangold type" against
Manfred when he attempted to offer constructive criticism concerning university improprieties and the rejection of an advanced
machine for mass production by incompetent Party officials that
so alienated Manfred from the socialist ideology that it drove

him to the ultimate step of abandoning his country. Never
before had a work of literature from the GDR dared to blaspheme
against the most sacred apparatus of the socialist system as
was the case with this accusation.

The new role model of the effective Party functionary is
depicted in the persons of Ernst Wendland and Egon Schwarzenbach.
Deeds instead of words, compassion instead of dogmatism are the
hallmark characteristics of these men. Their quiet resolve and
dedication to socialism are evident in their actions, not the
blare of useless slogans. Their method of operation is characterized by a humane relationship with their associates that
seeks to unite rather than to divide, to bind up the wounds
caused by interpersonal friction and other calamities rather
than to repudiate and chastise those who have erred. It is no
coincidence, therefore, that Wendland is the first to visit Rita
in the hospital following her breakdown and that Schwarzenbach
not only recruits Rita for her new career as a teacher but, as
the antithesis to Mangold, serves as the role model to be emu-
lated by all aspiring Party functionaries.

It is particularly noteworthy that Wendland, Schwarzenbach,
Meternagel and Rita, the most positive characters in this work,
far from fitting the mold of the traditional messianic supporters
of socialism are instead set apart from the others by their zeal
for truth and honesty and not for ideological considerations:
"'Mit Überstunden haben wir lange genug gearbeitet. Der Ausweg
ist: Jeder leistet soviel er kann, ehrlich'"(GH, p.60) Similarly, Schwarzenbach when faced with the dilemna of maintaining
blind allegiance to the Party at the cost of suppressing the
truth, chooses the latter: "'Wissen Sie, warum ich heute zu
Ihnen gekommen bin?' fragte er. 'Ich wollte wissen: Hat es
Sinn, die Wahrheit, die man kennt, immer und unter allen
Umständen zu sagen?' 'Das wollten Sie von mir hören?' 'Ja,'
sagt Schwarzenbach. 'Ich habe es von Ihnen gehört.' 'Was ist
denn los?' sagt Rita. 'Warum haben Sie daran gezweifelt?'"
(GH, p. 185) Meternagel, too, is not motivated by lofty Party
slogans in his unrelenting effort to produce more. Instead, he
wants to do what is "normal" which he defines as: "Normal ist,

was uns nützt, was unsereinen zu Menschen macht. Unnormal ist,
was uns zu Arschkriechern, Betrügern und Marschierern macht,
die wir lange genug gewesen sind."(GH, p.74)

It is clear, therefore, that Christa Wolf has departed from
the traditional concept of socialist partiality by subordinating
political ideology to the higher and much more noble principle
of truth. Yet, "Der geteilte Himmel" still abides by the concept of partiality. The new form of socialist partiality advocated in this work is not one imposed from above by the Communist Party but rather one adhered to out of personal conviction. This new socialist partiality is above all characterized
by a longing for a socialist society built upon a foundation of
truth, tolerance of criticism and a new humanity. The pursuit
of these noble principles, as Günther Dahlke points out, is well
worth the hardships and sacrifice endured by the inhabitants of
the GDR:

> Das Leben in unserer noch jungen Deutschen Demo-
> kratischen Republik ist auch in seiner Herbheit
> lebenswert, weil diese Herbheit einem edlen Kampf
> entspringt, dem Kampf um die Zukunft der Nation,
> einem Kampf, der auch solch bittere Widersprüche und
> schmerzhafte Konflikte, die uns heute noch bewegen,
> morgen in die Vergangenheit verbannen wird. Das
> Ringen um die Vollendung unseres neuen soziali-
> stischen Gemeinwesens schließt Opfer des Einzelnen
> nicht aus; aber um des Menschen und der Nation
> willen lohnt es, diese Opfer zu bringen.[8]

3. National Orientation

As evidenced by the unusually high sales figures and nation-
wide debate at all levels of society, it is unlikely that there
were more timely and more relevant issues on the minds of the
inhabitants of the GDR than those raised in "Der geteilte
Himmel." For the first time, a work written in the GDR dared
to take an honest look at the discrepancy between the reality
of life in that socialist country and the illusions depicted
in the ubiquitous Party slogans. Far too long the everyday
conditions in the GDR had been camouflaged behind a façade of

propaganda. Despite the efforts of the politicians to coverup "what was" by accentuating "what should be" the truth was known by all. Everyone was aware of the deceit perpetrated upon the people within and outside the borders of the GDR. It was time to tell the truth concerning life in this socialist country in order to free the people from the feeling of guilt suffered as a result of living a lie. This much needed catharsis was provided by Christa Wolf in this work through which she contributed immeasurably to the mental and spiritual health not only of Rita Seidel but an entire nation.

Immense fascination was generated in the entire nation by the frank description of the impediments, hardships and antagonism retarding the progress of socialism in general and the suffering and sacrifice willingly endured by some in their effort to advance the socialist order. For the first time, the reader was offered a balanced picture of a socialist society that inspired some individuals to support the principles of socialism on the basis of its achievements and promise for the future, while others repudiated the same system for its failures. The tragic consequences of such antithetical reactions to socialism are illustrated in the dissolution of a near perfect love relationship and escape of one member of this pair to the West while the other in desperation attempts to commit suicide in the GDR.

These were the crucial issues on the minds and in the hearts of the people of the GDR. They experienced the conditions depicted in "Der geteilte Himmel" daily. They were familiar with the problems plaguing the "Brigade Ermisch," the incompetence of politically appointed managers and directors within the society, the "Mangold-type" who made life miserable for the great majority of the people, and the constant stream of those who had thrown in the towel and "waren abgehauen."

Hardly anyone in the GDR had not endured similar firsthand tragic experiences as had befallen Rita and Manfred. Families were torn apart over the issue of siding with or against socialism. Countless families had lost one or more members of their family to the West as a result of irreconcilable differ-

ences. They empathized fully with Rita's agony and understood
the reasons for her act of desperation. In short, the tragic
experiences of Rita and Manfred had been played out on so many
occasions throughout the GDR that "Der geteilte Himmel" had
taken on a personal element with which nearly every citizen
of the GDR could readily identify.

The primary reason that the inhabitants felt so close to
this novel was its forthright portrayal of the causes leading
individuals to the difficult decision to escape to the West.
In "Der geteilte Himmel" the escapees were not depicted as war
mongers or Western saboteurs, as the propaganda machine asserted.
They were the mothers and fathers, the brothers and sisters,
the sons and daughters of ordinary citizens. Those who escaped
were good people who had become so disillusioned with socialism
that they had to leave. This is the reason for the great re-
morse felt by the friends and relatives left in the GDR. Thus,
Rita's breakdown is symbolic of many an actual breakdown experienced by GDR citizens who had lost loved ones to the West and
is evidence of the fact that every refugee represents a great
personal and national loss to the people of the GDR.

Despite these tragic losses Christa Wolf does not paint a
picture of doom and gloom for the future of the GDR. Instead,
she asserts that the people will simply have to work harder in
order to compensate for the void created by Manfred and six
million others who left the GDR. The people of the GDR must
overcome these obstacles through even greater personal sacrifice
and hard work, as exemplified by the efforts of Rolf Meternagel:

> Vor ihren Augen hatte ein Mensch einen schweren
> Packen auf sich genommen, von niemandem gezwungen,
> nicht nach Lohn fragend, hatte einen Kampf begonnen,
> der fast aussichtslos schien, wie nur je die bewunder-
> ten Helden alter Bücher; hatte Schlaf und Ruhe ge-
> opfert, war verlacht worden, gehetzt, ausgestoßen.
> Rita hatte ihn am Boden liegen sehen, daß sie dachte:
> Der steht nicht mehr auf. Er kam wieder hoch, jetzt
> etwas Furchterregendes, fast Wildes im Blick; gerade
> da traten, ihm selbst beinahe unerwartet, andere

neben ihn, sagten, was er gesagt hatte, taten, was
er vorschlug. Rita hatte ihn aufatmen und schließlich
siegen sehen, und das alles blieb ihr unvergeßlich.(GH, p.73)

Thus, the future of the GDR lies in the hands of its inhabitants. Herculean efforts are called for to transform the temporary shortcomings plaguing the GDR into the longed for moral
society which is the crowning point of the "Sog einer großen
menschlichen Bewegung."

4. The Typical

It is certainly to Christa Wolf's credit as a developing
writer that for the most part she refrained in this work from
depicting the usual good versus evil stereotypes so typical of
socialist realism literature in the early 1960's. In fact, it
is her portrayal of genuine, flesh and blood human beings instead of wooden "types" that explains the dramatic appeal of
this work to readers within the GDR and on the international
scene. Through this unexpectedly refreshing depiction of "life
behind the Iron Curtain" Christa Wolf contributed immensely to
raising the interest level in and respect for GDR literature
world-wide.

A closer look at the more important characters presented in
this work reveals that Erwin Schwarzenbach, Ernst Wendland,
Rita Seidel and even Manfred Herrfurth are depicted as multi-
faceted human beings. Only Manfred's parents and Mangold represent the destructive "types" from opposite ends of the political spectrum while Rolf Meternagel.is the incarnation of
the devoted socialist at any price.

Although Erwin Schwarzenbach is a member of the Communist
Party and successful recruiter of candidates to become teachers,
his impact in this novel is much stronger as a caring, compassionate person and dedicated family man. Indeed, it is his
personal warmth and humaneness, not his political beliefs, that
attract Rita to him during their first meetings in her village.
Thus, it is completely in keeping with his character that this
advocate of human kindness and understanding rebukes his comrade
for his insensitivity and callousness toward others:

'Wissen Sie,' sagte Schwarzenbach, immer noch

leise und zu Mangold, 'daß ich, Sohn eines Arbeiters, in den Werwolf gehen oder mich um-
bringen wollte, als der Krieg zu Ende ging?'
Schwarzenbach warf sein ganzes Leben in die Waag-
schale, für sie, seine Schüler.
'Damals,' sagte er, 'hatten wir Haß und Verach-
tung verdient und erwartet. Die Partei war nach-
sichtig und geduldig mit uns, wenn auch anspruchs-
voll. Seitdem halte ich etwas von diesen Eigen-
schaften: Nachsicht, Geduld. Revolutionäre Eigen-
schaften, Genosse Mangold. Sie waren nie darauf
angewiesen?'
Mangold zuckte die Achseln. Nachsicht, Geduld!
Wer habe dafür heute Zeit? - Das klang fast
bitter.(GH, pp.130-31)

Similarly, Ernst Wendland is much more than the embodiment
of the new type of capable manager so desperately needed if
the economy of the GDR is to flourish. As in the case of
Schwarzenbach, Wendland's success is more the result of his
benevolent human qualities rather than his managerial expertise. Furthermore, Wendland's triumphs in the work place are
tempered with his defeats in the private sphere. His wife was
unfaithful to him and subsequently left him all alone to care
for his son. Even though he is a genuinely kindhearted and
congenial person, Wendland does not have a single good friend.
Despite the apparent success and respect accorded him profes-
sionally, Wendland leads a less than enviable life in relative
loneliness and isolation.

Even Rita Seidel, the focal point of this novel, cannot be
viewed as a one-sided "type" who blindly chooses socialism
over a personal relationship with Manfred Herrfurth. More
than anything else Rita is the embodiment of a highly impres-
sionable, malleable human being who makes the important decisions
in her life with her heart and not her mind. Rather than debat-
ing the pros and cons of any choice before her, Rita Seidel
follows intuition and the dictates of her conscience as a guide
for her actions. Thus, her continued love for Manfred defies

all rational reasoning in that she is constantly made aware of personal characteristics in him that are antithetical to her own. Manfred is a cold, arrogant person while Rita exudes empathy and congeniality. Manfred is committed to his personal advancement; Rita is devoted to the improvement of life for all.

Seen from this perspective, Rita's relationship with Manfred may be built less on a foundation of true love than mutual convenience. Manfred desperately needs the warmth and understanding of another human being to counteract the cold, inhumane atmosphere experienced at home. Rita, on the other hand, feels a deep compassion for this loner who at the same time provides her an outlet for her natural desire to help her fellow man. It is this same desire to contribute to the betterment of life on a larger scale, not a political ideology per se, that draws her even closer to Meternagel, Schwarzenbach and Wendland and gradually distances her from the unrelenting selfishness exhibited by Manfred in his abscondence to the West. Rita Seidel, therefore, is by no means a staunch advocate of the socialist ideology. She is, instead, a genuinely empathetic person who sees the suffering of her fellow human beings and dedicates herself to do her part to bring about an improvement of these conditions.

The most remarkable and noteworthy change in "Der geteilte Himmel" is found in the depiction of the fugitive to the West. Whereas in the past the escapees to the West were summarily "cast" into the role of subversives driven by blind greed, Manfred is depicted as the product of a national socialist upbringing that has implanted antisocial characteristics in him. Nevertheless, even this unfavorable influence upon Manfred does not lead him to reject socialism outright. While as an outsider he focuses more keenly on the shortcomings of this political ideology than do adherents to the system, his criticism is offered with the intention of improving rather than destroying the system. In fact, this criticism of the new political order is Manfred's way of testing the credibility of the system and a desperate effort to gain entrance to a meaningful life.

It is to the discredit of the new socialist society that
Manfred's attempts to gain entrance to the system went unheeded
and his well-meaning efforts for reform were misunderstood and
rejected as evidence of continued subversive plots against the
state. To a considerable degree, therefore, Manfred is not
abandoning the GDR but is driven from his homeland by the insensitivity of the socialist system to the needs of one of its
citizens. It is only after Manfred's most crushing rejection,
the refusal to mass produce the Spinn Jenny, a decision motivated
by political rather than technical considerations, that he is
overcome by a complete sense of frustration and seeks mental
relief in the West.

Manfred Herrfurth, therefore, is no longer the "typical"
fugitive from the GDR. He is imbued with both positive and
negative characteristics. He is honest and courageous to the
point of defending his friend Martin Jung against unwarranted
political accusations. He can be warm and tender to Rita on
a strictly personal level. He tries to improve the system
through constructive criticism. When these efforts are met
with constant suspicion and rejection, he reciprocates by turning his back on those who repudiated him.

"Der geteilte Himmel" is not totally free of stereotypes,
however. Certainly Manglod and Manfred's parents are presented
as totally negative figures on the one hand while Rolf Meternagel
is the incarnation of the selfless servant to a higher cause.
Perhaps the most counterproductive and destructive character in
this novel is Mangold, the self-appointed, self-annointed high
priest of Party policy: "Er sprach über die Parteilinie, wie
Katholiken über die unbefleckte Empfängnis reden."(GH, p.130)
Oddly enough, the most vocal advocate of strict communist ideology not only fails to inspire the people with his political
pronouncements, but instead arouses disgust and loathing as a
result of his tirades.

Indeed, Mangold's rantings in the name of the Party have the
same destructive impact on the establishment of the socialist
society as the open hatred exhibited by Manfred's mother for
the new political system: "Warum ist mir früher nie die

Ähnlichkeit zwischen Frau Herrfurth und Mangold aufgefallen, dachte Rita."(GH, p.123) While one may expect opposition to the establishment of the new socialist order from this woman whose primary effort is directed to maintaining her physical appearance and listening with religious devotion to "Eine freie Stimme der freien Welt" while longing for the moment of liberation: "Wann würde diese Stimme die Verbindlichkeit aufgeben und zustoßen?"(GH, p.149), the real danger to socialism comes from the narrow-minded Mangold-type. Unless the Mangolds of the GDR change their "Maßlosigkeit" and "Ich-Bezogenheit" to "Nachsicht" and "Geduld"(GH, p.131), they will undermine the successful implementation of the new society as surely as the many "Herrfurths" left over from the era of national socialism.

While Mangold and the Herrfurths are depicted in a totally negative light without possessing a single redeeming quality, Rolf Meternagel is the stereotype of the new socialist personality who dedicates his entire being to the advancement of the new society. As such, he sacrifices his mental and physical well-being for the good of the nation. Even though he has suffered an unjust demotion as a result of a betrayal by his fellow workers, Meternagel forgives these perpetrators of this injustice and contributes to their spiritual regeneration by convincing them to increase their productivity in accordance with their ability. Always leading by example, Meternagel works himself into poor health and near exhaustion.

The unparalleled output in physical labor by Meternagel for the betterment of all is complemented by an unrivaled sense of honesty and integrity. Surrounded by meager furnishings while sharing "einen dünnen Kaffee" Meternagel's wife reveals to Rita the degree of her husband's commitment to principle and honesty:

'Er ist nicht wie andere Menschen,' sagt sie mutlos. 'Ich habe ja mitangesehen, wie er sich kaputtgemacht hat. Andere haben sich einen Fernseher und einen Kühlschrank hingestellt und ihrer Frau eine Waschmaschine. Wissen Sie, was er mit seinem Geld macht, seit die Mädels unsere Hilfe nicht mehr brauchen? Er spart es. Er denkt, ich weiß nicht,

wofür. Aber ich weiß: Er will die dreitausend Mark
zurückgeben, die er damals zuviel ausgezahlt hat.
Er ist verrückt, er ist wirklich verrückt. Fehlen
denn so einem Betrieb dreitausend Mark? Mir fehlen
sie.'(GH, p.197)

From a socialist perspective Meternagel's self-sacrifice is
seen as the most exemplary leadership and devotion to a noble
cause by one of its disciples. No personal suffering or adver-
sity can dissuade this true disciple of socialism from his goal
to work for the advancement of the "cause." A more objective
observer, however, might be tempted to ask: What real benefit
does Rolf Meternagel receive for all of his personal suffering?
How can Rolf Meternagel justify the pain and lifelong suffering
borne by his wife as a result of his struggle? When even Rita
Seidel is unable to find the "richtigen Worte" for a proper
response to such questions, Meternagel's wife provides a dis-
quieting reply: "'Ich weiß schon,' sagt sie still. 'Er muß
so sein, wie er ist.'"(GH, p.198)

5. The Positive Hero

Perhaps the most conspicuous change between the "Moskauer
Novelle" and "Der geteilte Himmel" is the turnabout in the
treatment of the positive hero. Whereas Christa Wolf's first
prose work contained a plethora of positive heroes, this novel
is totally devoid of a single textbook positive hero figure.
While one may justifiably argue that Rolf Meternagel, Erwin
Schwarzenbach, Ernst Wendland and Rita Seidel exhibit characteristics worthy of positive hero status, none of these characters fulfills all the criteria set forth for this distinction by
socialist realism guidelines.

Although Rolf Meternagel unquestionably was cast in the role
of positive hero in this work, he too falls short of attaining
that coveted status as prescribed by socialist realism tenets.
Even though Meternagel has undergone the called-for political
regeneration, the motivation for his unending, almost masochistic
sacrifices for the establishment of the new society is not nurtured by his faith in communism as prescribed by socialist realism tenets but rather by his fervent commitment to truth and an

insatiable desire to improve the lives of his fellow man through higher productivity. Productivity, not political rhetoric, is seen as the salvation for mankind by this man who keeps an accurate tally of the number of hours squandered by the members of the Ermisch brigade. Not once does this Faustian figure utter a single word relating to political ideology as the primary motivation for his efforts. Thus, Rolf Meternagel must be seen less as the incarnation of the positive hero as envisioned by socialist realism guidelines than the embodiment of human dedication to selfless sacrifice:

> Dies war wirklich geschehen...: Vor ihren Augen hatte
> ein Mensch einen schweren Packen auf sich genommen,
> von niemandem gezwungen, nicht nach Lohn fragend,
> hatte einen Kampf begonnen, der fast aussichtslos
> schien, wie nur je die bewunderten Helden alter Bücher;
> hatte Schlaf und Ruhe geopfert, war verlacht worden,
> gehetzt, ausgestoßen. Rita hatte ihn am Boden liegen
> sehen, daß sie dachte: Der steht nicht mehr auf. Er
> kam wieder hoch, jetzt etwas Furchterregendes, fast
> Wildes im Blick; gerade da traten, ihm selbst beinahe
> unerwartet, andere neben ihn, sagten, was er gesagt
> hatte, taten, was er vorschlug. Rita hatte ihn auf-
> atmen und schließlich siegen sehen, und das alles
> blieb ihr unvergeßlich.(GH, p.73)

Meternagel is indeed an inspiration to Rita and his fellow workers. However, this inspiration emanates from Meternagel's humanity, not his political persuasion. For this reason, Meternagel succeeded in attaining a far greater status than that of a positive hero. He is the embodiment of a first-rate HUMAN BEING.

Similarly, Erwin Schwarzenbach while exhibiting the most positive image of a communist in this work by projecting "Wärme, Weite und Bewegung" in all that he does, he also falls short of the requirements for positive hero status. Schwarzenbach, like Meternagel, knows that the hope for the new society does not lie in blind adherence to any political dogma but rather in a new "Vertrauen zur Klasse" that is based on the power to "über-

zeugen" rather than to "diktieren" to their fellow citizens.
This dedication to a new humanity enables him to rebuke Mangold
for his callous relationship with others as a result of his
adherence to cold political dogma.

The critical reason for Schwarzenbach's ineligibility for
positive hero status, however, is not found in his efforts to
transform insensitive Communist Party members into caring individuals and to call for reform in the system at all levels.
That in itself is viewed as a legitimate task for any true
proponent of communism. Schwarzenbach, however, commits the
cardinal sin of placing his faith for the establishment of the
new society in something greater than the communist ideology:
"Die reine nackte Wahrheit und nur sie, ist auf die Dauer der
Schlüssel zum Menschen."(GH, p.186) Such political heresy ex-
cludes an individual from positive hero status standing while
it entitles him to the stature attained by Rolf Meternagel.

Ernst Wendland is the third person who is a genuinely good
human being. As such, he embodies similar humane characteristics
as were exhibited by Meternagel and Schwarzenbach. Despite his
awesome responsibilities as plant manger, Wendland takes time to
befriend a temporary employee such as Rita Seidel. He listens
patiently to her personal problems and even offers to intercede
on Manfred's behalf to mass produce his Spinn Jenny. Throughout
his interaction with Rita, Manfred and his fellow workers,
Wendland never assumes a posture of superiority toward others.
Instead, he behaves just like any member of the group. He is
sensitive to the needs of others as exemplified by his willingness to ease the burdens of a friend:

'Wissen Sie, wo ich jetzt eigentlich sein müßte?
Auf einer Versammlung, in deren Rednerliste mein
Name steht.'
Warum erzählt er mir das? Wäre er doch in seine Versammlung gegangen... Und doch war es angenehm zu
wissen, daß dieser zuverlässige Mensch ihretwegen
leichtsinnung wurde. 'Wie wollen Sie sich morgen
entschuldigen?' fragte sie.
Er sagte: 'Ich werde sagen, daß ich unbedingt nach-

sehen muBte, ob das stimmt, was sie im Radio erzählen:
daB die Bäume blühen und die Vögel singen und irgendwo
in der Welt Leute herumlaufen, die glücklich sind.
Ich habe herausgefunden: Es stimmt. Nun können wir
weiter Versammlungen machen. - Übrigens ist es mein
erster Ausbrecher,' setzte er hinzu.(GH, p.152)
Wendland's personal attributes that are characterized by
"Einsicht und Güte" are complemented by a strength of conviction to buck the system when necessary. Thus, he boldly sends
a falsified telegram to a plant manager in Berlin in order to
procure needed parts to meet the production quota of his factory. Wendland is reprimanded by the political hierarchy for
these "egoistischen" methods with such accusatory terms as
"Anarchismus" and "Werksegoismus." It is clear, therefore,
that Wendland, like Meternagel and Schwarzenbach before him,
is prepared to go against political canon in order to ensure
continuity of production. Political considerations, therefore,
seem to play only a role of convenience for him. When he deems
it advantageous to play by the prescribed political rules,
Wendland abides by them. When they impede progress, they are
cast aside as illustrated by Wendland's reaction to the Party's
reprimand for his independent ways: "'Sie haben mir den Kopf
gewaschen, und ich habe schließlich stillgehalten. Was soll
man machen? Sie haben recht und ich hab recht. So was gibt's.'"
(GH, p.104) Anyone who challenges the authority of the Party
in such a self-assertive manner, no matter how great his personal achievements, cannot be considered for positive hero
standing according to socialist realism requirements. Therefore, Wendland merits the same distinctive stature that was
accorded to Meternagel and Schwarzenbach.

Finally, even Rita Seidel, the most congenial, likeable
character in the entire novel, does not fulfill the socialist
realism criteria as a positive hero. Although it is clear that
Rita will become a valuable, productive member of the GDR after
her convalescence, her past history leads the reader to believe
that her contributions to her homeland will emulate the examples provided by her closest friends and mentors--Meternagel,

Schwarzenbach and Wendland. Therefore, Rita's future characteristics can be predicted as mirroring the present character
traits described in her role models. It is, therefore, safe
to say that Rita will continue her development as a caring,
compassionate person who will be a dedicated worker for the
establishment of the new socialist society. However, like
Meternagel, Schwarzenbach and Wendland, her primary focus will
always be on the welfare of the people, not on adherence to
political ideology. In this way, the circle will be completed
in that this promising disciple will follow in the footsteps
of her mentors.

We have observed a drastic departure from the ideals presented
in the "Moskauer Novelle" to the real world portrayed in "Der
geteilte Himmel." Whereas the first prose work depicted an
advanced socialist society according to the Marxist/Leninist
blueprint, "Der geteilte Himmel" reveals a developing socialist
society riddled by internal strife, an absence of positive heroes
and a general disregard for official Party policy. It is no
wonder, therefore, that the political hierarchy heaped praises
upon Christa Wolf for her strict adherence to the concepts of
socialist realism in the "Moskauer Novelle," while the same
politicians berated the author of "Der geteilte Himmel" for her
abandonment of these principles with the sharp reprimand:
"Besinn dich auf dein Herkommen, besinn dich auf unser Fortkommen,
wenn du mit deiner klugen Feder der deutschen Arbeiterklasse,
ihrer Partei und der Sache des Sozialismus dienen willst."[9]

Chapter V

"Nachdenken über Christa T,:" The Quest for One's Self

During the second half of the 1960's there occurred a
fundamental change in the literature of the German Democratic
Republic. Lyric, dramatic and prose works suddenly shifted
their emphasis from the traditional subject matter that had
examined the transition from capitalism to the eventual "Ankunft"
in the advanced socialist society to a portrayal of life in the
contemporary GDR. Commensurate with this change in subject
matter, the idealistic depictions of projected achievements in
the earlier "Ankunftsliteratur" were accompanied by realistic
accounts of the difficulties and "non-arrivals" experienced by
a great number of GDR citizens.

As a result of continued hardships encountered in most segments of life in the GDR, the hope for personal fulfillment in
that socialist society grew ever dimmer. Consequently, GDR
writers as a whole turned from the public sphere to the private
domain in search of self-actualization. In this quest, GDR literature gradually abandoned the depiction of surface reality in
favor of ever frequent portrayals of internal conflicts torment-
ing ordinary citizens in the socialist society. The central
theme of this new literature revolved around the conflicting
demands made by the state on the individual for the attainment
of political goals and the equally persistent clamor of GDR
citizens for the right for personal fulfillment. Subsequently,
the pursuit of self-actualization was no longer sought in the
full integration of the individual within the overall socialist
framework but rather in a heretofore alien effort to come to
terms with one's self--"das Zu-sich-selbst-Kommen."

The impetus for this new literature that seriously trans-
gressed against the prevailing socialist realism guidelines came
from the proceedings of the Kafka conference held in Liblice
near Prague in May, 1963. Following heated debates about the
nature of Kafka's works and their possible destructive impact
on socialist realism literature, it was nevertheless agreed

that even such Kafkaesque phenomena as personal isolation and
alienation should play a legitimate role in socialist realism
works. As a result of the admittance of the formally despised
"heretic" into the socialist realism camp, there emerged a new
type of literature that departed from prescribed socialist realism guidelines and expanded its parameters to include the depiction of personal frustration and alienation experienced within
the socialist system, sought personal fulfillment through intro-
spection rather than from political amalgamation and departed
from the simplistic authorial mode of narration to embrace a
highly complicated narrative structure consisting of a montage
of stream of consciousness narration intertwined with flashbacks
and foreshadowings. This new structural format expressed more
accurately the internal anguish harrowing many characters in
GDR literature of the 1960's. The most important representatives of this new philosophical and literary output are Roger
Garaudy's "Realismus ohne Ufer," Robert Havemann's "Dialektik
ohne Dogma," Stefan Heym's manifest "Die Langeweile von Minsk,"
Wolf Biermann's "Die Drahtharfe," Werner Bräunig's "Rummelplatz,"
Eduard Claudius' "Wintermärchen auf Rügen," Gerd Bieler's
"Sternschnuppenwünsche," Manfred Bieler's "Das Kaninchen bin
ich," Peter Hacks' "Moritz Tassow," Hans Pfeiffer's "Begegnung
mit Herkules," Werner Heiduczek's "Abschied von den Engeln,"
Irmtraud Morgner's "Hochzeit in Konstantinopel," Günter de
Bruyn's "Buridans Esel," and Christa Wolf's "Nachdenken über
Christa T."

The response to Christa Wolf's third novel "Nachdenken über
Christa T." in 1968 rivaled the overwhelming success she had
attained with the publication of "Der geteilte Himmel" five
years earlier. Even though the authorities attempted to suppress
the impact of this novel upon the populace of the GDR by permitting only a limited edition of the work, "Nachdenken über Christa
T." became an immediate national and international success. Adam
Drzeminski, a Polish critic, hailed Christa Wolf's latest work as
the "Ereignis des Jahres 1969"[1] in the weekly journal "Polityka"
while a Soviet critic extolled the novel as a "moralisches
Vorbild" in the "Literaturnaja gazeta."[2] The world-wide appeal

of this novel is reflected by its subsequent translation into
Czech, Danish, Dutch, English, Finnish, French, Japanese,
Italian, Norwegian, Spanish and Swedish.

1. Objective Reflection of Reality

Whereas the focus of the "Moskauer Novelle" and "Der geteilte
Himmel" was on the establishment of an advanced socialist society,
"Nachdenken über Christa T." deals primarily with the unsuccessful quest for self-actualization within an established socialist
state. Even though the narrated time in this novel covers ap-
proximately twenty years from 1945 to 1965, external political
developments in the GDR play virtually no role in this work.
Instead, Christa Wolf focuses on the internal struggles of one
individual, Christa T., in her effort to escape from the group
mentality syndrome, to maintain her individuality, to live life
to the fullest and to gain a more complete understanding of her
"self." This struggle for a keener understanding of the inner
essence of a human being within a society geared toward the
promotion of group consciousness at the expense of self actualization is presented in a highly complicated first person stream
of consciousness format in which the narrator often merges with
the character of Christa T., thereby offering a dual perspective
on the attempt by Christa T. and the narrator to preserve the
"identity" of one GDR citizen from fading into oblivion.

It is important to note that one of the most fundamental prerequisites for the successful implementation of an advanced
socialist society is the regeneration of human mentality from
an "I" or individual to a "we" or group orientation. Accordingly,
in a socialist society the welfare of the group is always of
much greater importance than individual rights. Indeed, it
is a basic assumption that every individual in a socialist society will voluntarily abdicate his personal rights when these
are in conflict with those of the state. Thus, it follows that
every socialist society deters any tendencies toward individualism among its citizens and in a similar manner opposes literary
independence from prescribed socialist realism guidelines because
of their potential threat to the monolithic edicts issued by the
central government.

"Nachdenken über Christa T." must, therefore, be viewed not
only as the abandonment of but a direct challenge to the principle of objective reflection of reality in that this novel is
dedicated to the memory of a "loner" and "outsider" who rejected
the mass psychology syndrome of the "Hopp-Hopp Menschen" in
favor of a search for an answer to the question: "Was ist das:
Dieses Zu-sich-selber-Kommen?"[3] This question that was taken
from Johannes R. Becher's diary serves as the motto for this
work. It was written in 1947/48 by Becher while serving as
minister of culture in the Soviet Occupied Zone. Even Becher
was alarmed by the continued expropriation of individual and
artistic rights by the SED as necessary sacrifices for advancing
the establishment of the new socialist society. He feared that
this continued abdication of human rights for the purpose of promoting a greater common good would ultimately lead to "Schwermut
und zur Verzweiflung, da wir das Leben nicht leben, das uns zu
leben gegeben wäre."[4]

Becher's concerns over the loss of individual freedoms for
the sake of promoting socialist ideals are shared by Christa
Wolf to the degree that this work is intentionally written
"against the stream" of socialist realism tenets by glorifying
the efforts of one GDR citizen in her "Versuch, man selbst zu
sein."(CT, p.7) The search for one's "self" is so important
to Christa Wolf that this effort on the part of Christa T. must
be preserved from "Vergessenwerden," not to honor the deceased
Christa T. but to serve as a reminder to the living: "Und bloß
nicht vorgeben, wir täten es ihretwegen. Ein für allemal: Sie
braucht uns nicht. Halten wir also fest, es ist unseretwegen,
denn es scheint, wir brauchen sie."(CT, p.8) Why do the people
of the GDR need Christa T.? What distinguishes Christa T. from
her fellow citizens in the German Democratic Republic that entitles her to be remembered by posterity?

Christa T. is needed by the people of the GDR as a constant
reminder of the inherent danger associated with the loss of
human rights for any purpose. Any system that is founded upon
human conformity and regimentation for political ends represents
a threat to its citizens by curtailing individual development,

individual expression and self-actualization. Knowingly or
unknowingly the great majority of the inhabitants of the GDR
has abdicated its rights for personal fulfillment for the sake
of promoting the new socialist society. Only Christa T. dares
to be different. This "difference" is apparent from the first
day she appeared in school. Much to the surprise of her class-
mates the newcomer showed no interest in seeking acceptance by
the group: "Sie saß in der letzten Bankreihe und zeigte keinen
Eifer mit uns bekannt zu werden."(CT, p.10) Even more astonishing to the other pupils and the narrator are Christa T.'s totally
uncharacteristic responses to her teacher. Christa T. states
boldly that she does not like any school subjects and instead
prefers hikes through the forest. The "outsider" qualities
within the classroom are then repeated by further evidence of
non-conformity after school:

> So ging sie vor uns her, strakste erhobenen Hauptes
> auf der Rinnsteinkante entlang, hielt sich plötz-
> lich eine zusammengedrehte Zeitung vor den Mund
> und stieß ihren Ruf aus: Hooohaahooo, so ungefähr.
> Sie blies ihre Trompete, und die Feldwebel und
> Unteroffiziere vom Wehrbezirkskommando hatten
> gerade Pause und sahen sich kopfschüttelnd nach
> ihr um. Na, die aber auch, hat der Mensch Töne?
> Da siehst du nun, wie sie sein kann, sagte eine
> zu mir.
> Da sah ich's nun. Grinste dazu wie alle, wußte aber,
> daß ich nicht grinsen sollte.(CT, p.13)

An additional trait pointing to the "unusual" life style of
this ten-year-old girl is her practice to write down her daily
experiences for a highly unusual purpose: "Dichten, dicht machen,
die Sprache hilft. Was denn dicht machen und wogegen?"(CT, p.20)
The process of writing about her daily experiences even at this
early age is a desperate effort by Christa T. to seek an understanding of her "self." It is a means of introspection--a need
to confront herself as a human being: "Ja, so wird es sein.
Dies ist der Weg zu uns selber. So wäre diese Sehnsucht nicht
lächerlich und abwegig, so wäre sie brauchbar und nützlich."

(CT, p.33) Most of all, however, the act of writing affords
Christa T. the opportunity to set herself apart from the masses,
to emerge as an individual. This therapeutic function of the
writing process helps Christa T. overcome her fear, "einem
selbst könnte zustoßen, was gang und gäbe war; spurlos zu
verschwinden."(CT, p.35)

Christa T.'s attempts to maintain her individuality by
separating herself from the group mentality are motivated by
the conviction that a person cannot attain his full humanity by
adhering to a herd philosophy. Only a state of unrestrained
freedom offers a human being the opportunity for: "Leben,
erleben, freies großes Leben! O herrliches lebensgefühl, daß
du mich nie verläßt! Nichts weiter als ein Mensch sein."(CT,
p.37) In order to reach the full status of a "Mensch" Christa
T. is constantly driven to new experiences. Only by "... hinter
sich lassen, was man zu gut kennt, was keine Herausforderung
mehr darstellt. Neugierig bleiben auf die anderen Erfahrungen,
letzten Endes auf sich selbst in den neuen Umständen. Die
Bewegung mehr lieben als das Ziel..."(CT, p.43), can the human
being fully realize all of his potential.

Christa T. had embarked fully on the road to becoming an
individual who leaves "tracks" of her life as a result of her
insatiable desire to "see" and experience new things when she
was afflicted by a noticeable "Müdigkeit." This fatigue is not
caused by her unending desire to expand her horizons, however,
but rather by the strict limitations set to her quest for
independence:

> ...in den letzten Jahren haben wir sie nie anders als
> müde gesehen. Heute kann man ja fragen, was diese
> Müdigkeit verriet, damals unterblieb die Frage wegen
> Sinnlosigkeit. Die Antwort hätte weder ihr noch uns
> genützt. Soviel ist sicher: Niemals kann man durch
> das, was man tut, so müde werden wie durch das, was
> man nicht tut oder nicht tun kann. Das war ihr
> Fall. Das war ihre Schwäche und ihre geheime
> Überlegenheit.(CT, p.135)

Upon closer examination it is revealed that the recurring

fatigue afflicting Christa T. is caused by leukemia. This
physical ailment is symbolic of the spiritual suffering endured
by Christa T. The fatigue, the difficulty in breathing and
ultimately the cause of her death in a physical and spiritual
sense is the direct result of the constraints placed upon her.
This feeling of incarceration leads to utter frustration in
Christa T. that she will never experience "freedom"--to partake
of everything that life has to offer. Without this freedom,
Christa T. will never have the opportunity for self-actualization as Johannes R. Becher had feared:

> Alle ihre Versuche, den toten Kreis zu verlassen, der
> sich um sie gebildet hatte, kamen in schrecklichem
> Gleichmut nur immer wieder zu ihr zurück. Sie spürte,
> wie ihr unaufhaltsam das Geheimnis verlorenging, das
> sie lebensfähig machte: das Bewußtsein dessen, wer sie
> in Wirklichkeit war. Sie sah sich in eine unendliche
> Menge von tödlichen banalen Handlungen und Phrasen
> aufgelöst.(CT, p.153)

Christa T. ultimately succumbs to this "cancer," this confine-
ment of the human spirit, that snuffs out the opportunity for her
individual fulfillment. Nevertheless, her quest for greater
freedom and individuality as a member of a socialist society
lives on: "Christa T. wird zurückbleiben. Einmal wird man
wissen wollen, wer sie war, wen man da vergißt."(CT, p.180)
To ensure that this noble pursuit for self-actualization is not
forgotten, Christa Wolf has memorialized this search for individuality in a group-oriented society by the same process that
Christa T. used in her quest for her self: "Schreiben ist groß
machen. Nehmen wir uns zusammen, sehen wir sie groß."(CT, p.170)

2. Partiality

Soon after the publication of "Nachdenken über Christa T."
GDR critics launched a massive attack against this work on the
grounds that Christa Wolf had flagrantly violated the principle
of partiality in her latest publication. In an article of
May 14, 1969 in "Neues Deutschland" Heinz Sachs, the editor of
the Mitteldeutscher Verlag that had published this novel, seems
to apologize for publishing this work that advocates a life

style in clear violation of socialist realism guidelines:

Es wurde festgestellt, daß es innerhalb des Verlages ästhetische Auffassungen gibt, mit denen sich
nur ungenügend auseinandergesetzt wird. (...) Unbestreit-
bar liegt mit diesem Buch ein Versuch der Autorin vor,
Antworten zu suchen auf die Frage 'Wie soll man leben?'
Aber es ist nicht zu übersehen, daß die Heldin des
Romans so angelegt ist, daß eine Beantwortung dieser
Frage auf sozialistische Art schwerfällt, die es von
vornherein unmöglich erscheinen läßt, daß das Mädchen
Christa T. zum Vorbild werden kann. Zu dieser Helden-
wahl kommt, daß Christa Wolf die Möglichkeiten, die
die sozialistische Gesellschaft dem einzelnen bietet
(...) nicht zur Geltung bringt. Christa Wolf findet
keine Distanz zu ihrer Heldin. Pessimismus wird zur
ästhetischen Grundstimmung des Buches. Die Antwort,
die Christa Wolf letzten Endes findet, bleibt eine
allgemein-humanistische. Wenn aber sozialistische
Literatur ihre Funktion erfüllen und Weltgeltung finden soll, kann sie das nur, wenn sie auf allgemein be-
wegende Fragen spezifisch sozialistische Antworten
gibt. Gerade aber hier liegt das entscheidende Ver-
säumnis des Verlages in der Zusammenarbeit mit der
Autorin Christa Wolf.[5]

Max Walter Schulz was even more adamant in his objections to
this work. While praising Christa Wolf's literary talent, Schulz
condemns the novel for its anti-socialist tendencies in that it
advocates a quest for self-actualization outside the socialist
framework. Such a clear violation of the concept of partiality,
he asserts, threatens the most basic socialist assumptions concerning the "Aufgabe" of literature in a socialist society and
thereby undermines the very foundation of socialism:

Hier drängt sich ein offenes Wort über Christa Wolfs
'Nachdenken über Christa T.' auf. Wir kennen Christa
Wolf als eine talentierte Mitstreiterin unserer Sache.
Gerade deshalb dürfen wir unsere Enttäuschung über ihr
neues Buch nicht verbergen. Wie auch immer parteilich

140

die subjectiv ehrliche Absicht des Buches auch gemeint
sein mag: So wie die Geschichte nun einmal erzählt
ist, ist sie angetan, unsere LebensbewuBtheit zu be-
zweifeln, bewältigte Vergangenheit zu erschüttern, ein
gebrochenes Verhältnis zum Hier und Heute und Morgen
zu erzeugen. - Wem nützt das?[6]

Furthermore, warns Max Walter Schulz, such anti-socialist
tendencies as portrayed in "Nachdenken über Christa T." not only
demoralize ardent advocates of socialism within the GDR but provide hostile critics with the ammunition to attack the GDR and
its socialist ideology. He cites Reich-Ranicki's highly critical reviews of GDR literature and policy as a classic example of
such practices:

Wem nützt eine subjektiv ehrliche parteilich ge-
meinte Absicht, wenn sie streckenweise im literarischen Text und im Gesamteindruck die Doppelbö-
digkeit der Aussage so eindeutig provoziert, daB
sich die andere Seite nur zu wählen braucht, was
ihr beliebt, nur herauszulesen braucht, was sie
gern herauslesen möchte. Wir sind nun einmal noch
nicht allein auf der Welt, wir Sozialisten. Wir
lassen uns unser Urteil nicht vom Gegner diktieren.
Wenn aber ein Mann wie Reich-Ranicki, der Anna
Seghers' neuen groBen Roman aufs niederträchtigste
beschimpfte und besudelte, gleichzeitig das 'Nachdenken über Christa T.' so kommentiert: 'Sagen wir
klar. Christa T. stirbt an Leukämie, aber sie leidet
an der DDR'- dann muB uns das auch zu denken geben,
um so mehr, als eine alte Methode wieder einmal prak-
tiziert wird: Die DDR-Schriftsteller sind gegeneinan-
der auszuspielen. Wer eindeutig parteilich schreibt,
wird - je eindeutiger je schlimmer - ohne Ansehen der
literarischen Leistung literarisch disqualifiziert.
Wer dagegen den Anschein erweckt, mit dem Arbeiter-und-
Bauern-Staat und der Partei der Arbeiterklasse unzu-
frieden zu sein, rückt ohne weiteres Ansehen, wieviel
Augen der literarischen Qualität er tatsächlich ge-

worfen hat, gleich um zehn Felder vor.[7]

Werner Neubert also bemoans the drastic changes in Christa
Wolf's development as a writer. Whereas she had begun as an
ardent socialist realism advocate in "Moskauer Novelle" and
"Der geteilte Himmel," he observes a noticeable absence of
socialist realism tenets in "Nachdenken über Christa T." According to Neubert, Christa Wolf's latest work provides ample
evidence of her abandonment of open support for socialist ideology and an ever increasing tendency to dabble in the subjective
domain that is so odious to advocates of true socialist realism
literature:

> Es ist zu bedauern, daß der wesentliche Beitrag
> der Autorin, vielfältige Bezüge von Individuellem
> und Gesellschaftlichem intensiv zu fassen, in der
> neuen Erzählung 'Nachdenken über Christa T.' nicht
> ausgeweitet, sondern stark nach der Seite des Sub-
> jektiven hin reduziert wurde. Eine im Brechtschen
> Sinne gemeinte Vernachlässigung der Kausalität zwischen
> Psyche und Umwelt muß festgestellt werden. Sich
> leitmotivisch auf Johannes R. Becher berufend, hat
> Christa Wolf nicht - wie dieser es anstrebte - ein
> Bild des ganzen sozialistischen Menschen gewonnen;
> ein 'Zu-sich-selber-Kommen des Menschen' kann nicht
> als eine abstrakte, von der konkreten gesellschaft-
> lichen Praxis losgelöste Entwicklung verstanden
> werden.[8]

Are the accusations by these GDR critics justified? Did
Christa Wolf totally abandon the concept of partiality in this
novel? Has the author of "Nachdenken über Christa T." really
crossed the threshold from socialist realism literature to
literature?

Despite all the criticism of socialism offered in this work,
Christa Wolf does not break her allegiance to the GDR and its
political system. Indeed, she unabashedly defends socialism
as a political philosophy that is unequalled by any other form
of government:

> Denn die neue Welt, die wir unantastbar machen

wollten, und sei es dadurch, daB wir uns wie ir-
gendeinen Ziegelstein in ihr Fundament einmauer-
ten - sie gab es wirklich. Es gibt sie, und nicht
nur in unseren Köpfen, und damals fing sie für uns
an. Was aber immer mit ihr geschah oder geschehen
wird, es ist und bleibt unsere Sache. Unter den
Tauschangeboten ist keines, nach dem auch nur den
Kopf zu drehen sich lohnen würde...(CT, p.52)

However, as a fully integrated member of the GDR, Christa Wolf
reserves the right to point out shortcomings within that political system. Thus, while Christa Wolf is in full agreement with
the overall goals of socialism, she challenges the prevailing
attitude that the establishment of the new socialist society
can be built at any sacrifice, even the eradication of human
individuality:

Der Mechanismus, nach dem sich das alles bewegte -
aber bewegte es sich denn? -, die Zahnräder, Schnüre
und Stangen waren ins Dunkel getaucht, man erfreute
sich an der absoluten Perfektion und ZweckmäBigkeit
des Apparats, den reibungslos in Gang zu halten kein
Opfer zu groB schien - selbst nicht das: sich aus-
löschen. Schräubchen sein.(CT, p.57)

Furthermore, Christa Wolf wholeheartedly opposes current
tendencies to implement the socialist society by means of
coercion and duress of its citizens. While calling for an end
to such practices, she advocates policies that attract recalcitrant citizens of the GDR to socialism on the basis of its
advocacy of human equality and social justice. Above all, this
novel is an appeal to the political bureaucrats to abandon their
restrictive policies on individual freedom and to accord every
citizen of the GDR an opportunity to reach his full potential
as an individual:

Menschen, ja. Ich bin kein Einsiedler, Du kennst
mich. Aber kein Zwang darf dabeisein, es muB mich
zu ihnen drängen. Dann wieder muB ich allein sein
können, sonst leide ich. Ich will arbeiten, Du
weiBt es - mit anderen, für andere. Aber meine

Wirkungsmöglichkeiten sind, soviel ich sehe, schrift-
licher, mittelbarer Natur. Ich muß mich mit den
Dingen in Stille, betrachtend, auseinandersetzen
können... Das alles ändert nichts, unlösbarer Wider-
spruch, an meiner tiefen Übereinstimmung mit dieser
Zeit.(CT, p.71)

Finally, Christa Wolf takes issue with the all too common
practice in socialist countries in which the people are herded
together for mass demonstrations to exploit the mass psychology
syndrome for the purpose of promoting greater support for socialist policies while indiscriminately condemning capitalist
actions around the world. Such efforts to manipulate human
weaknesses are not only an insult to human intelligence but
accentuate the need of the populace to escape from these political shenanigans as was done by Christa T.:

 Aber auch die Fähigkeit, in einem Rausch zu leben,
ist ihr abgegangen. Die heftigen, sich überschla-
genden Worte, die geschwungenen Fahnen, die über-
lauten Lieder, die hoch über unseren Köpfen im Takt
klatschenden Hände. Sie hat gefühlt, wie die Worte
sich zu verwandeln beginnen, wenn nicht mehr guter
Glaube und Ungeschick und Übereifer sie hervorschleudern,
sondern Berechnung, Schläue, Anpassungstrieb.(CT, p.56)

The effect of this regimentation of GDR citizens has disas-
trous consequences. Not only does it stifle free expression in
the political arena concerning governmental policies, but it
retards the spiritual growth of the population as a whole.
Fearful of the political repercussions a voicing of their true
feelings would entail, GDR citizens prefer silence to advocacy,
adherence to the status quo to the introduction of bold initia-
tives, and mental stagnation to the pursuit of spiritual
growth:

Die Wahrheit ist: Wir hatten anderes zu tun. Wir
nämlich waren vollauf damit beschäfigt, uns unantast-
bar zu machen, wenn einer noch nachfühlen kann, was
das heißt. Nicht nur nichts Fremdes in uns aufneh-
men - und was alles erklärten wir für fremd! -, auch im

eigenen Innern nichts Fremdes aufkommen lassen, und
wenn es schon aufkam - ein Zweifel, ein Verdacht,
Beobachtungen, Fragen -, dann doch nichts davon anmer-
ken zu lassen. Weniger aus Angst, obwohl viele auch
ängstlich waren, als aus Unsicherheit. Eine Unsicherheit, die schwerer vergeht als irgend etwas anderes,
was ich kenne.(CT, p.52)

These are the reasons for the narrator's, and therefore by
implication Christa Wolf's, support for Christa T.'s escape from
the social and political restrictions imposed upon her, her quest
to be free, to partake of the infinite physical and mental experiences craved by the human being, and her effort to penetrate
the essence of her being as a result of this freedom. This
need for individuality and personal freedom is not permitted
by socialist ideology. On the contrary, the right to search
for one's self is expropriated in the name of socialism by narrow-
minded politicians: "...mir graut vor der neuen Welt der
Phantasielosen. Der Tatsachenmenschen. Der Hopp-Hopp-Menschen,
so hat sie sie genannt."(CT, p.52)

In order to overcome the current restrictions upon individual
rights by the bureaucrats and "Hopp-Hopp-Menschen," Christa Wolf
advocates individual action motivated by personal conviction:
"Wir müssen schon einiges dazu tun, um alle lebenswert zu leben.
Man muß bereit sein, eine gewisse Verantwortung zu übernehmen."
(CT, p.53) In essence Christa Wolf suggests nothing less than
a renewal of the "revolution" in order to make much needed mid-
course corrections to ensure that the advanced socialist society
affords every GDR citizen the right "ich [zu] sagen."

It is clear, therefore, that "Nachdenken über Christa T."
both adheres to and departs from the concept of partiality as
envisioned by the progenitors of socialist realism. On the one
hand Christa Wolf is firmly rooted to the principles of socialism as the best form of government; on the other hand, the
present form of socialism in the GDR is portrayed as a repressive system that stifles basic human rights which are defined
as the need for individuality and personal fulfillment. The
socialist system in the GDR, therefore, is badly in need of

reform. In order to become a viable political system, it must
assent to the desperate call of its citizens for greater independence in order to prevent Christa T.'s illness from reaching
epidemic proportions. Christa Wolf, therefore, has not abandoned
the concept of partiality in this novel, but she has transformed
it. Partiality to Christa Wolf no longer means blind support
of government policies. Instead, the new definition of partiality calls for constructive criticism in order to promote a true
socialist society. If Christa Wolf's prescription for a cure
of the current shortcomings is incorporated into the system,
then she is certain: "Nicht mehr lange wird an dieser Krankheit
gestorben werden."(CT, p.177)

    3. National Orientation

As had been the case for the "Moskauer Novelle" and "Der
geteilte Himmel," "Nachdenken über Christa T." continues the
depiction of life in a socialist society. Upon closer examination, however, one observes a noticeable change in Christa
Wolf's portrayal of everyday life in a socialist state in
these works. Whereas the "Moskauer Novelle" presented a near
idyllic portrait of life in a socialist state, "Der geteilte
Himmel" dealt with the hardships experienced by advocates of
socialism. As we will see, "Nachdenken über Christa T." addresses the crucial question: "How should one live in a socialist state?"

    Various critics have focused on specific aspects of this
novel in an attempt to provide their response to this question.
The East German critic Hermann Kähler in his analysis of this
work comes to the bold conclusion: "Eine autonome Persönlichkeit
ohne soziale Funktion ist eine... Illusion."[9] Roland Wiegenstein
on the other hand perceives the central issue in this novel as
a "Rückzug ins Private"[10] while Heinrich Mohr interprets the
work as a "zukunftssüchtiger Erinnerungsroman, ein Buch der
Utopie."[11] While each of these critics provides valuable insights for further reflection, Christa Wolf may have pointed
to the essence of her work in the "Selbstinterview" concerning
"Nachdenken über Christa T.:"

    Unsere Gesellschaft wird immer differenzierter.

> Differenzierter werden auch die Fragen, die ihre
> Mitglieder ihr stellen - auch in Form der Kunst.
> Entwickelter wird die Aufnahmebereitschaft vieler
> Menschen für differenzierte Antworten. Das Subjekt
> lebt immer souveräner in seiner Gesellschaft, die
> es als sein Werk empfindet: nicht nur denkt und
> weiß, sondern empfindet.[12]

According to Christa Wolf, it is the central purpose of this
novel to present a picture of the evolving socialist society in
terms of its changing patterns of life, attitudes and artistic
perceptions. Form and content of this novel, therefore, complement one another in advocating changes within the GDR from
a highly regimented society to a more tolerant state. Far from
achieving the hoped for political integration by means of restrictions imposed on personal freedoms, these practices have
fostered "loner" or "outsider" personalities in the mold of
Christa T. who are motivated by a desperate need to break out
of the group mentality in their effort to seek self fulfillment.
The extreme urgency for greater opportunities for self fulfillment is underscored by the repeated fusion of the character of
Christa T. with the narrator. In this format Christa Wolf
reveals her innermost convictions for more tolerance and understanding, for the need for human individuality and self-actualization:

> Später merkte ich, daß das Objekt meiner Erzäh-
> lung gar nicht so eindeutig sie, Christa T., war
> oder blieb. Ich stand auf einmal mir selbst
> gegenüber, das hatte ich nicht vorhergesehen.[13]

This work, however, goes far beyond a mere presentation of
contemporary life in the GDR according to the concept of national orientation. As was the case for Christa T., the act
of writing provides an outlet for Christa Wolf herself in her
effort "Die Dinge dicht zu machen." Like Christa T., Christa
Wolf can "nur schreibend über die Dinge kommen." Thus, the
process of writing serves as an exorcism for Christa Wolf. It
is the most effective way for her to confront difficult questions, to search for a meaning for life, and to penetrate the

essence of life itself:

> Ich schreibe, suchend. Es ergibt sich, daß ich
> eben dieses Suchen festhalten muß, so ehrlich wie
> möglich, so genau wie möglich, daß ich die abgeris-
> senen Fäden dieses Lebens aufnehmen und verlängern
> muß, daß ich die Tote noch einmal erschaffen muß,
> damit sie am Leben bleibt. Also dringe ich in die
> frühere Welt der Toten ein, versuche zu begreifen,
> warum sie mir fehlt, was mir an ihr fehlt.[14]

Thus, the GDR and its socialist society only provides the canvass upon which Christa Wolf reveals the eternal struggle confronting all human beings--whether to lead a life as a "Mitläufer" and "Anpasser" or whether to chart a course toward greater independence and self fulfillment. Christa Wolf has chosen the second path in this novel, motivated by the conviction that freedom and individuality are the only means by which adherents to any political ideology can come to an understanding of one's essence as a human being. This path to one's inner self is always painful and difficult, yet it must be pursued in an effort to search for the essence of life: "Obwohl zum Innehalten die Zeit nicht ist, wird einmal keine Zeit mehr sein, wenn man jetzt nicht innehält. Lebst du jetzt, wirklich? In diesem Augenblick, ganz und gar? Wann, wenn nicht jetzt?"(CT, p.98)

4. The Typical

During the Second Bitterfeld Conference in 1964 Christa Wolf shocked those in attendance by condoning a departure from the concept of the typical in socialist realism literature. In response to the complaint of a fourteen-year-old boy that youth literature in the GDR is characterized by sugar-coated superficialty which is "abweichend" from reality, Christa Wolf offers the following suggestion: "Nun habe ich tatsächlich nicht den Mut aufgebracht, diesem Jungen die Gesetze des Typischen in der Literatur zu erklären, sondern ich habe gesagt: 'Es sollte ruhig mal einer über das Abweichende schreiben.'"[15] As if to emphasize this rejection of the typical as a legitimate element of the literary process, Christa Wolf staunchly defended Werner Bräunig's novel "Rummelplatz" against Erich Honecker's attacks

as a work deviating from the depiction of typical elements by
focusing on negative aspects of GDR life during the eleventh
plenary session of the Central Committee of the SED:

> Dazu möchte ich aber sagen, daß die Kunst sowieso
> von Sonderfällen ausgeht und daß Kunst nach wie vor
> nicht darauf verzichten kann, subjektiv zu sein, das
> heißt, die Handschrift, die Sprache, die Gedankenwelt
> des Künstlers wiederzugeben. Ich möchte auch sagen,
> daß der Begriff des Typischen, der in der Diskussion
> mehrmals gebraucht wurde, auch seine sehr genaue
> Untersuchung verlangt, daß man nicht wieder zurück-
> fällt auf den Begriff des Typischen, den wir schon
> mal hatten und der dazu geführt hat, daß die Kunst
> überhaupt nur noch Typen schafft.[16]

"Nachdenken über Christa T." may thus be seen as the direct
implementation of these theoretical statements into practice in
that this work has been cleansed of the last vestiges of the
typical as required by socialist realism guidelines. Indeed,
Christa Wolf seems to have gone out of her way to portray a
"Sonderfall" in a highly "subjektiv" manner to underscore most
emphatically that she would no longer abide by the concept of
the typical in her works.

It comes as no great surprise, therefore, that this novel
does not offer a single "typical" character. In fact, the only
principle character in the work, Christa T., is the antithesis
of the "typical" character that the founders of socialist realism had in mind. Indeed, the figure of Christa T. represents
more than a rejection of the principle of the typical by Christa
Wolf; this character encompasses all the prerequisites for the
introduction of the "typically" "untypical."

As was the case for Bräunig's "Rummelplatz," this novel
focuses on the untypical, a "Sonderfall," a would-be writer,
who from her earliest childhood is destined to forsake the
external world for internal realism: "Nun war sie wohl für
immer in die andere Welt geraten, die dunkle, die ihr ja seit
je nicht unbekannt war - woher sonst ihr Hang, zu·dichten,
dichtzumachen die schöne, helle, feste Welt, die ihr Teil sein

sollte?"(CT, p.23)   The process of writing "zu dichten" is this
child's means of coping with "dichtzumachen" the real world.
The written word provides the mechanism for Christa T. to communicate her innermost thoughts to the external world.   The
essence of these thoughts revolves around the central idea to
reject the herd philosophy, exhibited by so many of the inhabitants of the GDR as illustrated by the medical student:

Der Kern der Gesundheit ist Anpassung.   - Das wiederholt er gleich noch mal, sie solle nur nicht die
Brauen heben, ob sie denn wirklich begreife, was das
heißt?
Nun, Christa T. verstand allzugut, sie glaubte auch
seinen entwicklungsgeschichtlichen Exkurs entbehren
zu können, aber er ist nicht zu unterbrechen.   Über-
leben, ist ihm klar geworden, sei das Ziel der Mensch-
heit immer gewesen und werde es bleiben.   Das heißt,
ihr Mittel zu jeder Zeit: Anpassung. Anpassung um
jeden Preis.(CT, p.109)

Except for the narrator, Christa T. does not make any converts to her "Weltanschauung." The pupils in the public school,
her fellow students at the university, her landlady, her circle
of friends during her final days and her own former students do
not really understand Christa T.'s reasons for "being different."
They perceive her as somewhat eccentric and pity her for her
obvious idiosyncracies. From the perspective of the group, it
is Christa T., not society, that is in need of adjustment and
correction.

The second reason for Christa T.'s reason for writing is her
search for self fulfillment that she can not achieve in the real
world. Indeed, the prescription for self-actualization offered
by socialist realism tenets calling for the amalgamation of the
individual into society by means of "Anpassung" is tantamount
to the destruction of the self. Therefore, repudiation of the
mass psychology syndrome and strict adherence to one's individuality is necessary for self fulfillment. Thus, the process of
writing serves as a means of dealing with an uncontrollable outer
reality, as an outlet for personal hopes and dreams and as a

means of self preservation. These functions of the writing
process are also contained in Christa T.'s thesis entitled
"Der Erzähler Theodor Storm" in which she attempts to deal with
the central issue: "...wie man denn - und ob überhaupt und
unter welchen Umständen - in der Kunst sich selbst verwirklichen
könne."(CT, p.94) Christa T. selects the works of Theodor Storm
as the basis for her investigation,

> ...weil sein Weltrerhältnis 'vorwiegend lyrisch' ist
> und weil eine solche Natur, in eine von Niedergangs-
> tendenzen und Epigonentum gezeichnete Zeit gestellt,
> besondere Anstrengungen nötig hat, um dennoch ihr
> Werk hervorzubringen. Diese Anstrengungen sind es
> also. Nicht, daB sie das Werk überschätzte, aber sie
> schätzt, daB es dennoch zustande kam. Nicht, daB
> sie den Idylliker verteidigte, die Provinz, die er
> besetzt hält, zu einem groBen poetischen Reich umzu-
> deuten suchte. Aber er hat, was er immerhin besitzt,
> wirklich erobert, und unter welchen Bedingungen!(CT, p.94)

Both Storm and Christa T., therefore, are faced with the
enormous task of preserving their integrity as writers and human
beings during less than ideal times. Theodor Storm's successful
struggle against his adversaries serves as a source of inspiration to Christa T. to continue her efforts to maintain her individuality. Although Christa T. does not succeed in becoming a
writer like Storm, the act of writing has served as the stimulus
for someone else to extol her effort to preserve her "self" as
worthy of emulation by her contemporaries in the GDR:

> Wenn ich sie erfinden müBte - verändern würde ich sie
> nicht. Ich würde sie leben lassen... Erfahrungen
> aufzeichnend, die die Tatsachen des wirklichen Lebens
> in ihr hinterlassen haben... Den Durst nicht löschen,
> den sie immer spürt... Würde sie die wenigen Blätter
> vollenden lassen, die sie uns hinterlassen wollte und
> die, wenn nicht alles täuscht, eine Nachricht gewesen
> wären aus dem innersten Innern, jener tiefsten Schicht,
> in die man schwerer vordringt als unter die Erdrinde
> oder in die Stratosphäre, weil sie sicherer bewacht

ist: von uns selbst. 'Einmal,' so schließt der Roman,
wird man wissen wollen, wer sie war, wen man da vergißt.
Wird sie sehen wollen, das verstände sie wohl... Wird
sie wohl!... Wird sie, also, hervorzubringen haben,
einmal... Wann, wenn nicht jetzt?(CT, p.170)
We have seen that Christa T.'s quest for self fulfillment
through a tenacious effort to preserve her individuality is in
gross violation of the principle of the typical which calls for
the integration of the individual into society. Furthermore,
the first person narrative of this novel, in which the narrator
often fuses with the character of Christa T., further emphasizes
the agreement of the narrator and author with the "Weltanschauung"
expressed by the heroine. It is undisputable, therefore, that
Christa Wolf has rejected the concept of the typical both in
theory and in practice in this novel.

5. The Positive Hero

Commensurate with the abandonment of the socialist realism
criterion of the typical, this novel is also totally devoid of
the concept of the positive hero. "Nachdenken über Christa T."
thus represents the first absolute break with this important
socialist realism concept in that not a single character of this
novel qualifies even remotely for positive hero status. Indeed,
this work goes far beyond mere repudiation of this crucial socialist realism requirement in that Christa T. represents the
incarnation of the anti-hero in GDR literature.

Christa T. fulfills the criteria for anti-hero status in
that she violates all of the formal requirements for the positive hero as prescribed by socialist realism regulations. Far
from portraying a character in complete harmony with herself
and society, Christa T. is a restless, listless individual who
cannot cope with the regimentation of life in the GDR. She
rejects the socialist tendency toward human and material collectivization as a threat to the preservation of individualism.
The loss of individuality, she fears, will ultimately result in
complete loss of personal satisfaction and self-actualization.

The second violation of the concept of the positive hero may
be attributed to the fact that Christa T. exhibits no traits of

"Vergnügen an der Meisterungsmöglichkeit des menschlichen
Schicksals." Far from depicting the prototype of a socialist
personality in complete command of his destiny, Christa T. is
a "Sternkind," predestined to succumb at an early age to a
disease that robs her of personal fulfillment in the private
and public sector. Instead of being the master of her fate,
therefore, Christa T. is the victim of seemingly uncontrollable
circumstances--the antithesis of the socialist realism version
of the positive hero.

The third infraction against the socialist realism projection
of the positive hero is Christa T.'s quest for individual rather
than collective fulfillment. Whereas a true positive hero is
dedicated to the common good through the advancement of the socialist society, Christa T. exists on the fringe of society and
is concerned only with her private needs. Instead of working
enthusiastically for the promotion of a "wir" consciousness,
Christa T.'s efforts are directed to transforming the herd syndrome into an "ich" mentality. This attitude is totally incom-
patible with socialist realism tenets and confirms her anti-hero
characteristics.

Finally, Christa T. is in total violation of the fourth
characteristic of a positive hero which calls for such a person
to serve as a "Wegweiser," "Antizipation" and "Aktivist" in the
establishment of the socialist society. Instead of serving as
a "Wegweiser" to the advanced socialist society, however, Christa
T. searches for an understanding of the inner self. Far from
offering herself as the "Antizipation" of the new socialist
"type," Christa T. is its antithesis who exists on the edge of
society driven by an inner restlessness and yearning to come
to grips with herself. Christa T. therefore, cannot be characterized as the "Aktivist," the hero striving for the establishment of the new socialist society, in that her primary concern
is the preservation of human rights within the socialist framework.

Chapter VI

"Kein Ort. Nirgends:" The Death of Socialist Realism

The year 1974 marked a high point in the official existence
of the German Democratic Republic. During this year the socialist nation celebrated its twenty-fifth anniversary as an independent state, its admittance to the United Nations, and the
issuance of a new Constitution. The GDR thus had reached political maturity and was officially recognized by the world
community as a sovereign state. Despite its formal entry into
the world arena, the GDR remained firmly rooted to the socialist ideology in terms of its political, social and literary
perspectives. Indicative of the unchanged conservative political dogma prevailing in the GDR in 1974 is the article "Der
Sozialismus - Macht des Friedens und der Menschlichkeit" in
which Hurt Hager, a member of the Central Committee of the SED,
warns against all forms of ideological compromise with the
West as diversionary tactics by the capitalists to dilute the
purity of socialism.[1]

Alexander Abusch and the deputy minister for culture Höpcke
issued similar warnings to the intellectual community of the
GDR on the occasion of the twenty-fifth anniversary of the German
Democratic Republic. In these declarations GDR authors were
reminded of the unchanged "Aufgabe" of literature in the fulfill-
ment of socialist ideals. GDR authors were exhorted to produce
socialist realism works characterized by a "Gestaltung des
Arbeiters und seiner charakteristischen Züge: Schöpferdrang,
BewuBtsein, Organisiertheit und Disziplin. Falsch sei eine
Literatur, die den Menschen in seiner Isolierung zeige, das
Individuum forme sich in der und durch die Gesellschaft."[2]
Rainer Kerndl joins this chorus of politicians who urges his
fellow countrymen to return to the purity of socialist realism
while deploring the growing tendency in GDR literature to por-
tray atypical characters who strive for individual fulfillment
rather than the attainment of social and political goals.[3]
Finally, Kurt Hager states unequivocally that the political,

social and literary directives in the GDR will continue to be
determined solely by the Central Committee of the Socialist
Unity Party and that literature, therefore, is expected to
perform its assigned role in the advancement of socialism:

> Die philosophische Erkenntnis und Begründung der
> allgemeinen Gesetzmäßigkeiten, nach denen sich der
> sozialistische Aufbau in allen Ländern vollzieht,
> sowie die Aufdeckung der spezifischen Bedingungen,
> unter denen diese in unserem Lande wirken, bildet
> einen entscheidenden Ausgangspunkt bei der Festle-
> gung der Politik der SED.[4]

Despite such admonitions by the political hierarchy to
adhere to the traditional socialist realism guidelines, the
most reknowned GDR authors continued to produce literature
that virtually ignored these declarations as evidenced by the
publication of works that further emphasized the antagonistic
relationship between the individual and society that characterized "Nachdenken über Christa T." Subsequent to that publication such works as Rolf Schneider's "Reise nach Jaroslaw,"
Wolfgang Joho's "Der Sohn," Volker Braun's "Unvollendete
Geschichte," Rainer Kunze's "Die wunderbaren Jahre," and Ulrich
Plenzdorf's "Die neuen Leiden des jungen W." now focused on the
rebellion by the youth of the GDR and their efforts to break
out of the restrictions and regimentation imposed upon them by
the political and social sectors. The timeliness of these
works was confirmed by a poll conducted by the FDJ magazine
"Forum" in which forty percent of the respondents shared the
criticism voiced by Edgar in Ulrich Plenzdorf's "Die neuen
Leiden des jungen W." and sixty percent of the youth questioned
could easily envision themselves as friends of the "Außenseiter"
who showed a total disdain for the restrictions imposed upon him
by society through his flagrant use of foul language, his hippy-
like appearance and total nonconformity in his behavior patterns.
It seems that the yearning for greater personal freedom depicted
in literature had indeed struck a responsive chord in the youth
of the GDR.

The second trend in GDR literature during the 1970's focused

on the re-emergence of the "Erinnerungsroman" in its return to
the Nazi era in an effort to obtain final absolution for the
sins committed during those dark days of German history. This
time the reexamination of the horrors of the Nazi past was not
motivated by political propaganda against the West but rather
by the sincere desire on the part of the authors of these works
to ascertain the truth about the possible involvement of their
friends and relatives in these transgressions against humanity.
Driven by an intense need for atonement for the past, the
authors of these works preferred the discovery of potential
wrongdoings to the gnawing uncertainty concerning the role
played by their loved ones during the Nazi era. The most important of the second generation "Erinnerungsromane" are Klaus
Schlesinger's "Michael," "Alte Filme," and "Berliner Traum,"
Helga Schütz' "Vorgeschichten oder Schöne Gegend Probstein,"
"Das Erdbeben bei Sangershausen," "Festbeleuchtung," and "Jette
in Dresden," Hermann Kant's "Der Aufenthalt," and Christa Wolf's
"Kindheitsmuster."

Although we will not analyze this novel by Christa Wolf as
a work of socialist realism criteria because it does not differ
appreciably from "Nachdenken über Christa T." in the progression
from socialist realism literature to literature per se, a brief
look at this novel may offer considerable insight into the
nature of these GDR "Erinnerungsromane."

"Kindheitsmuster" which appeared in 1976 attempts to answer
such gnawing questions of GDR citizens as: "Wie sind wir so
geworden, wie wir sind?" Who provided the role models for
children growing up during the Nazi era? What was the attraction of fascism that enabled it to command the loyalty of
millions of ordinary people? What resistance, if any, was
offered against Nazism by the German people? Such questions
are confronted in a highly complicated four-level narrative
format in an effort to come to grips with the suppressed experiences of the past in a personal yet impassionate manner.
Thus, the first level of narration in this novel consists of
accounts of actual survivors of the Nazi era to Nelly Jordan
during a trip to Landsberg an der Warthe which is now located

in Poland. These accounts are subsequently internalized by
the heroine in a process of self interrogation wherein Nelly
compares the accounts of the past with the narrative present
in the year 1971. Further reflection concerning the events of
the Nazi era are achieved by the third level of narration in
which the narrator contemplates the past during the process of
writing the novel within the years 1972-1975. Finally, the
fourth level of narration reveals the "Schwierigkeiten beim
Schreiben der Wahrheit" encountered by the narrator in recording
the experiences related to her by the various sources. This
four-level narrative format provides a means for intense reflection concerning the events of 1935-1945. As a result of this
literary exorcism the author, narrator and literary figures
have overcome the shame of the past and have attained a new
sense of dignity as human beings that enables them to confront
the future with confidence.

The pain and agony experienced by the narrator of this novel
in confronting once more the ignoble German past is indicative
of the torment endured by Christa Wolf herself in writing
"Kindheitsmuster." Despite the personal anguish experienced
by the author in reopening a wound that plagued an entire nation,
Christa Wolf was determined to bear any price for a restoration
of her integrity as a human being and writer:

> ...ich hatte seit Jahren das deutliche Gefühl, dass
> ich diesen Beitrag, den ich selber leisten muss, um
> danach anderes schreiben zu können, noch nicht ge-
> leistet habe. Es gibt da auch gewisse Gesetze der
> Berufsmoral. Wenn man eine bestimmte Sache noch
> nicht gesagt hat, darf man nicht zu anderem übergehen.[5]

The third trend in GDR literature of the 1970's was the
emergence of a "Frauenliteratur" in which women authors dealt
with the unique problems encountered by females in the GDR.
This trend marked a significant change from the earlier "Frauenliteratur" in which men had dealt with issues relating to women.
Thus, such works by male writers as Eberhard Paulitz' "Die
sieben Affären der Dona Juanita," Helfried Schreiter's "Frau
am Fenster," and Heiner Müller's "Zement" paved the way for the

woman's entry into the mainstream of literature. However, in the mid 1970's women authors in the GDR began to take the initiative in presenting their concerns to the public. As a result, the literature of the GDR was enriched by such works as Brigitte Reimann's "Franziska Linkerhand," Gerti Tetzner's "Karen W.," Irmtraud Morgner's "Trobadora Beatriz," Helga Schubert's "Lauter Leben," Christine Wolter's "Wie ich meine Unschuld verlor," and Maxie Wander's edition "Guten Morgen, du Schöne. Frauen in der DDR. Protokolle."

As was the overall trend in GDR literature of the 1970's, the "Frauenliteratur" also strove for greater personal freedom and the opportunity for self-fulfillment as "women" and human beings. The focus in these works, therefore, is no longer on admittance to and acceptance by society into various places of work or professions. Instead, women come to terms with their unique nature as a result of their sexual makeup. Physical and psychological characteristics of women as a result of biological factors are examined in a variety of surreal modes of narration and formats ranging from the fairy tale to science fiction. No matter what the format of these works, however, the ultimate goal of the "Frauenliteratur" is the promotion of a sense of liberation and self-actualization as a result of a clearer understanding of the unique nature of the species known as "woman."

Christa Wolf's most recent prose work "Kein Ort. Nirgends" which was published in 1979 is an important contribution not only to the continuing trend of "Frauenliteratur" but also serves as the revival of the "Künstlerroman" in the GDR.[6] As such, "Kein Ort. Nirgends" represents the first complete break with all five socialist realism characteristics and thereby marks the death of socialist realism in the longer prose works by Christa Wolf. A brief look at the theoretical writings of Christa Wolf will strengthen the proposition that the death of socialist realism in "Kein Ort. Nirgends" is not a chance occurrence but rather the result of an evolution in theory and practice from socialist realism literature to literature per se by this internationally acclaimed GDR writer.

Christa Wolf's beginnings as a socialist realism writer
during the early 1960's are characterized by a linear, authorial depiction of objective reality through which she illustrates the prescribed socialist realism criteria of objective
reflection of reality, partiality, national orientation, the
typical and positive hero in the "Moskauer Novelle" and "Der
geteilte Himmel." Beginning with "Nachdenken über Christa T.,"
however, we observe a noticeable shift from an outward or
objective to an inner or subjective authenticity.[7] In her
interview with Hans Kaufmann in 1974 Christa Wolf for the
first time alludes to the crucial component of "subjektive
Authentizität"[8] in her writing process.

In this interview inner authenticity is defined by Christa
Wolf as the intimate relationship between the author and his
work, the element of tension that exists between the narrator,
author and written product. This inseparability of the author
from his material during the creative process results in fundamental changes in the author and written product.[9] By means
of subjective authenticity, the author brings a fourth dimension
to his creative process in which "Erfahrung," "Erinnerung,"
"Vergessen," and "Gedächtnis" contribute to the creation of
literature characterized by "Erfindung," "Wirklichkeit,"
"Wahrheit," and "Realität."[10] These theoretical concepts are
indicative of Christa Wolf's abandonment of the restrictive
guidelines of socialist realism literature and point to her
intention to embrace a creative process according to universally
accepted standards which find a direct application in "Kein Ort.
Nirgends."

1. Objective Reflection of Reality

"Kein Ort. Nirgends" marks a complete break with the concept of objective reflection of reality in the longer prose
works of Christa Wolf in that this "Erzählung" for the first
time deals with a subject matter and historical time period
which are completely removed from the GDR experience. Whereas
the "Moskauer Novelle," "Der geteilte Himmel," "Nachdenken über
Christa T." and "Kindheitsmuster" all dealt with political and
social issues relating directly to life in the GDR, the narrated

time in "Kein Ort. Nirgends" is one Sunday afternoon in 1804 in Winkel and Rhein. Thus, political considerations play absolutely no role in this work which may be more aptly characterized as a discourse or polemic that depicts the conflict between the artist and society as well as the antagonistic relationship between man and woman as exemplified in the experiences of Heinrich von Kleist and Karoline von Günderrode.

In accordance with Christa Wolf's perception of subjective authenticity, the focus in this work is not on the outer action as evidenced by its virtual nonexistence but rather on the penetration of the inner selves of these two writers who cannot reconcile their artistic convictions with the conventions of society. The penetration of the inner world of Kleist and Günderrode is made possible by the use of interior monolog which permits the reader direct access to the thoughts of these two outsiders. Consequently, nearly the entire action in this work is conveyed as thought processes emanating from Kleist and Günderrode. Form and content, therefore, draw the reader to the inner sphere of Kleist and Günderrode which is the primary area of conflict in these two artists.

To a large extent "Kein Ort. Nirgends" may be viewed as an extension and refinement of "Nachdenken über Christa T." in that both works deal with the antagonistic relationship between the demands made by society on the individual and the efforts of the individual to procure greater independence outside the expected code of behavior imposed by the status quo. As was the case for Christa T., the stimulus for writing "Kein Ort. Nirgends" was provided by the premature deaths--in both cases suicides--of these two German writers as a result of their alienation from society. Karoline von Günderrode, a writer of poetry, prose and drama, committed suicide in 1806 at the age of twenty six in Winkel am Rhein. Heinrich von Kleist, the famous Prussian author, terminated his life in the Berliner Wannsee at the age of thirty-four in 1811. These are historical facts that are well known. Less well known, however, are the reasons for these desperate acts by these writers. "Kein Ort. Nirgends" is an effort to reveal some of the causes leading to these suicides.

A Sunday afternoon social at the home of Joseph Merten, a prominent businessman in Winkel am Rhein, provides both the setting for a fictitious meeting between Kleist and Günderrode and the background against which the rift between the artists and society is played out. While the local socialities and such celebrities as Savigny, a lawyer from Marburg, Clemens Brentano, his wife and sister Bettine enjoy the customary chit chat and conviviality at such affairs, Heinrich von Kleist literally stands apart from the group: "Darf man erfahren, was Sie uns entrückt?"[11] From the outset, therefore, Kleist is presented as an outsider who has great difficulty in assimilating himself into this social setting. Kleist is fully aware of his loner characteristics. He has criss-crossed the map of Europe in a desperate effort to find a place where political and social conventions are compatible with his personal and artistic convictions. All of these efforts end unsuccessfully: "Wo ich nicht bin, da ist das Glück."(KON, p.6) Finally, this unsuccessful odyssey by Kleist in search of a home that provides him a sense of tranquility and peace of mind ends in a mental "Zusammenbruch" that leaves him on the verge of committing suicide as a result of his irreconcilable differences with society as illustrated in the monolog from Kleist's "Guiscard:" 'Denn wer ertrüg der Zeiten Spott und Geisel... des Mächtigen Druck, der Stolzen Mißhandlungen...' (KON, P.16)

Kleist's enmity with society is the result of his "über-scharfen Gehör" which sensitizes him more keenly than the ordinary human being to the attempt by society to impose its standards upon individuals. Thus, Kleist is caught between the uncomfortable choice of closing his eyes to these repressive efforts or rebelling against the impositions of society by following the dictates of his conscience: "Er hat die Wahl - falls das eine Wahl zu nennen ist -, das verzehrende Ungenügen, sein bestes Teil, planvoll in sich abzutöten oder ihm freien Lauf zu lassen und am irdischen Elend zugrunde zu gehn. Sich Zeit und Ort nach eigner Notwendigkeit zu schaffen oder nach

gewöhnlichem Zuschnitt zu vegetieren."(KON, pp.38-39) Despite
the personal agony endured by Kleist in the process of incorporat-
ing his innermost hopes and dreams for a better, more sensitive
society into his works and the full konwledge that his most
intimate thoughts will be ignored by that entity as totally
irrelevant to real life, Kleist perseveres in his efforts even
at the risk of his physical and mental well-being: "Mörderische
Wohltat: Meinen, was man sagt, und von der eigenen Meinung
zerrissen werden."(KON, p.15)

The complete disregard shown by society as a whole for the
ideals advocated by Kleist in his works is depicted most point-
edly in the attitude exhibited by Savigny. In this lawyer's
view, literature and philosophy inherently deal with matters
that lie outside the realm of reality. Therefore, these concoc-
tions of the mind have no direct relevance for real life and
should not be considered for implementation in society:

DaB man die Philosophie nicht beim Wort nehmen, das
Leben am Ideal nicht messen soll - das ist Gesetz.
Bleibt zu fragen: Gilt es immer? Ausnahmslos?
Allerdings. Es ist das Gesetz der Gesetze, Kleist,
auf dem unsre menschlichen Einrichtungen in ihrer
notwendigen Gebrechlichkeit beruhn. Wer dagegen auf-
steht, muB zum Verbrecher werden. Oder zum Wahnsin-
nigen.(KON, pp.63-64)

This disregard shown by society for the ideals advocated by
the artists has a devastating effect on Kleist. He is
"gemütskrank" and constantly teeters on the edge of self-
annihilation: "Denn kein Mensch kann auf die Dauer mit der
Erkenntnis leben, daB, so stark wie sein Widerstand gegen das
Übel der Welt der Trieb in ihm ist, sich diesem Übel unbedingt
zu unterwerfen."(KON, p.69) Consequently, an irreconcilable
rift develops between society and the artist. While Kleist
pleads for greater independence and individuality as an essential prerequisite for human self actualization, the state advocates the suppression of individuality in favor of conformity
as a means of facillitating the realization of political ends.
This attempt by the state to quell individuality for the sake

of political expedience must be resisted at all cost: "Die
Menge, heiBt es. Soll ich meine Zwecke und Ansichten künstlich
zu den ihren machen?"(KON, pp.85-86)

As long as society and the state value only the short term,
pragmatic contributions of the sciences while the "truths"
presented by the artists and writers are dismissed as uncomfortable nuisances, Kleist insists on his right to follow the
"innere Vorschrift in meiner Brust, gegen welche alle äuBern,
und wenn sie ein König unterschrieben hätte, nichtswürdig sind."
(KON, p.86)

Kleist's existence on the brink of self annihilation as a
result of his alienation from society is not an isolated example
of the antagonistic relationship between the artist and society.
Karoline von Günderrode too is one of those "die 'ihre Stirn an
der gesellschaftlichen Mauer der Wirklichkeit wundrieben.'"
(KON, inside cover) As a woman and writer, Günderrode must
endure constant ridicule and social ostracism by her contemporaries for her dual transgression against the conventions of
her time. First, Günderrode has violated the prevailing social
code which frowns upon women who embark upon a profession that
is deemed to be a man's domain. Secondly, Günderrode, like
Kleist, is viewed with suspicion and apprehension for advocating
ideas in her works that challenge the prevailing mores of
society.

As was the case for Kleist, Günderrode's advocacy of
integrity and dignity for every human being through greater
individuality and freedom has brought her in conflict with
society. In an effort to escape the friction with her peers
as a result of the principles she advocates as a writer,
Günderrode has retreated to a convent where she is free to
pursue her literary career. Her presence at this soiree is,
therefore, one of her rare appearances in a social setting.
It is apparent from the outset that Günderrode does not fit into
this environment. Like Kleist, she is physically and spiritually
separated from the other guests: "Ein unsichtbarer Kreis ist
um sie gezogen, den zu übertreten man sich scheut."(KON, p.12)
While the other guests relish the opportunity to carry on the

163

customary small talk with their peers, Günderrode finds little
pleasure in these activities: "Die Frau, Günderrode, in den
engen Zirkel gebannt, nachdenklich, hellsichtig, unangefochten
durch Vergänglichkeit, entschlossen, der Unsterblichkeit zu
leben, das Sichtbare dem Unsichtbaren zu opfern."(KON, p.6)
Günderrode is fully aware of the dampening impact that her
presence has on the gaiety of this soiree. Consequently, she
regrets her decision to leave the serenity of the convent where
she was engaged in the agonizing process of committing her
deepest convictions to paper for this gathering in which the
dispersal of superficial amenities is the primary gauge for
social success. Indeed, Günderrode's attendance at this gathering represents little more than a circus attraction: "Man
läßt mich jetzt, duldet meine Entfernung, als Grille, verlangt
nichts weiter, als daß ich mich grillenhaft zeige, von Zeit zu
Zeit."(KON, p.9) A victim of the prevailing moral code imposed
upon women by a society dominated by men, Günderrode is forced
to lead her life as a woman and writer within narrow restrictions which severely stifle her development as a writer and
human being:

    Auffällige Gesten meidet sie, so lange es möglich
    ist. Sie hat das Unglück, leidenschaftlich und stolz
    zu sein, also verkannt zu werden. So hält sie sich
    zurück, an Zügeln, die ins Fleisch schneiden. Das
    geht ja, man lebt. Gefährlich wird es wenn sie sich
    hinreißen ließe, die Zügel zu lockern, loszugehn,
    und wenn sie dann, in heftigstem Lauf, gegen jenen
    Widerstand stieße, den die andern Wirklichkeit nennen
    und von dem sie sich, man wird es ihr vorwerfen,
    nicht den rechten Begriff macht.(KON, p.11)
The impact of these restrictions on Günderrode is so devastating that she is prepared to terminate her life rather than
to accede to the demands of society as an expected, submissive
"Hämmelchen." To underscore the seriousness of her intentions,
Günderrode always carries the means of self extinction in her
purse:

    Sie kennt die Stelle unter der Brust, wo sie den

Dolch ansetzen muß, ein Chirurg, den sie scherzhaft
fragte, hat sie ihr mit einem Druck seines Fingers
bezeichnet. Seitdem, wenn sie sich sammelt, spürt
sie den Druck und ist augenblicklich ruhig. Es wird
leicht sein und sicher, sie muß nur achten, daß sie
die Waffe immer bei sich hat.(KON, p.10)

Compounding Günderrode's difficulties in procuring her rights
as a woman and author against the will of society is the fact
that even Clemens Brentano voices his opposition to a woman
entering the literary profession. Clemens Brentano's prejudice
against women entering the writing profession manifests itself
in his review of Günderrode's poetry. He is hard-pressed to
acknowledge that the intense emotion found in Günderrode's
poems, which are so close to his own perceptions, could have
been written by a woman. Brentano even goes so far as to accuse
Günderrode of arrogance and narcissism for seeking entrance to
the writing profession: "Er staune, sagt er, wie sie so von
einem festen Bewußtsein des eignen Wertes durchdrungen sei;
wie sie es sich herausnehme, in einem für ihr Geschlecht
ungewöhnlichen Maße gerecht zu sein. Sie sei hochmütig, ob
sie das wisse.(KON, p.35)

Even at the risk of confirming Brentano's accusations and
attributing to herself characteristics of a "Spröde, Zimperliche,
Unweibliche,"(KON, p.28) Günderrode does not submit to the
pressure exerted upon her: "Clemens, sagt sie endlich, lassen
Sie es genug sein. Daß ich schreiben muß, steht mir fest. Es
ist eine Sehnsucht in mir, mein Leben in einer bleibenden Form
auszusprechen."(KON, p.31)

It is apparent, therefore, that Karoline von Günderrode is
even a greater social outcast than Heinrich von Kleist. Günderrode must not only deal with the constant reproach by society
in general for her transgressions against the mores of her time,
but she must also endure the chiding of her fellow artists for
desiring to enter a profession they consider a man's domain.
Despite the chorus of disapproval from all sides, Günderrode
defends her actions as essential for the preservation of her
sanity:

Hörst du, Savigny, ich weiß mir nichts Besseres.
Gunda sagt, es sei dumm, sich von einer so kleinen
Kunst, wie es die meine sei, bis auf diesen Grad
beherrschen zu lassen. Aber ich liebe diesen Fehler, wenn es einer ist. Er hält mich oft schadlos
für die ganze Welt. Und er hilft mir glauben an die
Notwendigkeit aller Dinge, auch an die meiner eignen
Natur, so anfechtbar sie ist. Sonst lebte ich nicht,
lieber Savigny, das mußte ich dir einmal sagen.
Und nun soll zwischen uns nie wieder die Rede
davon sein.(KON, p.77-78)

Thus, Günderrode, like Kleist, exists on the edge of society.
She is completely misunderstood by her contemporaries and is
looked upon as an eccentric who is barely tolerated: "Unheimlich
bin ich ihnen, doch können sie nicht sagen, warum. Ich weiß
es: Ich bin unter ihnen nicht heimisch."(KON, p.46)

It is only fitting, therefore, that the very characteristics
for which Kleist and Günderrode are shunned by society serve
as the source of magnetic attraction for each other. As the
rift between the "Außenseiter" and society widens, the bond of
trust and friendship between Kleist and Günderrode intensifies.
The antagonistic relationship between the artists and society
is presented symbolically in that the two opposing forces literally part company. While the socialites stroll along the
"downstream" bank of the Rhine, Kleist and Günderrode proceed
in the "upstream" direction. Arm in arm, the two artists
share their innermost thoughts with one another. For the first
time Kleist has found someone else who understands the anguish
that he suffers as a result of his refusal to compromise his
principles as a writer and human being for a harmonious relationship with society: "...-irgend etwas an dieser Frau entzieht
ihm wie ein Magnet die angreifbarsten Geständnisse-,..."(KON,
p.141) Karoline von Günderrode, on the other hand, confesses
to Kleist the unbearable humiliation endured by women as a
result of the restrictions imposed upon them by society and
calls for a united effort by women to bring about the freedom
and independence to which every human being is entitled:

Sie sagt, nach ihrer Beobachtung gehöre zum Leben
der Frauen mehr Mut als zu dem der Männer. Wenn
sie von einer Frau höre, die diesen Mut aufbringe,
verlange es sie danach, mit ihr bekannt zu sein.
Es sei nämlich dahin gekommen, daß die Frauen, auch
über Entfernungen hinweg, einander stützen müßten,
da die Männer nicht mehr dazu imstande seien.(KON,
pp.118-119)

By sharing their most intimate hopes and dreams for a more
humane world, Kleist and Günderrode transcend the artificial
barrier that existed between them as "man" and "woman" and
acquire a mutual respect for each other as human beings. Kleist,
in particular, has undergone a metamorphosis in that his earlier
perception of women as mere weaklings has undergone a radical
change as a result of his encounter with Günderrode: "In
dieser Frau, denkt er, könnte ihr Geschlecht zum Glauben an
sich selber kommen."(KON, p.149) Thus, these two artists--one
a man, the other a woman--have overcome centuries of distrust
and bigotry toward each other by sharing a common goal: "Unser
unausrottbarer Glaube, der Mensch sei bestimmt sich zu vervoll-
domm[n]en,..."(KON, p.150) In pledging their mutual commitment
to advancing this objective at all cost, Kleist and Günderrode
have already come very close to the realization of their dream:
"Näher sind sie sich nie als in dieser Minute."(KON, p.150)

It is absolutely clear, therefore, that Christa Wolf abandoned the socialist realism concept of objective reflection of
reality in this work in that the subject matter of "Kein Ort.
Nirgends" does not contain the remotest allusion to a transformation from capitalism to socialism. Indeed, this work is
totally apolitical in the narrow sense of the term in that
partisan politics plays no role in this polemic. Thus, the
subject matter associated with the concept of objective reflection of reality has been replaced with a topic typical of Western writers in which the personal anguish and alienation experienced in the "Küntler-Bürger" and "Mann-Frau" conflicts
are emphasized. Instead of adhering to socialist realism
guidelines, the content of "Kein Ort. Nirgends" is more remi-

niscent of the works of such Western writers as Thomas Mann
and Franz Kafka while the highly complicated stream of consciousness format resembles the works of such authors as James
Joyce, Henry James, Virginia Woolf, Samuel Beckett, Hermann
Broch, Martin Walser, Max Frisch and Uwe Johnson. Form and
content in "Kein Ort. Nirgends," therefore, are evidence of
the total rejection of the concept of objective reflection of
reality and its subsequent replacement with a subject matter
and format that are characteristic of universal literary concerns.

2. Partiality

As was the case for the concept of objective reflection of
reality, "Kein Ort. Nirgends" is a clear repudiation of the
socialist realism notion of partiality in that it discards
Lenin's mandate to produce literature that serves the "Millionen und aber Millionen Werktätigen," advances the goals of the
"proletarischen Sache," and is "offen mit dem Proletariat
[verbunden]." Instead of dealing with issues that are of
direct relevance for a proletarian audience as advocated by
Lenin, this work examines conflicts and concerns that are of
primary interest to the hated "oberen Zehntausend." Thus,
Christa Wolf has not only rejected the concept of partiality
but has embraced the odious bourgeois literary characteristics
which the concept of partiality was designed to expunge.

The subject matter of "Kein Ort. Nirgends" which focuses
on the conflict between the individual and society and the
antagonistic relationship between the sexes does not conform
to the socialist realism mandate to promote a mutually beneficial partnership between the writers and the state. Instead
of advocating a subservient role for literature to the political
hierarchy as advocated by the concept of partiality, "Kein Ort.
Nirgends" champions the quest for greater individuality and
self-actualization as human beings. Thus, the complete absence
of any "Übereinstimmung mit den Zielen und Aufgaben der
marxistisch-leninistischen Partei," as advocated by Werner
Jehser, Kurt Hager and Erwin Pracht, is further proof of the
rejection of the principle of partiality in this work. Finally,

this polemic is totally devoid of any evidence of Christa Wolf's support for the "Gesamtwillen und Gesamtplan" of the SED and a "bewuBte Klassenverbundenheit" with the proletariat as demanded by Klaus Träger.

Instead of espousing socialist ideology as was done in the "Moskauer Novelle" and "Der geteilte Himmel," as stipulated by the concept of partiality, "Kein Ort. Nirgends" deals with supra political problems that torment human beings in every society. Thus, the central issue presented in this work-- whether to strive for a degree of individuality and self- actualization through the adherence to personal conviction as was exhibited by Kleist and Günderrode or whether to lead a "Larven" existence as practiced by the "Mitläufer" in society-- confronts every thinking human being. This question by itself is in violation of the concept of partiality which demands adherence to partisan politics at any cost. Christa Wolf's advocacy of a quest for greater freedom and individuality in spite of the resulting persecution by society must be viewed as a direct repudiation of the concept of partiality.

Far from advocating the elimination of individuality for the purpose of promoting a monolithic approach to the establish- ment of a socialist society as mandated by the principle of partiality, "Kein Ort. Nirgends" champions the antithesis of this socialist realism tenet--the quest for individuality and human rights. Kleist and Günderrode serve as the role models for this struggle for their time and all subsequent "AuBenseiter" in every society. This new subject matter transcends the narrow restrictions of socialist realism and instead takes on the qualities that characterize first-rate literature through the ages.

3. National Orientation

"Kein Ort. Nirgends" marks the first complete break with the concept of national orientation in a longer prose work by Christa Wolf in that all elements of this socialist realism formulation have been discarded. Whereas the progenitors of the concept of national orientation in the Soviet Union and the German Democratic Republic perceived national orientation as the

creation of literature that presented customs, traditions and
socio-political concerns common to a specific nation with the
expressed purpose of promoting greater zeal and unity in the
advancement of national goals, "Kein Ort. Nirgends" focuses
on the rift between two artists and their society. Far from
dealing with a topic that is a "direkter Ausdruck des
Volkswillens" as envisioned by the architects of national
orientation, this work examines a conflict that is of primary
interest to the elite. Furthermore, this polemic concerning
the unbridgeable chasm between Kleist and Günderrode on the
one hand and society on the other takes place outside the framework of the GDR experience, thereby further reducing the impact
of this work on the ordinary GDR citizen which is in direct
violation of the intent of the concept of national orientation.
The most serious transgression against the concept of national
orientation in "Kein Ort. Nirgends," however, lies in its
presentation of issues that have no direct relevance to the
nation-wide interests of the broad spectrum of the GDR. To
the average GDR reader the physical and mental anguish experienced by Kleist and Günderrode as a result of their alienation
from society is little more than an interesting historical
phenomenon. It does not address the crucial issues pertaining
to the immediate problems in establishing the advanced socialist
society. Thus, the subject matter of "Kein Ort. Nirgends"
lies totally outside the legitimate parameters of national
orientation and as such must be viewed as a conscious rejection of this concept by Christa Wolf.

The form of "Kein Ort. Nirgends" exhibits a similar rejection of the criteria of national orientation. In order to
achieve the greatest possible impact upon the broad masses, a
crucial characteristic of national orientation is its adherence
to a simple form. As formulated by Brecht in 1938, national
orientation or "Volkstümlichkeit" in socialist realism literature
was to be expressed in a manner that is "...den breiten Massen
verständlich, ihre Ausdrucksform aufnehmend und bereichernd..."[12]
The campaign against formalism and the "Bitterfelder Weg" are
concrete examples of the efforts undertaken by GDR authorities

to abide by the principles of national orientation with the
expressed goal "den 'kleinen Kreis der Kenner' zu einem großen
Kreis der Kenner zu machen."

In sharp contrast to the simplicity in form advocated by
Brecht as the most effective means to pursue the goals of
socialist realism, "Kein Ort. Nirgends" is written in a highly complicated stream of consciousness format that totally
rejects the linear, authorial mode of narration. By abandoning
the outer authenticity for an inner subjectivity that is
expressed through extensive use of interior monolog, Christa
Wolf has returned to the hated formalism which GDR authorities
opposed with such vehemence during the "Formalismus Kampagne"
of the early 1950's. The complicated mode of narration in
"Kein Ort. Nirgends" that challenges the ability of the most
sophisticated readers to understand this work clearly is not
intended for consumption by the great masses. Thus, the drastic
change in the form of "Kein Ort. Nirgends" is further indication
of Christa Wolf's calculated transition from a writer of socialist realism literature to an author of universally recognized
literature.

As was the case for the concepts of objective reflection of
reality and partiality, "Kein Ort. Nirgends" has also been
cleansed of the concept of national orientation in form and
content. Neither the subject matter nor the mode of presentation thereof is intended for consumption by the broad masses
of the GDR. Instead, this work marks the return to traditional
literature in that both form and content address the concerns
of the enlightened reader in a most compelling and challenging
manner.

4. The Typical

Friedrich Engels, W.I. Lenin and Makcim Gorki envisioned
the concept of the typical as an integral part of the overall
framework of socialist realism literature in advancing socialism. By focusing on "typische Charaktere unter typischen
Umständen" the advocates of this concept hoped to evoke an
image of "der bekannte Unbekannte" who strove to bring about
the new socialist order. Such "typical" proponents of social-

ism were to serve as positive role models to the public at
large by virtue of exhibiting true socialist characteristics
that would stimulate the process of regeneration of mankind
from adherents to the old order to promoters of the new
socialist society. "Kein Ort. Nirgends," however, contains
none of the criteria of the typical as espoused by the progenitors of this concept. Indeed, the subject matter, main
characters and form of this work may be characterized as the
antithesis of the concept of the typical as advanced by the
advocates of socialist realism, thereby emphasizing the ultimate
rejection of this concept by Christa Wolf.

"Kein Ort. Nirgends" deviates from all previous longer
prose works by Christa Wolf in that for the first time the
subject matter of this work does not directly relate to the
GDR. By selecting a historical setting that precedes the
founding of the GDR by nearly a century and a half, Christa
Wolf deliberately distances herself from the typical subject
matter expected of socialist realism works. For the first time,
therefore, partisan politics plays absolutely no role in a
longer prose work by this author. Indeed, socialist ideology,
the cornerstone of the "Moskauer Novelle," "Der geteilte Himmel,"
"Nachdenken über Christa T." and "Kindheitsmuster" has been
replaced with a new anti-socialist subject matter--the depiction of increased alienation between individuals and society
as a result of the stifling effect of the restrictions placed
upon the human need for self-actualization. Christa Wolf's
advocacy of greater individual rights in spite of the resulting
alienation from society as illustrated by the examples of Kleist
and Günderrode is in direct violation of the concept of the
typical which glorifies the establishment of harmonious relationships between individuals and society whithin the framework
of socialism.

This quest for individual rights at the risk of incurring
the wrath of society is illustrated by two completely "atypical"
characters as envisioned by socialist realism advocates. Indeed,
Kleist and Günderrode, the archetypes of the "outsider," embody
all the characteristics which the "typical" characters of

socialist realism oppose. Both Kleist and Günderrode value
their personal freedom as artists and human beings so much that
they are willing to endure social ostracism, mental and physical
suffering and even death for their beliefs. Kleist criss-crosses
the map of Europe in a desperate effort to find a society that
permits him the necessary freedom to strive for self fulfillment. Günderrode, on the other hand, seeks to escape persecution by society for her rebellion against the prevailing restrictions imposed upon women by entering a convent. When Kleist's
and Günderrode's efforts for self-actualization fail and they
discover that in this world there is "Kein Ort. Nirgends"
that tolerates their quest for unrestricted freedom, these
"Außenseiter" prefer to end their lives rather than to continue
an existence that deprives them of the opportunity for self-
fulfillment as human beings.

This atypical subject matter coupled with its atypical
characters finds it expression in a most atypical form. Whereas
socialist realism tenets call for simple authorial narration
in order to be readily understood by the average reader for
whose benefit socialist realism works are intended, "Kein Ort.
Nirgends" is characterized by an extremely complicated stream
of consciousness format that challenges the intellectual skills
of the most experienced reader. Often entire sections must
be reread in order to ascertain their meaning. This complex
form is in direct violation of typical socialist realism modes
of expression which strive for simplicity in order to be easily
understood by the broad masses. By relinquishing the simple
authorial mode of narration so characteristic of her earliest
prose and instead turning to Western formalism as the predominant
mode of expression, Christa Wolf has given notice that the
concept of the typical as it applies to modes of narration will
no longer be adhered to in her works.

    5. The Positive Hero

As was the case for the concepts of objective reflection of
reality, partiality, national orientation and the typical,
"Kein Ort. Nirgends" also disregards the last criterion prescribed for socialist realism literature. In this work the

figure of the positive hero who functions as the ultimate
symbol of the ideals of communism by depicting an individual
who is in harmony with himself, who functions as a "Wegweiser"
and "Antizipation" of the "neue Mensch" who believes in the
"Meisterungsmöglichkeit des menschlichen Schicksals durch die
Gesellschaft" has been supplanted by the figures of Kleist and
Günderrode, two "Aussenseiter" who commit suicide as a result
of their alienation from society. This displacement of the
socialist realism positive hero with its antithesis is indicative of Christa Wolf's total rejection of the most symbolic
criterion of this literary phenomenon and, therefore, by implication the entire framework of socialist realism.

As "Vorgänger" with "Blut im Schuh" Kleist and Günderrode
have replaced the socialist realism version of the positive
hero with its antithesis as seen form a socialist realism perspective. While the positive hero depicted individuals who
were "...herausgehoben...aus jeder individuellen Enge und
Bedrängnis," this work portrays two characters who succumb to
the "Enge und Bedrängnis" imposed upon them by society. In
stark contrast to the traditional positive hero who strove
for the establishment of a "wir" syndrome, Kleist and Günderrode attempt to break out of the "herd" philosophy and strive
for self fulfillment through the acquisition of greater independence. Self-actualization characterized by a sense of
integrity and regard for human dignity--not political or social
consideration--is the primary concern for these new heroes.
So noble is the quest for these principles that Kleist and Günderrode are prepared to sacrifice their personal well-being and
endure the persecution of society for the attainment of these
goals:

> Günderrode, sagt er, aber ist es uns nicht geboten,
> innezuhalten, eh sich solche Sätze in uns bilden!
> Ja, sagt die Frau. Das ist uns geboten.
> Und?
> Und wir müssen das Gebot übertreten.
> Warum?
> Das weiß man nicht.(KON, p.124)

The quest for personal freedom and greater regard for the dignity of the human being advocated in "Kein Ort. Nirgends" runs counter to the highest goals prescribed by socialist realism tenets in which such efforts are always subservient to political ends. Thus, the character traits exhibited by Kleist und Günderrode fit more closely into the mold of traditional Western literature in that their unwavering pursuit of self fulfillment transcends all considerations for personal welfare. This struggle "der dem Geist aller Zeiten strikt zuwiderläuft" (KON, pp.150-51) is both timeless and timely for every society and political ideology and, therefore, elevates "Kein Ort. Nirgends" from the self-serving level of socialist realism unto the plateau of true literature.

Conclusion

This study has shown how the East-West conflict following
World War II led to the division of Germany into a capitalist
and a socialist state as a direct consequence of the increasing
enmity between the two super powers. It soon became apparent
that the arts and sciences in the German Democratic Republic
would become totally subservient to the political process as
part of a calculated effort to bring about a regeneration of
the inhabitants of the GDR from bourgeois capitalism to socialism. The blueprint for the subordination of the arts to political
needs was provided by Wladimir I. Lenin and Friedrich Engels.
Joseph Stalin refined the exploitation of literature for political
ends in the early 1930's through the introduction of the concept
of "socialist realism" in which artists were to assume the role
of "Ingenieure der menschlichen Seele" for the establishment of
the new socialist society. This function of literature was
subsequently transplanted to the GDR following the occupation
of that territory by the Soviet Union.

Following the Soviet model, socialist realism literature in
the GDR is identified by five main characteristics: 1) Objective
Reflection of Reality, 2) Partiality, 3) National Orientation,
4) The Typical, and 5) The Positive Hero. By adhering to these
criteria, works of socialist realism carry out the "Auftrag"
to advance the precepts of socialism as a "Wegweiser" to the
transition from capitalism to communism.

Christa Wolf, one of the most eminent contemporary writers
of the GDR, began her literary career as a loyal Party member
and strict adherent to the concepts of socialist realism. Her
first novel "Moskauer Novelle" can be labelled a model of socialist realism in that it abides by all five criteria of that literary movement. Consequently, this work may be classified as
refined literary propaganda in that its primary purpose is the
promotion of stronger ties of friendship between the inhabitants
of the GDR and USSR. Fourteen years after the publication of
this work, Christa Wolf acknowledges the lack of literary merit
of the "Moskauer Novelle" and attributes it to youthful naivité.

The second decade in the existence of the German Democratic
Republic was accompanied by a greater sense of maturity and
confidence in the viability of the fledgling socialist nation.
This new state of mind was reflected in the "Ankunftsliteratur"
that focused on the achievements of the GDR under socialism.
The new-found sense of security, however, also fostered a
yearning for greater freedom of expression among the artists
and writers. "Der geteilte Himmel," the second work by Christa
Wolf, marks a breakthrough in the quality of GDR literature as
a result of its deviation from the strict guidelines of socialist
realism. Instead of presenting another "expected" portrait of
a utopian socialist order, "Der geteilte Himmel" represents
an unprecedented realistic account of life in the GDR that is
characterized by a "verschleierten Himmel," "Unrast," and
"Schatten." While this work still abides by the characteristics
of objective reflection of reality, partiality, and national
orientation, these concepts are no longer characterized by
political subservience but rather by honesty and truth. Of
greatest singnificance is the abandonment of the socialist
realism elements of the typical and the positive hero and their
replacement with genuine flesh and blood characters. This
gradual abandonment of socialist realism concepts and their
replacement with universally recognized literary criteria
earned Christa Wolf international acclaim.

Christa Wolf's third novel, "Nachdenken über Christa T.,"
continues the trend away from socialist realism by abandoning
the public sphere for an examination of the private domain, the
self, in the search for self-actualization. Thus, such Kafkaesque
phenomena as personal isolation and alienation are depicted in
such uncharacteristic socialist realism forms as stream-of-
consciousness, extensive use of interior monolog, and a complicated collage of flashbacks and foreshadowings.

Form and content of this work, therefore, represent not only
an abandoment of, but even a direct challenge to, the principles
of socialist realism. "Nachdenken über Christa T." may be
characterized as a direct repudiation of the concepts of objective reflection of reality and partiality in that Christa T.

openly rebels against the socialist realism mentality of the
"Hopp-Hopp-Menschen" and seeks fulfillment in discovering the
essence of her being. The concept of national orientation also
has been transformed in this novel in that the GDR no longer
serves as the center piece for the evolving socialist society.
Instead, the socialist state only serves as the vanvass upon
which Christa Wolf reveals the eternal struggle confronting all
human beings--whether to lead a life as a "Mitläufer" and
"Anpasser" or whether to chart a course for greater independence
and self fulfillment. Finally, this work marks a complete rejection of the elements of the typical and the positive hero in
that Christa T. represents the inauguration of the socialist
anti-hero in the novels of Christa Wolf through her rejection
of the herd syndrome and its replacement with the quest for individuality and self fulfillment.

"Kein Ort. Nirgends" marks the complete break with all five
socialist realism criteria. This work has been cleansed from
all the traditional socialist realism characteristics which
advocate a transition from capitalism to communism. Political
consideration no longer play a role in this novel. Instead,
the inner torment of two "Außenseiter" teetering on the edge of
self annihilation is examined. These typically Western motifs
are depicted in a stream-of-consciousness format that is
reminiscent of such Western writers as James Joyce, Henry James,
Virginia Woolf, Samuel Beckett, Hermann Broch, Martin Walser,
Max Frisch and Uwe Johnson. Thus, the abandonment of all five
socialist realism guidelines in "Kein Ort. Nirgends" and their
replacement with a typically Western form and content can
justifiably be labelled as the death of socialist realism in
the novels of Christa Wolf.

ENDNOTES

CHAPTER I

[1] Wolfgang Emmerich, "Die Literatur der DDR," in Deutsche Literaturgeschichte, eds. Wolfgang Beutin et. al. (Stuttgart: J.B. Metzlersche Verlagsbuchhandlung, 1979), p. 343.

[2] Ibid., p. 353.

[3] Um die Erneuerung der deutschen Kultur. 1. Zentrale Kulturkonferenz der KPD vom 3. bis 5. Februar 1946 in Berlin, 1946, p. 52.

[4] Grundsätze und Ziele der Sozialistischen Einheitspartei Deutschlands - Protokoll des Vereinigungsparteitages der SPD und KPD 1946, Berlin, 1946.

[5] For a more detailed history of the changing role of the "Kulturbund" see G. Friedrich, Der Kulturbund zur demokratischen Erneuerung Deutschlands - Geschichte und Funktion (Köln, 1952) and Hans Dietrich Sander Geschichte der Schönen Literatur in der DDR (Freiburg: Verlag Rombach, 1972).

[6] Friedrich Engels to Margaret Harkness, April 1888, cited in Zur Theorie des sozialistischen Realismus, Institut für Gesellschaftswissenschaften beim ZK der SED, ed. (Berlin: Dietz Verlag, 1974), p. 98.

[7] W.I. Lenin, "Parteiorganisation und Parteiliteratur," cited in Zur Theorie des sozialistischen Realismus, p. 538.

[8] W.I. Lenin, "Entwurf einer Resolution über proletarische Kultur," cited in Zur Theorie des sozialistischen Realismus, p. 211.

[9] Hans Dietrich Sander, "Die Literatur und Ihre Planer," in Literatur der DDR, Arbeitskreis der Collegia Politica an Deutschen Universitäten, 1970, p. 5.

[10] Wilhelm Pieck, Um die Erneuerung der deutschen Kultur, Typescript with personal entries. Wilhelm Pieck Archiv des Instituts für Marxismus-Leninismus, Berlin.

[11] Einheit, 6/1949.

[12] H. Bühl, Dieter Heinze, Hans Koch and F. Staufenbiel, eds., Kulturpolitisches Wörterbuch (Berlin: Dietz Verlag, 1970), p. 331.

[13] Otto Grotewohl, 1951 during the "Formalismus-Kampagne," cited in Jean Gomez, Entwicklung und Perspektiven der Literaturwissenschaft in der DDR (Paris, 1978), pp. 51-52.

[14] Hans-Georg Hölsken, Jüngere Romane aus der DDR im Deutschunterricht. Ein Beitrag zur Politischen Bildung (Hannover, 1969), p. 12.

[15] Wolfgang Joho, "Unsere Nationale Aufgabe," Neue deutsche Literatur, 9, No. 1(1961), 536.

[16] Walter Ulbricht, "Schlußwort zur I. Bitterfelder Konferenz," Kritik in der Zeit: Der Sozialismus seine Literatur - ihre Entwicklung, ed. Klaus Jarmatz (Halle/Saale: Mitteldeutscher Verlag, 1970), p. 460.

[17] "Kulturelle Aufgaben im Rahmen des Zweijahrplanes. Entschließung der I. Parteikonferenz der SED (Auszug), Kritik in der Zeit, p. 147.

[18] Cited in Sander, Literatur der DDR, p. 6.

[19] Ibid., p. 7.

[20] Emmerich, Deutsche Literaturgeschichte, p. 357.

[21] Cited in Sander, Literatur der DDR, p. 17.

[22] Alfred Kurella, "Erfahrungen und Probleme sozialistischer Kulturarbeit," In Kulturkonferenz 1960; Protokoll der vom ZK vom 27.-29. April im VEB Elektrokohle, Berlin, abgehaltenen Konferenz, Berlin/DDR, p. 15 ff.

[23] "Die Tiefe und Breite in der Literatur," in Kritik in der Zeit, p. 493.

[24] Anna Seghers speaking at the Writers' Congress, Moscow, 15-26 December 1954, quoted by Sigrid Bock, "Einleitung," in Über Kunstwerk und Wirklichkeit by Anna Seghers, I (Berlin: Akademie Verlag, 1970-71). 59.

[25] Emmerich, Deutsche Literaturgeschichte, p. 374.

[26] "Schlußwort zur I. Bitterfelder Konferenz," in Kritik in der Zeit, pp. 462-63.

[27] Emmerich, Deutsche Literaturgeschichte, p. 374.

[28] Programm der Sozialistischen Einheitspartei Deutschlands, (Berlin, 1963), pp. 135-36.

[29] Cited in Peter Orlow, "Die Bitterfelder Sackgasse," Die Orientierung, No. 1 (1970), p. 28.

[30] Zweite Bitterfelder Konferenz, Berlin 1964, p. 120.

[31] Ibid.

[32] Zur Theorie des sozialistische Realismus, p. 670.

[33] Cited in Orlow, p. 13.

[34] Erich Honecker, Bericht des Zentralkomitees an den VIII. Parteitag der Sozialistischen Einheitspartei Deutschlands, (Berlin, 1972), p. 75.

[35] Ibid., p. 76.

[36] Junge Welt, May 29, 1973.

[37] Konrad Franke, Die Literatur der Deutschen Demokratischen Republik (Zürich: Kindler Verlag, 1974), p. 187.

[38] Die Verantwortung des Schriftstellers in den Kämpfen unserer Zeit. Materialien zum VIII. Schriftsteller Kongreß der DDR (München: Damnitz Verlag, 1978), pp. 183-84.

[39] Ibid., p. 182.

[40] Ibid., p. 185.

[41] Zur Theorie des sozialistischen Realismus, pp. 670-71.

CHAPTER II

[1] Compare: Ulf Konrad Eggers, Aspekte zeitgenössischer Realismustheorie (Bonn: Bouvier Verlag Herbert Grundmann, 1976); Ulf Eisele, Realismus und Ideologie (Stuttgart: Metzler, 1976); Walter Fähnders and Martin Rector, Linksradikalismus und Literatur I. (Hamburg: Rowohlt, 1974); Walter Fähnders, Proletarisch-revolutionäre Literatur der Weimarer Republik (Stuttgart: Metzler, 1977); Friedrich Gaede, Realismus von Brant bis Brecht (München: Francke Verlag, 1972); Wilhelm Girnus, Grundlagen der marxistisch-leninistischen Ästhetik - Autorenkollektiv (Berlin-Ost: Dietz Verlag, 1962); Klaus Jarmatz, Forschungsfeld Realismus: Theorie, Geschichte, Gegenwart (Berlin: Aufbau-Verlag, 1975); Hans Koch, Marxismus und Ästhetik (Berlin-Ost: Dietz Verlag, 1961); Georg Lukács, Essays über Realismus (Berlin-Ost: Aufbau-Verlag, 1948); Frank Trommler, Sozialistische Literatur in Deutschland (Stuttgart: Alfred Kröner Verlag, 1976); Helmuth Widhammer, Die Literaturtheorie des deutschen Realismus (Stuttgart: Metzler, 1977); Helmuth Widhammer, Realismus und klassizistische Tradition (Tübingen: Max Niemeier Verlag, 1972).

[2] See "Friedrich Engels an MiB Harkness," in Marxismus und Literatur, ed. Fritz J. Raddatz, I (Reinbeck: Rowohlt, 1969), pp. 157-59.

[3] P. Rožkov, "O socijalisticeskom realizme," in Novyj mir, 9 (September 1933), 215.

[4] Frank Trommler, cited in Realismustheorien in Literatur, Malerei, Musik und Politik, eds. Reinhold Grimm and Jost Hermand

(Stuttgart, 1975), p. 69; see also R. Garaudy, L'itineraire
d'Aragon (Paris: Gallimard, 1961), pp. 277-78.

5 Edward Mozejko, Der sozialistische Realismus - Theorie,
Entwicklung und Versagen einer Literaturmethode (Bonn: Bouvier
Verlag Herbert Grundmann, 1977), p. 134.

6 Ibid., pp. 141-42.

7 Hans Koch, "Stichworte zum sozialistischen Realismus,"
Weimarer Beiträge, 6, No. 1 (1970), 10.

8 Ernst Fischer, Zeitgeist und Literatur (Europa Verlag, 1964),
p. 80.

9 H. Ermolaev, Soviet Literary Theories 1917-1934. The
Genesis of Socialist Realism (Berkeley: Univ. of California
Press, 1963), pp. 5-144.

10 S. Lukic, "Jedan pogled na teoriju i praksu socijalistickog
realizme," Delo, 10 (October 1970), 1143.

11 Pervyj vsesojuznyi S'ezd sovetskich pisatelej 1934.
Stenograficeskij otcet (Moskva, 1934), p. 716.

12 M. Gorkij, "O sovetskoj literature," In Pervyj vsesojuznyi
S'ezd sovetskich pisatelej, pp. 5-19.

13 H. Markiewics, "Realizm, naturalizm, typowosc," In
Glówne problemy wiedzy o literature (Krákow: Wydawnictwo
Literackie, 1965), p. 229.

14 For a more detailed account of the liberal trend in the
arts from 1945-1948 see Hans Dietrich Sander, Geschichte der
Schönen Literatur in der DDR (Freiburg: Verlag Rombach, 1972),
p. 92 ff.

15 Ibid., p. 95.

16 Der erste BundeskongreB - Protokoll der ersten Bundeskonferenz des Kulturbundes zur demokratischen Erneuerung
Deutschlands am 20. und 21. Mai 1947 in Berlin, Berlin (Ost)
1947, p. 54 ff. 101, 159.

17 Sander, Geschichte der Schönen Literatur in der DDR, p. 99.

18 A. Abusch, Literatur im Zeitalter des Sozialismus -
Beiträge zur Literaturgeschichte 1921-1966 (Berlin-Ost, 1967),
p. 575 ff.

19 A. Kantorowicz, Deutsches Tagebuch, II., p. 218.

20 Hans Koch, "Kunst und Wirklichkeit. Der neue Gegenstand,"
in Zur Theorie des sozialistischen Realismus, p. 410.

[21] Klaus Jarmatz, "Die Theorie des Kunstfort-Schritts--Bestandteil der Theorie des sozialistischen Realismus," in Zur Theorie des sozialistischen Realismus, p. 737.

[22] Mozejko, pp. 34-35.

[23] Erhard John, "Leninische Widerspiegelungstheorie und Ästhetik," Weimarer Beiträge, 1 (1972), 33.

[24] Cited in Gomez, p. 11.

[25] John, p. 36.

[26] Erwin Pracht in Zur Theorie des sozialistischen Realismus, p. 383.

[27] Ibid., p. 366.

[28] Erwin Pracht, Einführung in den sozialistischen Realismus (Berlin: Dietz Verlag, 1975), p. 167.

[29] W.I. Lenin, cited in Zur Theorie des sozialistischen Realismus, p. 567.

[30] W.I. Lenin, cited in Wolfgang Powroslo, Literatur der DDR im Unterricht (Düsseldorf: Pädagogischer Verlag Schwann, 1977), p. 34.

[31] Ibid.

[32] See G. Kuničyn, "V.I. Lenin o partijnosti i svobode turocestva," in Lenin i literatura, eds. L. Timofeev and V.R. Sčerbina (Moskva: Izd. chud. lit., 1963), pp. 32-97.

[33] See V.R. Sčerbina, Lenin i voprosy literatury (Moskva, 1961).

[34] Mozejko, p. 89.

[35] L. Sobolev, "Literatura i naša sovremennost," in Pervyj ucreditel'nyj s'ezd pisatelej Rossijskoj Federacii 7-13 dekabrja 1958 goda (Moskva: Sovetskaja Rossija, 1959), p. 32.

[36] Werner Jehser, In Zur Theorie des sozialistischen Realismus, p. 555.

[37] Werner Jehser, "Sozialistische Parteilichkeit als zentrale ideologische Kategorie des sozialistischen Realismus und seiner Theorie," Weimarer Beiträge, No. 3 (1970), 74.

[38] Pracht, Einführung in den sozialistischen Realismus, p. 333.

[39] Ibid., pp. 333, 74.

[40] Claus Träger, Studien zur Realismustheorie und Methodologie der Literaturwissenschaft (Frankfurt, 1972), pp. 146, 91.

[41] Ibid., p. 125.

[42] Pracht, Einführung in den sozialistischen Realismus, p. 333.

[43] Mozejko, p. 92.

[44] A. Puškin, cited in Mozejko, p. 92.

[45] V. Belinskij, "Dejanija Petra Velikogo, Mudrogo Preobrazitelja Rossii," Stat'ja II, In Izbrannye filozofskie socinenija, eds. M.T. Jovcuk and Z.V. Smirnova, I (Moskva: Gos. Izd. Polit. Lit., 1948), pp. 336-39.

[46] L. Timofeev, O snovy teorie literatury (Moskva: Prosvescenie, 1966), pp. 120-21.

[47] Pracht, Einführung in den sozialistischen Realismus, p. 353.

[48] Bertolt Brecht, Schriften zur Literatur und Kunst, Bd.II (Berlin und Weimar, 1966), p. 60.

[49] Hans Koch, In Zur Theorie des sozialistischen Realismus, p. 262.

[50] Heinz Blumensath and Christel Uebach, Einführung in die Literaturgeschichte der DDR, Ein Unterrichtsmodell (Stuttgart, 1975), p. 65.

[51] Michail Chraptschenko, "Probleme der modernen Ästhetik," Sinn und Form, 5 (1970), 1162.

[52] Sozialistischer Realismus, Positionen. Probleme. Perspektiven, eds., Erwin Pracht and Werner Neubert (Berlin-Ost, 1970), p. 228.

[53] Brecht, "Volkstümliche Literatur," Schriften zur Literatur und Kunst, Bd.II, pp. 72-73.

[54] Cited in Theorie des sozialistischen Realismus, pp. 600-601.

[55] Ibid., p. 601.

[56] Ibid., p. 602.

[57] Ibid., p. 603.

[58] Ibid.

[59] For a detailed analysis of the theoretical preconditions of the "typical" in the Soviet Union see B. Küppers, Die Theorie vom Typischen in der Literatur (München: Otto Sagner, 1966), p. 354.

[60] Mozejko, p. 97.

[61] L. Timofeev, O snovy teorii literatury (Moskva: Prosvescenie, 1971), pp. 121, 162.

[62] Zur Theorie des sozialistischen Realismus, p. 603.

[63] Ibid., pp. 603-604.

[64] Mozejko, p. 100.

[65] Ibid.

[66] J.R. Becher, Verteidigung der Poesie. Vom Neuen in der Literatur (Berlin, 1952), p. 346 ff.

[67] Bertolt Brecht, Schriften zum Theater, Bd.7 (Berlin and Weimar, 1964), p. 341.

[68] Cited in Gomez, p. 52.

CHAPTER III

[1] Hermann Kähler, "Christa Wolf erzählt," Weggenossen, ed. Institut für Gesellschaftswissenschaften beim Zentralkomitee der SED (Leipzig: Reclam, 1975), p. 214.

[2] Max Walter Schulz in Gomez, p. 176.

[3] Christa Wolf, "Um den neuen Unterhaltungsroman," in Neues Deutschland, 9/16, 1952.

[4] Louis Fürnberg, "Brief an Christa Wolf," in Louis Fürnberg. Ein Lesebuch für unsere Zeit, ed. Hans Böhm (Berlin: Aufbau, 1974), p. 420.

[5] Christa Wolf, "Einiges über meine Arbeit als Schriftsteller," in Junge Schriftsteller der DDR Selbstdarstellungen, ed. Wolfgang Paulick (Leipzig, 1965), p. 14.

[6] Christa Wolf, "Über Sinn und Unsinn von Naivität," in Eröffnungen. Schriftsteller über ihr Erstlingswerk, ed. Gerhard Schneider (Berlin: Aufbau, 1974), p. 165.

[7] Alfred Kurella, "Aus der Praxis des sozialistischen Realismus. Das Moskauer Schriftstellergespräch vom Dezember 1963," in Sowjetwissenschaft. Kunst und Literatur, 4 (1946), 343 f.

[8] Christa Wolf, ed. Proben junger Erzähler (Leipzig, 1959), p. 4.

[9] Ibid.

[10] Christa Wolf, "Kann man eigentlich über alles schreiben?," in Neue deutsche Literatur, 6 (1958), 13 f.

[11] Christa Wolf, "Probleme des zeitgenössischen Gesellschafts-romans - Bemerkungen zu dem Roman Im Morgennebel von Ehm Welk," Neue deutsche Literatur, 1 (1954), 145.

[12] Christa Wolf, Moskauer Novelle (Halle: Mitteldeutscher Verlag, 1961), p. 6. References to this work will henceforth be indicated by MN and page number.

[13] The "Bund Deutscher Mädchen"(BDM) was the equivalent of the "Hitler Jugend"(HJ) for girls.

[14] Christa Wolf, "Fragen an Konstantin Simonow," Neue deutsche Literatur, 21, No. 12 (1973), 15.

[15] Christa Wolf, "Über Sinn und Unsinn von Naivität," in Christa Wolf Materialienbuch, ed. Klaus Sauer (Darmstadt: Luchterhand, 1979), pp. 24-33.

[16] Ibid., p. 27.

[17] Ibid.

[18] Ibid.

[19] Ibid., pp. 27-28.

[20] Ibid., pp. 28-29.

CHAPTER IV

[1] Walter Ulbricht, cited in Frank Trommler, "DDR- Erzählung und Bitterfelder Weg," Basis, 3 (1972), 61.

[2] Eva Strittmatter, "Literatur und Wirklichkeit," Neue deutsche Literatur, 7 (1962), 35.

[3] K. Hager, "Parteilichkeit und Volksverbundenheit unserer Literatur und Kunst. Rede auf der Beratung des Politbüros des Zentralkomitees und des Präsidiums des Ministerrats mit Schrift-stellern und Künstlern am 25. 3. 1963," Neues Deutschland, 3/30, 1963.

[4] Louis Aragon, cited in Sander, Geschichte der Schönen Literatur in der DDR, p. 205.

[5] Walter Ulbricht, cited in Sander, Geschichte der Schönen Literatur in der DDR, p. 209.

[6] Stephan, p. 33. For a more complete listing of reviews of this novel, see 'Der geteilte Himmel' und seine Kritiker,

ed. Martin Reso (Halle: Mitteldeutscher Verlag, 1965).

[7] Christa Wolf, Der geteilte Himmel (Halle: Mitteldeutscher Verlag, 1973), p. 7. References to this work will henceforth be indicated by GH and page number.

[8] Günther Dahlke, "Geteilter Himmel und Geteilte Kritik," Sinn und Form, 16, No. 2 (1964), 317.

[9] See Chapter III, footnote 2.

CHAPTER V

[1] Adam Krzeminski, "Rytm pokoleniowy," Polityka, 17. No. 5 (1969). Cited in Alexander, Christa Wolf, p. 91.

[2] Ibid.

[3] Christa Wolf, Nachdenken über Christa T. (Neuwied und Berlin: Luchterhand, 1979), p. 5. References to this work will henceforth be indicated by CT and page number.

[4] Johannes R. Becher, Tagebuch 1950, Eintragungen 1951 (Berlin: Aufbau, 1969), p. 224.

[5] Hans Sachs, "Verleger sein heißt ideologisch kämpfen," Neues Deutschland, 5/14, 1969.

[6] Max Walter Schulz, "Das Neue und das Bleibende in unserer Literatur," Neue deutsche Literatur, 9 (1969), 47.

[7] Ibid., 48.

[8] Werner Neubert, et. al., "Zu einigen Entwicklungsproblemen der sozialistischen Epik 1963-1968/69," Neue deutsche Literatur, 9 (1969), 156.

[9] Hermann Kähler, "Christa Wolfs Elegie," Sinn und Form, 21 (1969), 256.

[10] Roland Wiegenstein, "Verweigerung der Zustimmung?," Merkur, 23 (1969), 780.

[11] Heinrich Mohr, "Produktive Sehnsucht. Struktur, Thematik und politische Relevanz von Christa Wolfs Nachdenken über Christa T.," Basis, 2 (1971), 232 f.

[12] Cited in Hermann Kähler, Weggenossen, p. 223.

[13] Ibid.

[14] Christa Wolf, "Auf den Grund der Erfahrungen kommen," Sonntag, 2/18, 1968.

[15] Christa Wolf, cited by Klaus Sauer, "Der lange Weg zu sich Selbst - Christa Wolf's Frühwerk," Materialienbuch, p. 77.

[16] "Gute Bücher - und was weiter? Diskussionsbeitrag auf dem 11. Plenum des ZK der SED, 16. bis 18. 12. 1965," in Dokumente zur Kunst-, Literatur und Kulturpolitik der SED, ed. Elimar Schubbe (Stuttgart, 1972), p. 1009.

CHAPTER VI

[1] Kurt Hager, "Der Sozialismus - Macht des Friedens und der Menschlichkeit," Neues Deutschland, 1/19, 1974.

[2] Neues Deutschland, 9/1, 1974.

[3] Neues Deutschland, 11/21, 1974.

[4] Neues Deutschland, 4/17, 1974.

[5] "Diskussion mit Christa Wolf," Sinn und Form, 28, No. 4 (1976), 862.

[6] Christa Wolf's latest prose works Kassandra (Darmstadt: Luchterhand, 1983) and Voraussetzungen einer Erzählung: Kassandra (Darmstadt: Luchterhand, 1983) appeared after the completion of this work.

[7] For a more detailed investigation of this trend, see Alice Kingsbury, "The Writings of Christa Wolf: From Objective to Subjective Authenticity," Diss. Michigan State University 1981; see also, John Erickson, "Der Wandel der Erzähltechnik im DDR-Roman," Diss. University of Minnesota 1981.

[8] Hans Kaufmann, "Gespräch mit Christa Wolf," Weimarer Beiträge, 6 (1974), 90-112.

[9] See Alexander Stephan, Christa Wolf, Autorenbücher 4 (München: Verlag Edition Text und Kritik, 1979), pp. 7-22.

[10] Compare Karin MᶜPherson, "In Search of the New Prose: Christa Wolf's Reflections on Writing and The Writer in The 1960's and 1970's," New German Studies, 9, No. 1 (1981), 1-13.

[11] Christa Wolf, Kein Ort. Nirgends (Darmstadt: Luchterhand Verlag, 1979), p. 15. References to this work will henceforth be indicated by KON and page number.

[12] See Chapter II, section on "National Orientation."

SELECTED BIBLIOGRAPHY

I. Primary Works by Christa Wolf

A. Theoretical Writings (Essays, Reviews, Interviews)

"Abgebrochene Romane." In Situation 66 - 20 Jahre Mitteldeutscher Verlag. Halle: Mitteldeutscher Verlag, 1966, pp.
156-59.

"Achtung, Rauschgifthandel." Neue deutsche Literatur 3
(February 1955), 136-40.

Afterword to Erzählungen, by Anna Seghers. Berlin: Luchterhand, 1970.

Afterword to Das siebte Kreuz, by Anna Seghers. Leipzig:
Reclam Verlag, 1971, pp. 411-22.

"Anmerkungen zu Geschichten." In Aufstellen eines Machinen-
gewehrs im Wohnzimmer der Frau Kamptschik, by Anna Seghers.
Neuwied: Luchterhand, 1970, pp. 157-64.

"Anna Seghers über ihre Schaffensmethode. Ein Gespräch." In
Über Kunstwerk und Wirklichkeit, by Anna Seghers. Vol.
II: Erlebnis und Gestaltung, ed. Sigrid Bock. Berlin:
Akademie Verlag, 1971, pp. 24-29.

"Auf den Grund der Erfahrungen kommen. Eduard Zak sprach mit
Christa Wolf." Sonntag 7 (1968), pp. 6-7.

"Auf den Spuren der Zeit." Neue deutsche Literatur 7 (June
1960), 126-9.

"Autobiographie und Roman." Neue deutsche Literatur 5 (October
1957), 142-3.

"Autoren-Werkstatt: Christa Wolf. Gespräch mit Joachim
Walther." Die Weltbühne (9 January 1973), pp. 51-55.

"Bei Anna Seghers." In Lesen und Schreiben. Aufsätze und
Prosastücke, by Christa Wolf. 3rd ed. Darmstadt: Hermann
Luchterhand Verlag, 1978, pp. 112-18.

"Beispiele ohne Nutzanwendung." Moderna Sprak No. 72 (1978),
265-69.

"Besiegte Schatten?" Neue deutsche Literatur 3 (September
1955), 137-41.

"Ein Besuch." In Lesen und Schreiben. Aufsätze und Prosastücke, by Christa Wolf. 3rd ed. Darmstadt: Hermann
Luchterhand Verlag, 1978, pp. 149-180.

"Bibliotheca Universalis." In Das Reclam Buch. Mitteilungen
    des Verlages Philipp Reclam jun., Sonderheft Nr. 52.
    Leipzig: Verlag Philipp Reclam jun., 1978.

"Botschaft wider die Passivität." Neue deutsche Literatur 6
    (February 1958), 144-45.

"Brecht und andere." In Lesen und Schreiben. Aufsätze und
    Prosastücke, by Christa Wolf. 3rd ed. Darmstadt: Hermann
    Luchterhand Verlag, 1978, pp. 54-56.

"Briefwechsel Gerti Tetzner - Christa Wolf." In "Was zählt,
    ist die Wahrheit. Briefe von Schriftstellern der DDR."
    Neue deutsche Literatur 22 (August 1975), 121-28.

"Christa Wolf spricht mit Anna Seghers." Neue deutsche Lite-
    ratur 12 (June 1965), 7-18.

Contribution to "Thomas Mann - Wirkung und Gegenwart." In
    Anlaß des hundertsten Geburtstages. Frankfurt: S. Fischer
    Verlag, 1975, pp. 63-64.

"Dankrede nach der Verleihung des Bremer Literaturpreises am
    Donnerstag [26.1.1978], 12 Uhr, im Bremer Rathaus." In
    Mitteilungen der Pressestelle des Senats der Freien
    Hansestadt Bremen. Bremen, 1978, pp. 1-6.

"Das wird man bei uns anders verstehen. UZ-Gespräch mit der
    bekannten DDR-Autorin Christa Wolf." Unsere Zeit (2
    November 1974).

"Deutschland unserer Tage." Neues Deutschland No. 77 (18 March
    1961).

"Deutsch sprechen." In Lesen und Schreiben. Aufsätze und
    Prosastücke, by Christa Wolf. 3rd ed. Darmstadt: Hermann
    Luchterhand Verlag, 1978, pp. 9-18.

"Diese Lektion wollen wir gründlich lernen." In "Chile -
    Gesang und Bericht. Beiträge von Alejo Carpentier, Julio
    Cortazar, Christa Wolf, Stephan Hermlin, Inge und Eduard
    Klein." Neue deutsche Literatur 22 (February 1975), 53.

Discussion at the "Konferenz junger Schriftsteller in Halle.
    Neue deutsche Literatur 9 (August 1962), 132-35.

"Diskussion mit Christa Wolf." Sinn und Form 28 (1976), 861-88.

"Einiges über meine Arbeit als Schriftsteller." In Junge
    Schriftsteller der Deutschen Demokratischen Republik in
    Selbstdarstellungen, ed. Wolfgang Paulick. Leipzig:
    Bibliographisches Institut, 1965, pp. 11-16.

"Ein Erzähler gehört dazu." Neue deutsche Literatur 8 (October
    1961), 129-33.

"Erziehung der Gefühle?" Neue deutsche Literatur 6 (November 1958), 129-35.

Foreword to In diesen Jahren: Deutsche Erzähler der Gegenwart, ed. Christa Wolf. Leipzig: Verlag Philipp Reclam jun., 1956, pp. 3-4.

Foreword to Guten Morgen, du Schöne. Frauen in der DDR, by Maxie Wander. Darmstadt: Hermann Luchterhand Verlag, 1978.

Foreword to Larifari und andere Erzählungen, by Juri Kasakow. Berlin: Kultur und Fortschritt, 1966, pp. 5-11.

Foreword to Proben junger Erzähler, ed. Christa Wolf. Leipzig: Reclam Verlag, 1959, pp. 3-4.

Foreword to Wir, unsere Zeit. Gedichte aus zehn Jahren, ed. Christa and Gerhard Wolf. Berlin: Aufbau Verlag, 1959, pp. 9-12.

Foreword to Wir, unsere Zeit. Prosa aus zehn Jahren, ed. Christa and Gerhard Wolf. Berlin: Aufbau Verlag, 1959, pp. 11-13.

"Fortgesetzter Versuch." In Über Anna Seghers. Ein Almanach zum 75. Geburtstag, ed. Kurt Blatt. Berlin: Aufbau, 1975, pp. 19-25.

"Fragen an Konstantin Simonow." Neue deutsche Literatur 20 (December 1973), 5-20.

"Freiheit oder Auflösung der Persönlichkeit?" Neue deutsche Literatur 5 (April 1957), 135-42.

"Fünfundzwanzig Jahre." In Lesen und Schreiben. Aufsätze und Prosastücke, by Christa Wolf. 3rd ed. Darmstadt: Hermann Luchterhand Verlag, 1978, pp. 23-25.

"Gedächtnis und Gedenken - Fred Wander." In Lesen und Schreiben. Aufsätze und Prosastücke, by Christa Wolf. 3rd ed. Darmstadt: Hermann Luchterhand Verlag, 1978, pp. 135-146.

"Gegenwart und Zukunft." In "Schriftsteller über Erfahrungen, Pläne und Probleme: Gegenwart und Zukunft." Neue deutsche Literatur 18 (January 1971), 68-70.

"Glauben an Irdisches." In Lesen und Schreiben. Aufsätze und Prosastücke, by Christa Wolf. 3rd ed. Darmstadt: Hermann Luchterhand Verlag, 1978, pp. 83-111.

"Gute Bücher - und was weiter?" Neues Deutschland (19 December 1965).

"Hans Kaufmann. Gespräch mit Christa Wolf." Weimarer Beiträge 6 (1974), 90-112.

"Kann man eigentlich über alles schreiben?" Neue deutsche
Literatur 6 (June 1958), 3-16.

"Komplikationen, aber keine Konflikte." Neue deutsche Literatur 2 (June 1954), 140-45.

"Krista Wolf beseduet so studentami." Internationalnaja
literatura 9 (1964), pp. 280-81.

"Land, in dem wir leben. Die deutsche Frage in dem Roman 'Die
Entscheidung' von Anna Seghers." Neue deutsche Literatur 8 (May 1961), 49-65.

"Eine Lektion über Wahrheit und Objektivität." Neue deutsche
Literatur 6 (July 1958), 120-23.

"Die Literatur der neuen Etappe. Gedanken zum III. Sowjetishen
Schriftstellerkongreß." Neues Deutschland, No. 167 (20
June 1959).

"Literatur und Zeitgenossenschaft." Neue deutsche Literatur
7 (March 1959), 7-11.

"Literaturkritik ohne Netz." Neues Deutschland (4 April 1964).

"Die Literaturtheorie findet zur literarischen Praxis." Neue
deutsche Literatur 3 (November 1955), 159-60.

"Max Frisch, beim wiederlesen oder: Vom Schreiben in Ich-Form."
Text und Kritik 47/48 (1957), 7-12.

"Menschen und Werk." Neue deutsche Literatur 3 (September
1955), 143-49.

"Menschliche Konflikte in unserer Zeit." Neue deutsche Literatur 3 (July 1955), 139-44.

"Notwendiges Streitgespräch. Bemerkungen zu einem internationalen Kolloquium." Neue deutsche Literatur 12 (March
1965), 97-104.

"Nun ja! Das nächste Leben geht aber heute an." Sinn und
Form 32 (1980), 392-418.

"Nur die Lösung: Sozialismus." Neues Deutschland (4 September
1968).

"Pocemu ja pisu." Internationalnaja literatura No. 2 (1964),
232-33.

"Popularität oder Volkstümlichkeit?" Neue deutsche Literatur
4 (January 1956), 115-24.

"Probe Vietnam." In Lesen und Schreiben. Aufsätze und Prosastücke, by Christa Wolf. 3rd ed. Darmstadt: Hermann
Luchterhand Verlag, 1978, pp. 26-28.

"Probleme des zeitgenössischen Gesellschaftsromans. Bemerkungen zu dem Roman 'im Morgennebel' von Ehm Welk." Neue deutsche Literatur 2 (January 1954), 142-50.

"Der Realitäten Kraft zerbricht des Klischees. Schriftstellerin Christa Wolf über die Lesungen von DDR-Autoren in West-Berlin." Neue Zeit (22 August 1964).

"Eine Rede." In Lesen und Schreiben. Aufsätze und Prosastücke, by Christa Wolf. 3rd ed. Darmstadt: Hermann Luchterhand Verlag, 1978, pp. 19-22.

Review of Dieter Noll's "Die Abenteuer des Werner Holt." Sonntag No. 46 (1960).

"Schicksal einer deutschen Kriegsgeneration." Sonntag No. 50 (1962).

"Die schwarzweiBrote Flagge." Neue deutsche Literatur 3 (March 1955), 148-52.

"Selbstinterview." In Lesen und Schreiben. Aufsätze und Prosastücke, by Christa Wolf. 3rd ed. Darmstadt: Hermann Luchterhand Verlag, 1978, pp. 76-80.

"Der Sinn einer neuen Sache - Vera Inber." In Lesen und Schreiben. Aufsätze und Prosastücke, by Christa Wolf. 3rd ed. Darmstadt: Hermann Luchterhand Verlag, 1978, pp. 57-60.

"Sozialistische Literatur der Gegenwart." Neue deutsche Literatur 7 (May 1959), 3-7.

Speech at the Second Bitterfeld Conference. Protokoll der von der Ideologischen Kommission beim Politbüro des ZK der SED und dem Ministerium für Kultur am 24. und 25. April im Kulturpalast des Elektrochemischen Kombinats Bitterfeld abgehaltenen Konferenz. Berlin: Dietz Verlag, 1964, pp. 224-34.

Speech at the Seventh Writers' Congress. VII. SchriftstellerkongreB der Deutschen Demokratischen Republik. Protokoll (Arbeitsgruppen). ed. Schriftstellerverband der Deutschen Demokratischen Republik. Berlin: Aufbau-Verlag, 1973, pp. 147-52.

"Suche nach dem Menschen. Christa Wolf über ihren neuen Roman im Gespräch mit Heinz Ludwig Arnold." Vorwärts (3 February 1977).

"Tagebuch - Arbeitsmittel und Gedächtnis." In Lesen und Schreiben. Aufsätze und Prosastücke, by Christa Wolf. 3rd ed. Darmstadt: Hermann Luchterhand Verlag, 1978, pp. 61-75.

"Über Sinn und Unsinn von Naivität." In Eröffnungen. Schriftsteller über ihr Erstlingswerk, ed. Gerhard Schneider.
Berlin: Aufbau-Verlag, 1974, pp. 167-74.

"Um den neuen Unterhaltungsroman." Neues Deutschland No. 169
(20 July 1952), 6.

"Unsere Meinung." Neue deutsche Literatur 6 (January 1958),
4-6.

"Vom erfüllten Leben." Neue deutsche Literatur 7 (February
1959), 140-42.

"Vom Standpunkt des Schriftstellers und von der Form der Kunst."
Neue deutsche Literatur 5 (December 1957), 119-24.

"Warum singt der Vogel nicht? Fortsetzung einer öffentlichen
Diskussion in der 'Schwarzen Pumpe' über Gegenwartsliteratur." Neues Deutschland No. 270 (14 November 1957).

"...wenn man sie durch Arbeit mehrt." Berliner Zeitung No. 95
(1961).

"Zu einem Datum." In Lesen und Schreiben. Aufsätze und Prosastücke, by Christa Wolf. 3rd ed. Darmstadt: Hermann
Luchterhand Verlag, 1978, pp. 181-220.

"Die zumutbare Wahrheit - Ingeborg Bachmann." In Lesen und
Schreiben. Aufsätze und Prosastücke, by Christa Wolf.
3rd ed. Darmstadt: Hermann Luchterhand Verlag, 1978,
pp. 121-134.

B. Fiction

"Blickwechsel." In Gesammelte Erzählungen, by Christa Wolf.
2nd ed. Darmstadt: Hermann Luchterhand Verlag, 1980,
pp. 5-23.

"Dienstag, der 27. September." In Gesammelte Erzählungen,
by Christa Wolf. 2nd ed. Darmstadt: Herman Luchterhand
Verlag, 1980, pp. 24-40.

Der geteilte Himmel. Halle: Mitteldeutscher Verlag, 1963.

"Juninachmittag." In Fahrt mit der S-Bahn. Erzähler der DDR,
ed. Lutz-W. Wolff. München: Deutscher Taschenbuchverlag,
1971, pp. 229-46.

Kein Ort. Nirgends. 4th ed. Darmstadt: Hermann Luchterhand
Verlag, 1980.

Kindheitsmuster. Darmstadt: Hermann Luchterhand Verlag,
1979.

"Kleiner Ausflug nach H." In Gesammelte Erzählungen, by
Christa Wolf. 2nd ed. Darmstadt: Hermann Luchterhand
Verlag, 1980.

Moskauer Novelle. In An den Tag gebracht. Prosa junger
Menschen. Halle: Mitteldeutscher Verlag, 1961, pp.
145-222.

Nachdenken über Christa T. Berlin: Luchterhand, 1969.

"Neue Lebensansichten eines Katers." In Gesammelte Erzählungen,
by Christa Wolf. 4th ed. Berlin: Hermann Luchterhand
Verlag, 1980.

"Selbstversuch." In Gesammelte Erzählungen, by Christa Wolf.
2nd ed. Darmstadt: Hermann Luchterhand Verlag, 1980.

"Unter den Linden." In Gesammelte Erzählungen, by Christa
Wolf. 2nd ed. Darmstadt: Hermann Luchterhand Verlag,
1980.

C. Collections

Gesammelte Erzählungen. 2nd ed. Darmstadt: Luchterhand
Verlag, 1980.

Lesen und Schreiben. Aufsätze und Prosastücke. 3rd ed.
Darmstadt: Hermann Luchterhand Verlag, 1978.

Unter den Linden. Drei unwahrscheinliche Geschichten.
Darmstadt: Hermann Luchterhand Verlag, 1974.

II. Secondary Material on Christa Wolf and GDR Literature

Abusch, Alexander. Humanismus und Realismus in der Literatur.
Leipzig. 1972.

_____. Literatur im Zeitalter des Sozialismus-Beiträge
zur Literaturgeschichte 1921-1966. Berlin (Ost): Aufbau-
Verlag, 1967.

_____. Tradition und Gegenwart des sozialistischen
Humanismus. Berlin (Ost), 1971.

Arnold, Heinz Ludwid, ed. Handbuch zur deutschen Arbeiterliteratur
I. München: Edition Text und Kritik, 1977.

Arvon, Henri. L'Esthetique marxiste. Paris, 1970.

Bathrick, David. "The Politics of Culture: Rudolf Bahro and
Opposition in the GDR." New German Critique. 15 (Fall
1978), 3-24.

Becher, Johannes R. Tagebuch 1950, Eintragungen 1951. Berlin: Aufbau, 1969.

_____. Über Literatur und Kunst. Berlin (Ost), 1962.

_____. Verteidigung der Poesie. Vom Neuen in der Literatur. Berlin, 1952.

Beckermann, Thomas. "Das Abenteuer einer menschenfreundlichen Prosa." Text und Kritik 46 (1975), 25-32.

Behn, Manfred. DDR- Literatur in der Bundesrepublik Deutschland. Meisenheim am Glan: Verlag Anton Hain, 1977.

_____, ed. Wirkungsgeschichte von Christa Wolfs 'Nachdenken über Christa T.' Königstein: Athenäum Verlag, 1978.

Benjamin, Walter. "Geschichtsphilosophische Thesen." Illuminationen Ed. Siegfried Unseld. Frankfurt, 1961, pp. 268-281.

Berghahn, Klaus L. "Volkstümlichkeit und Realismus." Nochmals zur Brecht-Lukacs Debatte. Basis 4 (1973), 7-37.

Beutin, Wolfgang, ed. et al. Deutsche Literaturgeschichte. Stuttgart: J.B. Metzlersche Verlagsbuchhandlung, 1970.

Bilke, Jörg B. "Auf den Spuren der Wirklichkeit: DDR- Literatur: Traditionen, Tendenzen, Möglichkeiten." Der Deutschunterricht 21 (1969), 24-60.

_____. "DDR- Literatur: Tradition und Rezeption in Westdeutschland." Deutschunterricht 21 (1969) Beilage.

_____. "Die Germanistik der DDR: Literaturwissenschaft in gesellschaftlichem Auftrag." Die deutsche Literatur der Gegenwart. Ed. Manfred Durzak. Stuttgart, 1971. pp. 366-385.

_____. "Die verdrängte Wirklichkeit: DDR- Literatur Herbst 1976." Deutsche Studien 14 (1976), 384-93.

_____. "Review of Kindheitsmuster." Neue deutsche Hefte 24 (1977), 373-77.

_____. "Zumutbare Wahrheiten?: Christa Wolfs Essayband Lesen und Schreiben." Basis 4 (1973), 192-200.

Blumensath, Heinz and Christa Uebach. Einführung in die Literaturgeschichte der DDR, Ein Unterrichtsmodell. Stuttgart: 1975.

Bock, Sigrid. "Christa Wolf: Kein Ort. Nirgends." Weimarer Beiträge 26 (1980), 145-57.

_____. "Christa Wolf: Kindheitsmuster." Weimarer Beiträge 23 (1977), 102-130.

_____. "Neuer Gegenstand-neues Erzählen." Weimarer Beiträge 19 (1973), 93-116.

Bohrer, K.H. "Review of Nachdenken über Christa T." Monat 21 (1969).

Bonk, Jürgen. "Christa Wolf: 'Der geteilte Himmel.'" In: Willi Bredel/Jürgen Bonk. Junge Prosa der DDR, by L. Bock. Berlin: Volk und Wissen Verlag, 1964.

Brandt, Sabine. "Der sozialistische Realismus." Deutschland. Kulturelle Entwicklung seit 1945. Ed. Paul Schallück. München, 1969, pp. 62-78.

Brauneck, Manfred, ed. Der deutsche Roman im 20. Jahrhundert, I. Bamberg: C.C. Buchners Verlag, 1976.

Brecht, Bertolt. Schriften zur Literatur und Kunst. Bd.II. Berlin und Weimar, 1966.

_____. Schriften zum Theater. Bd.VII. Berlin und Weimar, 1964.

_____. Über Realismus. Ed. Werner Hecht. Leipzig, 1968.

Brettschneider, Werner. Zwischen literarischer Autonomie und Staatsdienst. Die Literatur in der DDR. Berlin: Erich Schmidt Verlag, 1972. (Improved and enlarged edition 1974).

Brewer, Jim. "A Working Bibliography for the Study of the GDR." New German Critique 2 (1974), 124-51.

Bühl, H., Dieter Heinze, Hans Koch, F. Staufenbiel, eds. Kulturpolitisches Wörterbuch. Berlin: Dietz Verlag, 1970.

Chraptschenko, Michail. "Probleme der modernen Ästhetik." Sinn und Form 5 (1970).

Cosentino, Christine. "Eine Untersuchung des Sozialistischen Realismus Im Werke Christa Wolfs." German Quarterly 47 (1974), 245-61.

Cwojdrak, Günther. "Nachdenken über Prosa. Christa Wolf: Lesen und Schreiben." Sinn und Form 24 (1972), 1293-99.

Dahlke, Günther. "Geteilter Himmel und Geteilte Kritik." Sinn und Form 16 (1964), 307-17.

Demetz, Peter. Marx, Engels und die Dichter. Frankfurt/Main, 1969.

Der erste Bundeskongreß - Protokoll der ersten Bundeskonferenz
des Kulturbunds zur demokratischen Erneuerung Deutschlands
am 20. und 21. Mai 1947 in Berlin. Berlin (Ost), 1947.

"Der geteilte Himmel" und seine Kritiker. Dokumentationen. Ed.
Martin Reso. Halle: Mitteldeutscher Verlag, 1965.

Die Verantwortung des Schriftstellers in den Kämpfen unserer
Zeit. Materialien zum VIII. Schriftsteller Kongreß der
DDR. München: Damnitz Verlag, 1978.

Diersch, Manfred and Walfried Hartinger, eds. Literatur und
Geschichtsbewusstsein: Entwicklungstendenzen der DDR-
Literatur in den sechziger und siebziger Jahren. Berlin:
Aufbau, 1976.

Dittman, G. "Auseinandersetzung mit der Gegenwart. 'Der geteilte
Himmel' im Literaturunterricht." Deutschunterricht (DDR) 6
(1966).

Durzak, Manfred. "Der Moderne Roman. Bemerkungen zu Georg
Lukacs' Theorie des Romans." Basis 1 (1970), 26-48.

Eggers, Ulf Konrad. Aspekte Zeitgenössischer Realismustheorie.
Bonn: Bouvier Verlag Herbert Grundmann, 1976.

Einheit. 6/1949.

Einhorn, Barbara. Der Roman in der DDR 1949-1969. Kronberg/Ts.:
Scriptor Verlag, 1978.

Emmerich, Wolfgang. "Die Literatur der DDR." Deutsche Literaturgeschichte. Eds. Wolfgang Beutin, et. al. Stuttgart:
J.B. Metzlersche Verlagsbuchhandlung, 1979.

_____. "Identität und Geschlechtertausch." Basis 8 (1978),
127-54.

Ermolaev, H. Soviet Literary Theories 1917-1934. The Genesis
of Socialist Realism. Berkeley: Univ. of California Press,
1963.

Ester, Hans. "Review of Kindheitsmuster." Deutsche Bücher 7
(1977), 200-02.

Feitknecht, Thomas. Die sozialistische Heimat. Zum Selbstverständnis neuerer DDR-Romane. Bern, 1971.

Fischer, Ernst. Zeitgeist und Literatur. Wien: Europa Verlag,
1964.

Franke, Konrad. Die Literatur der Deutschen Demokratischen
Republik. Zürich: Kindler Verlag, 1974.

_____. "Ihrer Generation voraus." Frankfurter Hefte 7 (1970), 524-25.

Friedrich, G. Der Kulturbund zur demokratischen Erneuerung Deutschlands - Geschichte und Funktion. Köln, 1952.

Fürnberg, Louis. Ein Lesebuch für unsere Zeit. Ed. Hans Böhm. Berlin: Aufbau, 1974.

Garaudy, R. L'itineraire d'Aragon. Paris: Gallimard, 1961.

Geerdts, Hans-Jürgen, ed. Deutsche Literatur in einem Band. Berlin (Ost), 1967.

_____. Literatur der DDR in Einzeldarstellungen. Stuttgart Alfred Kröner Verlag, 1972.

_____. Literatur der Deutschen Demokratischen Republik. Einzeldarstellungen. Berlin (Ost), 1974.

Gerlach, Ingeborg. Der schwierige Fortschritt. Kronberg/Ts.: Scriptor Verlag, 1974.

_____. Bitterfeld. Kronberg/Ts.: Scriptor Verlag, 1974.

Girnus, Wilhelm. Von der unbefleckten Empfängnis des Ästhetische Berlin (Ost), 1972.

Gomez, Jean. Entwicklung und Perspektiven der Literaturwissen- schaft in der DDR. Paris, 1978.

Greif, Hans-Jürgen. Christa Wolf: "Wie sind wir so geworden wie wir heute sind?" Bern: Peter Lang, 1978.

Grimm, Reinhold and Jost Hermand, eds. Methoden der Literatur- wissenschaft. Darmstadt, 1973.

_____. Realismustheorien in Literatur, Malerei, Musik und Politik. Stuttgart, 1975.

Grundsätze und Ziele der Sozialistischen Einheitspartei Deutsch- lands - Protokoll des Vereinigungsparteitages der SPD und KPD 1946. Berlin, 1946.

Gumtau, Helmut. "Forschungsreise in die Vergangenheit." Der Tagesspiegel. April 3, 1977.

Haase, Horst. "Nachdenken über ein Buch." Neue deutsche Literatur 17 (1969), 174-85.

Haase, Horst, Hans-Jürgen, Erich Kuhne and Walter Pallus, eds. Geschichte der deutschen Literatur von den Anfängen bis zur Gegenwart, XI: Literatur der Deutschen Demokratischen Republik. Berlin: Volk and Wissen, 1976.

Hager, K. "Der Sozialismus - Macht des Friedens und der Menschlichkeit." Neues Deutschland, 1/19, 1974.

_____. "Parteilichkeit und Volksverbundenheit unserer
Literatur und Kunst. Rede auf der Beratung des Politbüros
des Zentralkomitees und des Präsidiums des Ministerrats
mit Schriftstellern und Künstlern am 25. 3. 1963." Neues
Deutschland, 3/30, 1963.

Hamm, Peter. "Der Blick in die westdeutsche Ferne. Zwei DDR-
Autoren beschreiben Republikflüchtlinge und solche, die
es werden wollen." Zeit, 3/27, 1964.

Hedlin, Irene Artis. The Individual in a New Society. Bern:
Peter Lang, 1977.

Heise, Rosemarie. "Das große Thema. Christa Wolf Der geteilte
Himmel." Neue deutsche Literatur 21 (1973).

Helmecke, Monica. "Kindheitsmuster." Sinn und Form 29 (1977),
678-81.

Hille, Ursula. "Review of Kindheitsmuster." Arbeiten zur
deutschen Philologie 12 (1978), 141-49.

Hohendahl, Peter Uwe. "Ästhetik und Sozialismus. Zur neueren
Literaturtheorie der DDR." Jahrbuch der deutschen Schiller-
gesellschaft 18 (1974), 606-41.

Hollis, Andrew. "Timelessness and the Game: Christa Wolf's
'Juninachmittag' und Joachim Walther's 'Wochenende im
Grünen.'" New German Studies 7 (1979), 145-67.

Hölsken, Hans Georg. "Zwei Romane: Christa Wolfs Der geteilte
Himmel und Hermann Kants Die Aula. Voraussetzung und Deutung."
Deutschunterricht 5 (1969), 61-99.

_____. Jüngere Romane aus der DDR im Deutschunterricht.
Ein Beitrag zur Politischen Bildung. Hannover, 1969.

Honecker, Erich. Bericht des Zentralkomitees an den VIII.
Parteitag der Sozialistischen Einheitspartei Deutschlands.
Berlin, 1972.

Huebener, Theodore. The Literature of East Germany. New York:
Ungar, 1970.

Huyssen, Andreas. "Auf den Spuren Ernst Blochs: Nachdenken
über Christa Wolf." Basis 5 (1975), 100-16.

Jackson, Neil and Barbara Saunders. "Christa Wolf's Kindheitsmuster. An East German Experiment in Political Autobiography."
German Life and Letters 4 (1980), 319-29.

Jäger, Manfred. "Die Literaturkritikerin Christa Wolf." Text

200

und Kritik 46 (1975), 42-49.

_____. Sozialliteratur. Funktion und Selbstverständnis
der Schriftsteller in der DDR. Düsseldorf, 1973.

Jarmatz, Klaus, ed. Kritik in der Zeit. Der Sozialismus - seine
Literatur - ihre Entwicklung. Halle (Saale), 1970.

Jehser, Werner. "Sozialistische Parteilichkeit als zentrale
ideologische Kategorie des sozialistischen Realismus und
seiner Theorie." Weimarer Beiträge 3 (1970).

Joho, Wolfgang. "Notwendiges Streitgespräch - Bemerkungen zu
einem internationalen Kolloquium." Neue deutsche Literatur
3 (1965), 88-112.

_____. "Unsere Nationale Aufgabe." Neue deutsche Literatur
1 (1961), 10-14.

John, Erhard. "Leninische Widerspiegelungstheorie und Ästhetik."
Weimarer Beiträge 1 (1972).

Jovcuk, M.T. and Z.V. Smirnova. Izbrannye filozofskie socinenija.
Moskva: Gos. Izd. Polit. Lit., 1948.

Junge Welt, 5/29, 1973.

Kähler, Hermann. "Christa Wolfs Elegie." Sinn und Form 21
(1969), 251-61.

_____. "Christa Wolf erzählt." Weggenossen. Ed. Institut
für Gesellschaftswissenschaften beim Zentralkomitee der
SED. Leipzig: Reclam, 1975, pp. 5, 214-32.

Kane, B.M. "In Search of the Past: Christa Wolf's Kindheitsmuster." Modern Languages 59 (1978), 19-23.

Kant, Hermann. "Review of Kindheitsmuster." Sonntag, No. 14
(1965).

Karl, Günther. "Experiment in Streitgespräch." Neues Deutschland
9/5, 1965.

Kaufmann, Hans. "Gespräch mit Christa Wolf." Weimarer Beiträge
6 (1974), 90-113.

_____. "Zu Christa Wolfs poetischem 'Prinzip.'" Weimarer
Beiträge 6 (1974), 113-25.

Kersten, Heinz. "Christa Wolfs Nachdenken über Christa T.
Zu einem literatischen und einem kulturpolitischen Ereignis."
Frankfurter Rundschau, 6/21, 1969.

_____. "Poesie unter geteilten Himmel." Der Monat (1964),
83-92.

Ketelsen, Uwe K. "Das sozialistische Menschenbild als dramen-
theoretisches Problem in der DDR Literatur." Basis 5
(1975), 65-79.

Kloehn, Ekkehard. "Christa Wolf: Der geteilte Himmel. Roman
zwischen sozialistischem Realismus und kritischem Realismus."
Deutschunterricht (BRD) 20 (1968), 43-56.

Knoll, Renate. "Das 'Innerste Innere' Christa Wolf und die Tradition des 18. Jahrhunderts. Eine phänomenologische Skizze."
Text und Kontext 1 (1979), 146-65.

Koch, Hans. Marxismus und Ästhetik. Berlin (Ost), 1962.

_____. "Stichworte zum sozialistischen Realismus." Weimarer
Beiträge 1 (1970), 10-38.

_____. Coordinator. Zur Theorie des sozialistischen
Realismus. Ed. Institut für Gesellschaftswissenschaften
beim ZK der SED. Lehrstuhl für marxistisch-leninistische
Kultur- und Kunstwissenschaften. Berlin (Ost), 1974.

Köhn, Lothar. "Erinnerung und Erfahrung Christa Wolfs Begründung
der Literatur." Text und Kritik 46 (1975), 14-24.

Korff, F.W. "Association zu Christa Wolf." Neue deutsche Hefte
146 (1975), 327-330.

Krogmann, Werner. "Moralischer Realismus - Ein Versuch über
Christa Wolf." Amsterdamer Beiträge 20 (1978), 233-61.

Kunert, Günter. "Von der Schwierigkeit des Schreibens." Text
und Kritik 46 (1975), 11-13.

Kuppers, B. Die Theorie vom Typischen in der Literatur. München:
Otto Sagner, 1966.

Kurella, Alfred. "Aus der Praxis des sozialistischen Realismus.
Das Moskauer Schriftstellergespräch vom Dezember 1963."
Sowjetwissenschaft. Kunst und Literatur 4 (1946).

_____. "Erfahrungen und Probleme sozialistischer
Kulturarbeit." Kulturkonferenz 1960; Protokoll der vom
ZK der SED dem Ministerium für Kultur und dem Deutschen
Kulturbund vom 27.-29. April in VEB Elektrokohle, Berlin,
abgehaltenen Konferenz, Berlin/DDR.

Lamse, Mary Jane. "Kindheitsmuster in Context: The Achievement
of Christa Wolf." University of Dayton Review 15 (1981),
49-56.

Lenin, W.I. Über Kultur und Kunst. Berlin (Ost), 1960.

Linn, Marie-Luise. "Doppelte Kindheit: Zur Interpretation zu
Christa Wolfs Kindheitsmuster." Deutschunterricht 30

(1978), 52-66.

Love, Myra. "Christa Wolf and Feminism: Breaking the Patriarchal Connection." New German Critique 16 (1979), 31-35.

Ludwig, Nadeshda. Die Entstehung des sozialistischen Realismus und seine Entfaltung in der russischen sowjetischen Literatur bis 1934. Potsdam, 1962.

Lukacs, Georg. Die Eigenart des Ästhetischen (2 vol.). Neuwied, 1969.

_____. Essays über Realismus. Neuwied, 1971.

_____. Probleme der Ästhetik. Neuwied, 1969.

Lukic, S. "Jedan pogled na teoriju i praksu socijalistickog realizma." Delo 10 (1970), 1143.

Lützeler, Paul Michael. "Goethes 'Faust' und der Sozialismus. Zur Rezeption des klassischen Erbes in der DDR." Basis 5 (1975), 31-54.

Manger, Philip. "Auf der Suche nach dem ungelebten Leben: Christa Wolf - Unter den Linden." Alemander von Bormann, Karl R. Mandelkow and A. Touber. Wissen aus Erfahrungen. Werkbegriff und Interpretation heute. Festschrift für Hermann Meyer zum 65. Geburtstag. Tübingen: Niemeier, 1968.

Mannack, Eberhard. Zwei deutsche Literaturen? Zu G. Grass, U. Johnson, H. Kant, U. Plenzdorf und C. Wolf. Mit einer Bibliographie der Schönen Literatur in der DDR (1968-1974). Kronberg: Athenäum Verlag, 1977.

Markiewicz, H. "Realizm, naturalizm, typowosc." Glowne problemy wiedzy o literature. Krakow: Wydawnictwo Literackie, 1965.

Marx, Karl and Friedrich Engels. Studienausgabe in vier Bänden. Ed. Iring Fetscher. Frankfurt/Main, 1966.

Mayer, Hans. "Christa Wolf/Nachdenken über Christa T." Neue Rundschau 1 (1970), 180-86.

McGauran, Fergus. "Gebrochene Generationen: Christa Wolf und Theodor Storm." German Life and Letters 31 (1978), 328-35.

McPherson, Karin. "In Search of the New Prose: Christa Wolf's Reflections on Writing and the Writer in The 1960's and 1970's. New German Studies 1 (1981), 1-13.

Meyer, Frauke. "Zur Rezeption von Christa Wolfs Nachdenken über Christa T." Alternative 18 (1975), 26-31.

Michaelis, Rolf. "Der doppelte Himmel. Christa Wolfs zweites

Buch: Nachdenken über Christa T./Der umstrittene Roman
aus der DDR." Frankfurter Allgemeine Zeitung, 5/28, 1969.

_____. "Recht auf Trauer." Zeit 12/27, 1974.

Mohr, Heinrich. "Produktive Sehnsucht: Struktur, Thematik und
politische Relevanz von Christa Wolfs Nachdenken über
Christa T." Basis 2 (1971), 191-233.

Mozejko, Edward. Der sozialistische Realismus - Theorie,
Entwicklung und Versagen einer Literaturmethode. Bonn:
Bouvier Verlag Herbert Grundmann, 1977.

Neubert, Werner, et. al. "Zu einigen Entwicklungsproblemen der
sozialistischen Epik 1963-1968/69." Neue deutsche Literatur
9 (1969).

Neues Deutschland. 4/17, 1974.

Neues Deutschland. 9/1, 1974.

Neues Deutschland. 11/21, 1974.

Nieraad, Jürgen. "Pronominalstrukturen in realistischer Prosa:
Beobachtungen zur Erzählebene und Figurenkonturen bei
Christa Wolf." Poetica 10 (1978), 485-506.

_____. "Subjektivität Als Thema Und Methode Realistischer
Schreibweise." Literaturwissenschaftliches Jahrbuch 19
(1978), 289-316.

Nitsche, Hellmuth. "Quo Vadis Christa Wolf?" Arbeiten zur
Deutschen Philologie 5 (1970), 155-71.

Nolte, Jost. "Die schmerzhaften Erfahrungen der Christa T."
In Grenzgänge. Berichte über Literatur. by Jost Nolte.
Vienna: Europaverlag, 1972, pp. 176-81.

Orlow, Peter. "Die Bitterfelder Sackgasse." Die Orientierung
1 (1970), 1-95.

Pareigis, Gottfried. Kritische Analyse der Realitätsdarstellung
in Ausgewählten Werken des 'Bitterfelder Weges.' Kronberg/
Ts.: Scriptor Verlag, 1974.

Parkes, K.S. "An All-German Dilemma: Some Notes on the
Presentation of the Theme of the Individual and Society in
Martin Walser's Halbzeit and Christa Wolf's Nachdenken
über Christa T." German Life and Letters 28 (1974-75),
58-64.

Paulick, Wolfgang, ed. Junge Schriftsteller der DDR Selbstdarstellungen. Leipzig, 1965.

Pawel, Ernst. "The Quest for Christa T." New York Times Book
    Review. 1/3, 1971.

Pervyj vsesojuznyi S'ezd sovetskich pisatelej 1934. Stenografi-
    ceskij otcet. Moskva, 1934.

Pieck, Wilhelm. Um die Erneuerung der deutschen Kultur. Type-
    script with personal entries. Wilhelm Pieck Archiv des
    Instituts für Marxismus-Leninismus, Berlin.

Plavius, Heinz. "Gewissensforschung: Christa Wolf. Kindheits-
    muster." Neue deutsche Literatur 25 (1977), 139-51.

_____. "MutmaBungsmut." Neue deutsche Literatur 22
    (1974), 154-57.

_____. "Tendenzen und Probleme der Prosa." Neue deutsche
    Literatur 1 (1976), 28-37.

Powroslo, Wolfgang. Literatur der DDR im Unterricht. Düsseldorf:
    Pädagogischer Verlag, Schwann, 1977.

Pracht, Erwin. Einführung in den sozialistischen Realismus.
    Berlin: Dietz Verlag, 1975.

_____. "Versuch einer Gegenstandsbestimmung der Theorie
    des sozialistischen Realismus." Weimarer Beiträge 6
    (1970), 25-47.

Pracht, Erwin and Werner Neubert, eds. Sozialistischer
    Realismus. Positionen. Probleme. Perspektiven. Berlin
    (Ost), 1970.

PreiBler, Helmut. "Konferenz Junger Schriftsteller in Halle."
    Neue deutsche Literatur 7 (1962), 28-50.

Probst, Gerhard F. "Thematization of Alterity in Christa Wolf's
    Nachdenken über Christa T." University of Dayton Review
    13 (1978), 25-35.

Programm der Sozialistischen Einheitspartei Deutschlands.
    Berlin, 1963.

Promies, Wolfgang. "Dass wir aus dem vollen leben...: Versuch
    über Christa Wolf." Eds. Heinz L. Arnold and Theo Buck.
    Positionen im deutschen Roman der sechziger Jahre. München:
    Boorberg, 1974, pp. 110-26.

Raddatz, Fritz J. "DDR Literatur und Marxistische Ästhetik."
    Germanic Review 43 (1968), 40-60.

_____. Traditionen und Tendenzen. Materialien zur Literatur
    der DDR. Frankfurt/Main: Suhrkamp, 1972.

Raddatz, Fritz J. "Zur Entwicklung der Literatur in der DDR."
Die deutsche Literatur der Gegenwart. Ed. Manfred Durzak.
Stuttgart, 1971, pp. 337-65.

_____, ed. Marxismus und Literatur. Eine Dokumentation
in drei Bänden. Reinbeck: Rowohlt, 1969.

Reich-Ranicki, Marcel. Deutsche Literatur in West und Ost.
München: Piper, 1963.

_____. "The Writer in Divided Germany." To Find Something
New. Ed. Henry Grosshans. Pullman, Washington: Washington
State Univ. Press, 1969, pp. 138-45.

_____. Zur Literatur der DDR. München: Piper, 1974.

Reinig, Christa. "Der ungeteilte Himmel." Spiegel 3 (1965),
70-1.

Reso, Martin, ed. 'Der geteilte Himmel' und seine Kritiker.
Halle: Mitteldeutscher Verlag, 1965.

Richter, Hans. "Review of Kindheitsmuster." Sinn und Form 29
(1977), 667-78.

Rožkov, P. "O socijalisticeskom realizme." Novy mir 9 (1933).

Sabouk, Sava. "Der sozialistische Realismus und das Problem
der künstlerischen Wahrheit." Weimarer Beiträge 1 (1975),
75-99.

Sachs, Hans. "Verleger sein heiBt ideologisch kämpfen." Neues
Deutschland. 5/14, 1969.

Salisch, Marion von. Zwischen Selbstaufgabe und Selbstverwirk-
lichung: Zum Problem der Persönlichkeitsstruktur im Werk
Christa Wolfs. Stuttgart: Klett, 1975.

Sander, Hans Dietrich. Geschichte der Schönen Literatur in der
DDR. Freiburg: Verlag Rombach, 1972.

_____. Literatur der DDR. Arbeitskreis der Collegia
Politica an Deutschen Universitäten, 1970.

Sander, Volkmar. "Erinnerungen an die Zukunft: Christa Wolfs
Nachdenken über Christa T." Eds. Ralph Ley, Maria Wagner,
Joanna Ratych and Kenneth Hughes. Perspectives and
Personalities: Studies in Modern German Literature Honoring
Claude Hill. Heidelberg: Winter, 1978.

Sauer, Klaus, ed. Christa Wolf Materialienbuch. Darmstadt:
Luchterhand, 1979.

Sčerbine, V.R. Lenin i voprosy literatury. Moskva, 1961.

Schlenstedt, Dieter. "Ankunft und Anspruch. Zum neueren Roman in der DDR." Sinn und Form 3 (1966), 814-35.

_____. "Motive und Symbole in Christa Wolfs Erzählung 'Der geteilte Himmel.'" Weimarer Beiträge 10 (1964), 77-104.

_____. "Strukturwandel in der neueren Prosa der DDR." Text und Kontext 1 (1979), 3-31.

_____. Wirkungsästhetische Analysen. Berlin: Akademie-Verlag, 1979.

Schleyer, Winfried. "Zur Funktion des Komischen bei Friedrich Dürrenmatt und Peter Hacks." Der Deutschunterricht 2 (1978), 67-77.

Schmitt, Hans-Jürgen, ed. Die Expressionismus-Debatte. Materialien zu einer marxistischen Realismus-Konzeption. Frankfurt/Main, 1973.

_____. Einführung in Theorie, Geschichte und Funktion der DDR-Literatur. Stuttgart: Metzler, 1975.

Schneider, Gerhard, ed. Eröffnungen. Schriftsteller über ihr Erstlingswerk. Berlin: Aufbau, 1974.

Schoeller, Wilfried F. "Nachdenken über Christa W." Weltwoche. 4/27, 1977.

Schoeps, Karl H. "Wandel und Erinnerung: Christa Wolfs Erzählung 'Blickwechsel' als Paradigma ihrer Erzählstruktur." German Quarterly 52 (1979), 518-525.

Schubbe, Elimar, ed. Dokumente zur Kunst- Literatur- und Kulturpolitik der SED. Stuttgart, 1972.

Schuhmann, Klaus. "Aspekte des Verhältnisses zwischen Individuum und Gesellschaft in der Gegenwartsliteratur der DDR." Weimarer Beiträge 7 (1975), 5-36.

Schultz, Gerda. "Ein überraschender Erstling." Neue deutsche Literatur 9 (1961), 128-31.

Schulz, Max Walter. "Das Neue und das Bleibende in unserer Literatur." Neue deutsche Literatur 9 (1969).

Seghers, Anna. "Für Christa Wolf." Sinn und Form 31 (1979), 282-83.

_____. Über Kunstwerk und Wirklichkeit. Berlin: Akademie Verlag, 1970-71.

Seiler, Bernd W. "Nachdenken über Theodor S.: 'Innerlichkeit' bei Storm und Christa Wolf." Schriften der Theodor-Storm-

Gesellschaft 27 (1978), 9-25.

Simons, Elizabeth. "Das Andersmachen, von Grund auf." Weimarer
Beiträge 15 Sonderheft Issue (1969), 183-204.

_____. "Über den sozialistischen Realismus." Weimarer
Beiträge 3 (1970), 40-74.

Sobolev, L. "Literatura i naša sovremennost." Pervyj
učreditel'nyj s'ezd pisatelej Rossijskoj Federacii 7-13
dekabrja 1958 goda. Moskva: Sovetskaja Rossija, 1959.

Sontheimer, Kurt and Wilhelm Bleek. Die DDR Politik.
Gessellschaft. Wirtschaft. Hamburg, 1972.

Spender, Stephen. "Review of A Model Childhood by Christa
Wolf." Ursule Molinaro and Hedwig Rappolt, trans. The
New York Times Book Review. 10/12, 1980, 11, 34.

Spinner, Kaspar H. "Prosaanalysen: Aus Christa Wolf, Nachdenken
über Christa T." Literatur und Kritik 90 (1975), 614-21.

Steinbach, Dietrich. "Die neue Literatur der DDR." Deutschunterricht 2 (1978), 100-24.

Stephan, Alexander. "Auswahlbibliographie zu Christa Wolf."
Text und Kritik 46 (1975), 5-55.

_____. Christa Wolf, Autorenbücher 4. München: Verlag
Edition Text und Kritik, 1979.

_____. "Die 'subjektive Authentizität' des Autors: Zur
ästhetischen Position von Christa Wolf." Text und Kritik
46 (1975), 33-41.

_____. "Die wissenschaftlich-technische Revolution in
der Literatur der DDR." Deutschunterricht 2 (1978), 18-34.

_____. "Review of Kindheitsmuster. Biddy Martin, trans.
New German Critique 11 (1977), 178-82.

Strittmatter, Eva. "Literatur und Wirklichkeit." Neue deutsche
Literatur 7 (1962).

Sutschkow, Boris. Historische Schicksale des Realismus. Berlin
(Ost), 1972.

Thomassen, Christa. Der lange Weg zu uns selbst: Christa
Wolfs Roman 'Nachdenken über Christa T.' als Erfahrungs-U.
Handlungsmuster. Kronberg/Ts.: Scriptor Verlag, 1977.

Timofeev, L. O snovy teorie literatury. Moskva: Prosvescenie,
1966.

_____. O snovy teorie literatury. Moskva: Prosvescenie,

1971.

Timofeev, L. and V.R. Sčerbina, eds. Lenin i literatura.
Moskva: Izd. chud lit., 1963.

Träger, Claus. Studien zur Realismustheorie und Methodologie
der Literaturwissenschaft. Frankfurt, 1972.

Trommler, Frank. "DDR- Erzählung und Bitterfelder Weg." Basis
3 (1972), 61-97.

_____. "Ideologische und ästhetische Aspekte beim
Interpretieren von DDR-Literatur." Der Deutschunterricht
2 (1978), 5-34.

_____. "Von Stalin zu Hölderin. Über den Entwicklungs-
roman in der DDR." Basis 2 (1971), 141-90.

Um die Erneuerung der deutschen Kultur. 1. Zentrale Kulturkonferenz
der KPD vom 3. bis 5. Februar 1946 in Berlin, 1946.

Wallman, Jürgen P. "Christa Wolf: Nachdenken über Christa T."
Neue Deutsche Hefte 16 (1969), 149-55.

_____. "Über die Schwierigkeit, ich zu sagen." Die Tat.
179 (8/1, 1970).

Walwei-Wiegelmann, Hedwig, ed. Neuere DDR-Literatur. Texte
und Materialien für den Deutschunterricht. Paderborn, 1973.

Weber, Heinz Dieter. "Die Wiederkehr des Tragischen in der
Literatur der DDR." Der Deutschunterricht 2 (1978), 79-99.

Weimann, Robert, ed. Tradition in der Literaturgeschichte.
Berlin (Ost), 1972.

Welzig, Werner. Der deutsche Roman im 20. Jahrhundert.
Stuttgart: Alfred Kröner Verlag, 1970.

Whitley, John. "Quest for Christa T." Sunday Times. 5/16,
1971.

Wiegenstein, Roland. "Verweigerung der Zustimmung?" Merkur
23 (1969).

Wiese, Benno von. Deutsche Dichter der Gegenwart: Ihr Leben
und Werk. Berlin: Schmidt, 1973.

Wirkungsgeschichte von Christa Wolfs 'Nachdenken über Christa T.'
Ed. Manfred Behn. Königstein/Ts.: Athenäum, 1978.

Zak, Edward. "Tragisches Erlebnis in optimistischer Sicht.
Zu Christa Wolfs Erzählung 'Der geteilte Himmel.'" Sonntag
20 (1963).

Zehm, Günter. "Nachdenken über Christa W." Welt der Literatur 3/27, 1969.

Zweite Bitterfelder Konferenz. Berlin, 1964.

Burns, Rob
THE QUEST FOR MODERNITY
The Place of Arno Holz in Modern German Literature

Francfort/M., Berne, Las Vegas, 1981. 278 pp.
European University Papers: Series 1, German Language and Literature. Vol. 431
ISBN 3-8204-6225-2   br. sFr. 69.–

The work of Arno Holz embraces a wide diversity of literary forms ranging from activist poetry and Naturalist prose to formalism and experimental writing. By tracing Holz's persistent concern with form and relating him to literary developments in the twentieth century this study assesses the claim made by Holz himself and reiterated by literary criticism in the sixties that he was the real pioneer of modernism in German literature.
Contents: «Buch der Zeit» – Consequential Naturalism – Phantasus.

Marshall, Alan
THE GERMAN NATURALISTS AND GERHART HAUPTMANN
Reception and Influence

Frankfurt/M., Berne, 1982. 418 pp.
Historisch-kritische Arbeiten zur Deutschen Literatur. Vol. 2
ISBN 3-8204-7148-0   pb. sFr. 89.–

European University Studies: Series 1, German Language and Literature. Vol. 556
ISBN 3-8204-7149-9   pb. sFr. 89.–

Gerhart Hauptmann's relationship to Naturalism has repeatedly been a subject of controversy. To clarify his position, this study analyses both published and unpublished opinions of his contemporaries within Naturalism. Following an outline of Naturalism based on the authors' own views of the often conflicting concepts related to the movement, emphasis is placed upon Naturalist critical response to Hauptmann's early works and upon the works of other Naturalist dramatists in relation to Hauptmann, underlining the authors' dependence upon his dramas as a model for literary success.
Contents: The Naturalistic Outlook – Hauptmann's Outlook – Critical Reception (Breakthrough, Hauptmann and Holz, Years of Success) – Productive Reception (Hirschfeld, Rosmer, Dreyer, Rosenow, etc.).

Verlag Peter Lang Bern · Frankfurt a.M. · New York
Auslieferung: Verlag Peter Lang AG, Jupiterstr. 15, CH 3000 Bern 15
Telefon (0041/31) 32 11 22, Telex verl ch 32 420